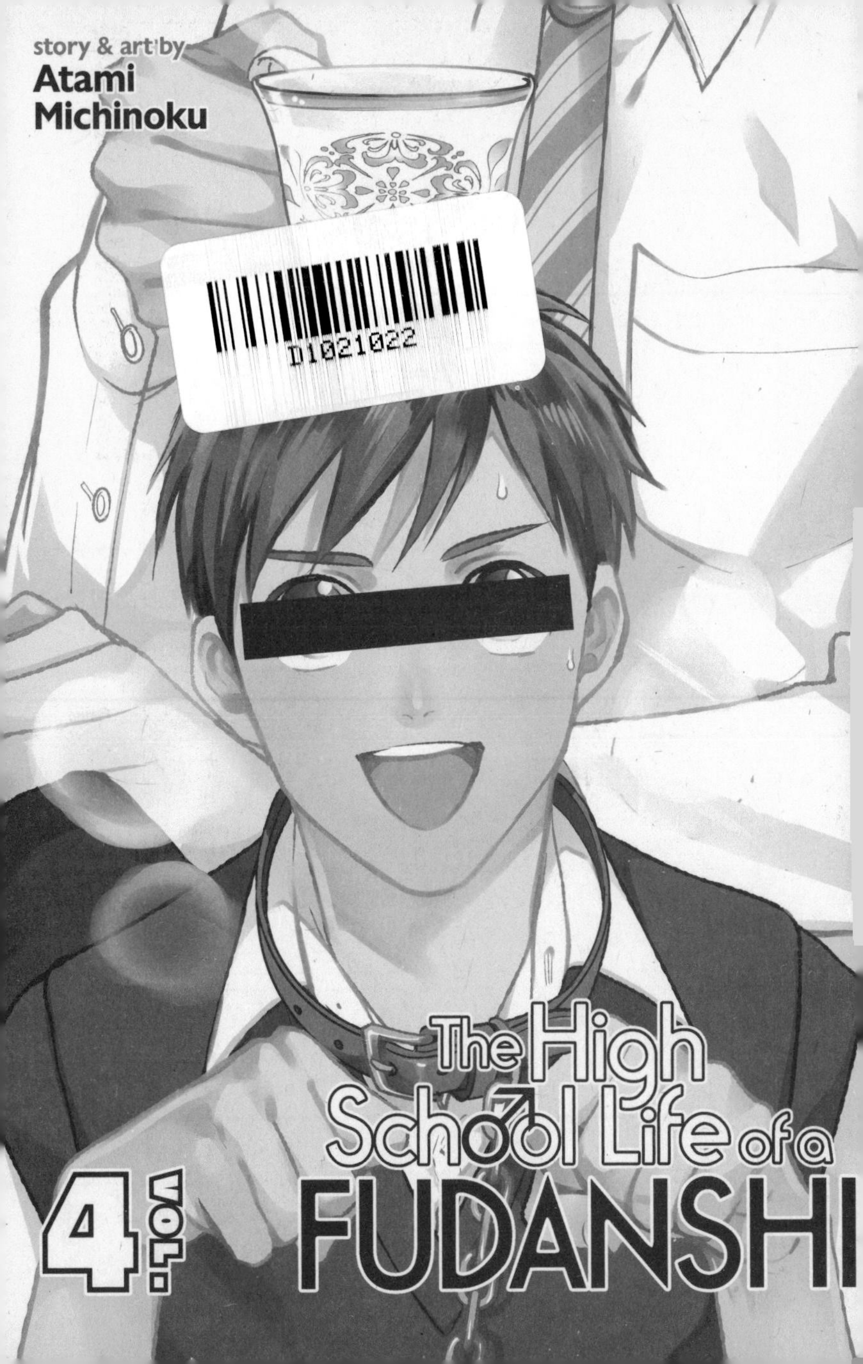
story & art by
Atami Michinoku
The High School Life of a
FUDANSHI
vol. 4

SEVEN SEAS ENTERTAINMENT PRESENTS

The High School Life of a FUDANSHI

story and art by ATAMI MICHINOKU VOLUME 4

TRANSLATION
Ryan Peterson

ADAPTATION
Lianne Sentar

LETTERING AND RETOUCH
Ray Steeves

LOGO DESIGN
Karis Page

COVER DESIGN
KC Fabellon

PROOFREADER
Dayna Abel
Danielle King

EDITOR
Jenn Grunigen

PRODUCTION ASSISTANT
CK Russell

PRODUCTION MANAGER
Lissa Pattillo

EDITOR-IN-CHIEF
Adam Arnold

PUBLISHER
Jason DeAngelis

THE HIGH SCHOOL LIFE OF A FUDANSHI VOL. 4

First published in Japan in 2017 by ICHIJINSHA Inc., Tokyo.
English translation rights arranged with ICHIJINSHA Inc., Tokyo, Japan.

Seven Seas books may be purchased in bulk for promotional, educational, or business use. Please contact your local bookseller or the Macmillan Corporate and Premium Sales Department at 1-800-221-7945, extension 5442, or by e-mail at MacmillanSpecialMarkets@macmillan.com.

ISBN: 978-1-626927-87-2

Printed in Canada

First Printing: November 2018

10 9 8 7 6 5 4 3 2 1

FOLLOW US ONLINE: *www.sevenseasentertainment.com*

READING DIRECTIONS

This book reads from ***right to left***, Japanese style. If this is your first time reading manga, you start reading from the top right panel on each page and take it from there. If you get lost, just follow the numbered diagram here. It may seem backwards at first, but you'll get the hang of it! Have fun!!

1
2
3
4
5
6
7
8
9

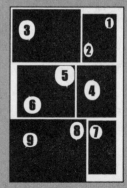

CHAPTER 26
Homeroom Romance

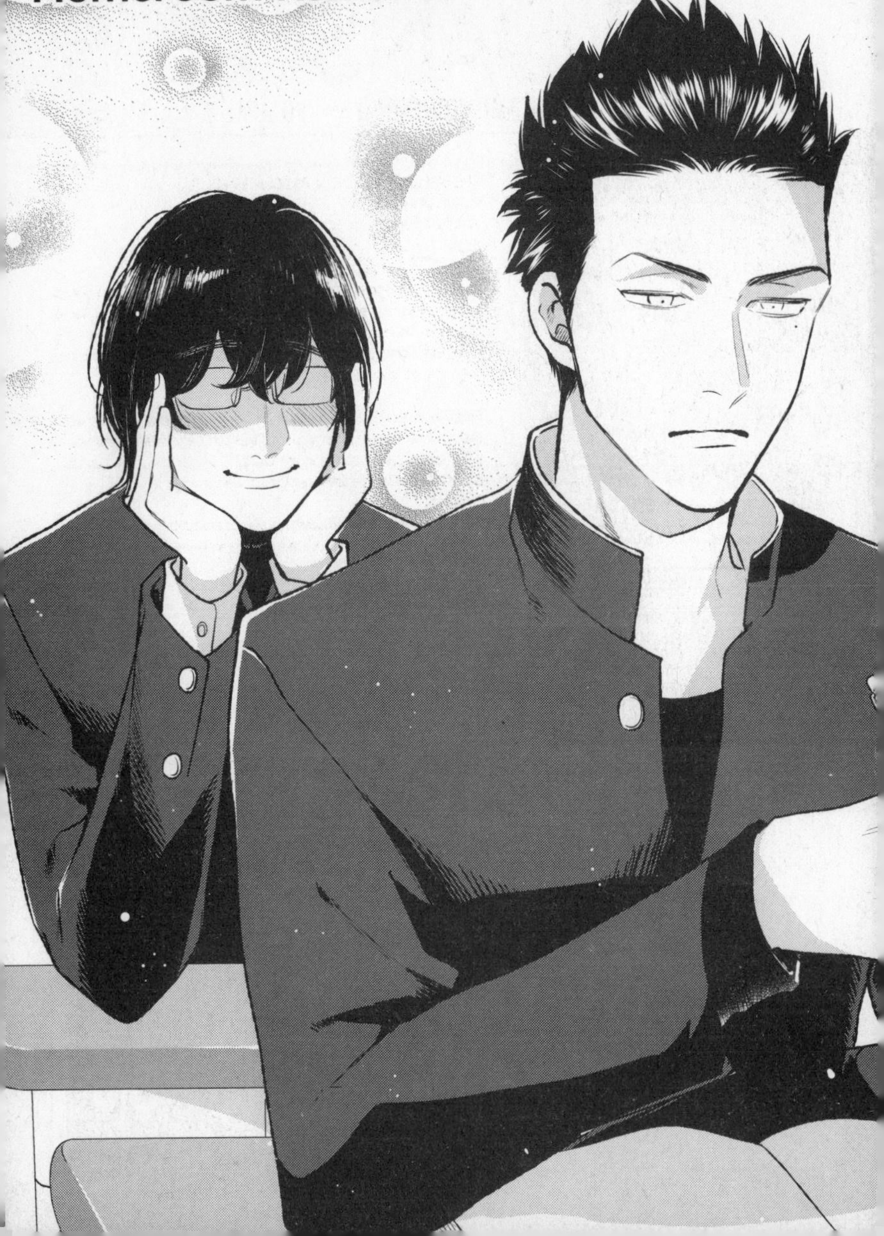

LETTING IT SLIP

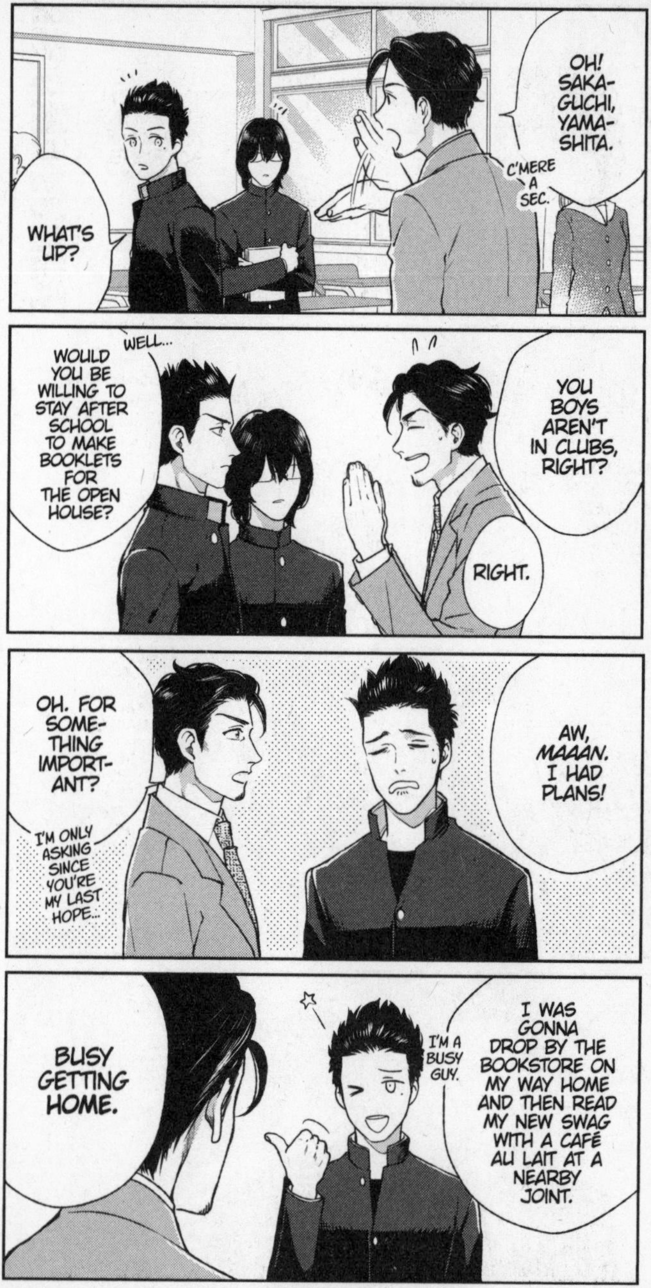
OH! SAKA-GUCHI, YAMA-SHITA.
C'MERE A SEC.
WHAT'S UP?
YOU BOYS AREN'T IN CLUBS, RIGHT?
RIGHT.
WELL...
WOULD YOU BE WILLING TO STAY AFTER SCHOOL TO MAKE BOOKLETS FOR THE OPEN HOUSE?
AW, MAAAN. I HAD PLANS!
OH. FOR SOME-THING IMPORT-ANT?
I'M ONLY ASKING SINCE YOU'RE MY LAST HOPE...
I WAS GONNA DROP BY THE BOOKSTORE ON MY WAY HOME AND THEN READ MY NEW SWAG WITH A CAFÉ AU LAIT AT A NEARBY JOINT.
I'M A BUSY GUY.
BUSY GETTING HOME.

HIS OWN AGENDA

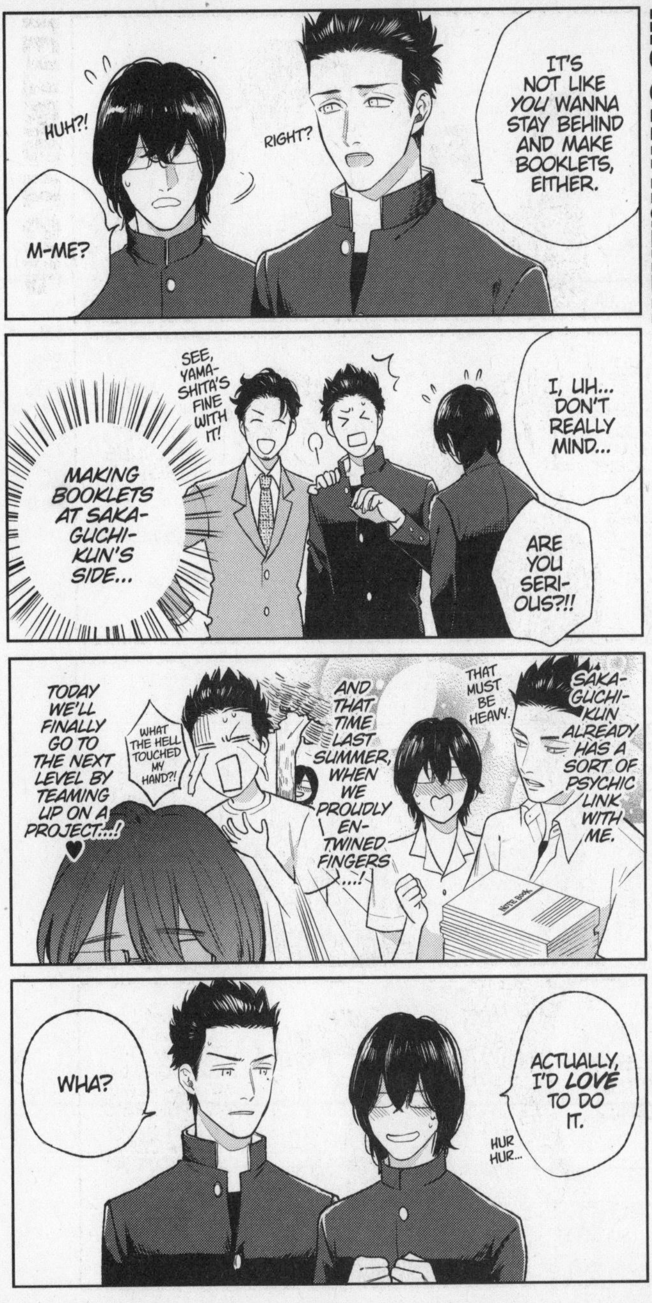
IT'S NOT LIKE *YOU* WANNA STAY BEHIND AND MAKE BOOKLETS, EITHER.
RIGHT?
HUH?!
M-ME?
I, UH... DON'T REALLY MIND...
ARE YOU SERI-OUS?!!
SEE, YAMA-SHITA'S FINE WITH IT!
MAKING BOOKLETS AT SAKA-GUCHI-KUN'S SIDE...
SAKA-GUCHI-KUN ALREADY HAS A SORT OF PSYCHIC LINK WITH ME.
THAT MUST BE HEAVY.
AND THAT TIME LAST SUMMER, WHEN WE PROUDLY EN-TWINED FINGERS...!
WHAT THE HELL TOUCHED MY HAND?!
TODAY WE'LL FINALLY GO TO THE NEXT LEVEL BY TEAMING UP ON A PROJECT...! ♥
NOTE Book
ACTUALLY, I'D *LOVE* TO DO IT.
HUR HUR...
WHA?

MELTING ME WITH HIS GAZE

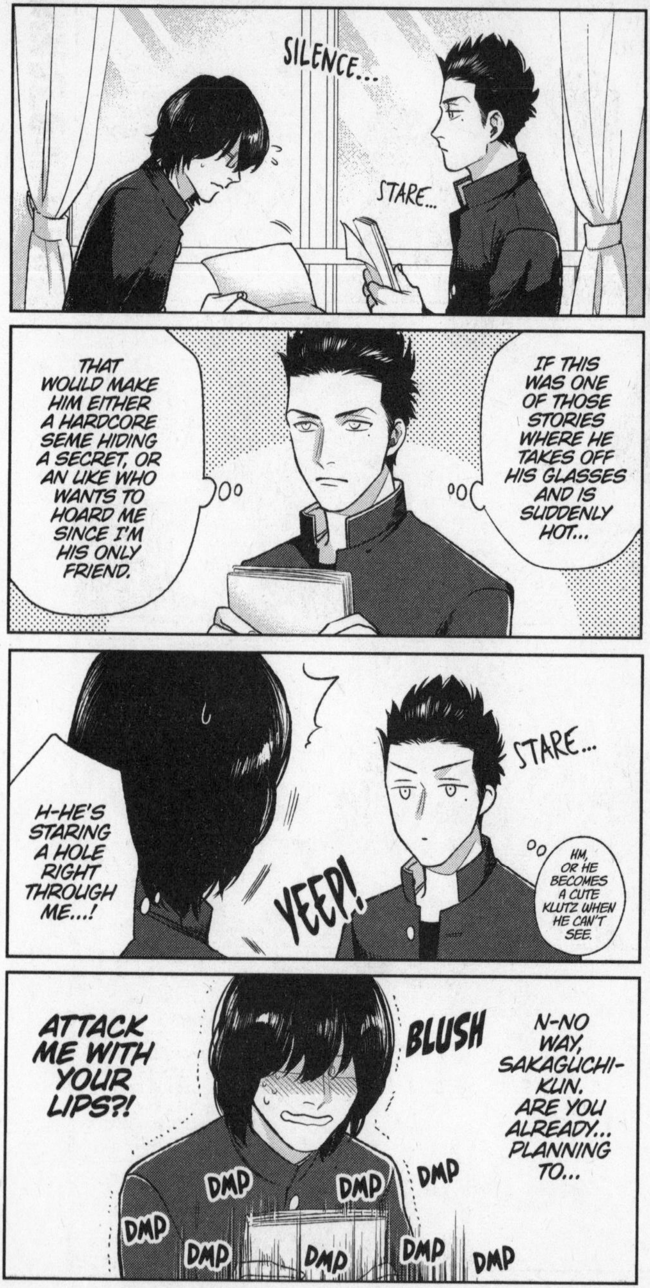

SILENCE...
STARE...
IF THIS WAS ONE OF THOSE STORIES WHERE HE TAKES OFF HIS GLASSES AND IS SUDDENLY HOT...
THAT WOULD MAKE HIM EITHER A HARDCORE SEME HIDING A SECRET, OR AN UKE WHO WANTS TO HOARD ME SINCE I'M HIS ONLY FRIEND.
STARE...
HM, OR HE BECOMES A CUTE KLUTZ WHEN HE CAN'T SEE.
YEEP!
H-HE'S STARING A HOLE RIGHT THROUGH ME...!
N-NO WAY, SAKAGUCHI-KUN. ARE YOU ALREADY... PLANNING TO...
BLUSH
ATTACK ME WITH YOUR LIPS?!
DMP
DMP
DMP
DMP
DMP
DMP
DMP
DMP

WHAT'S IN A NAME

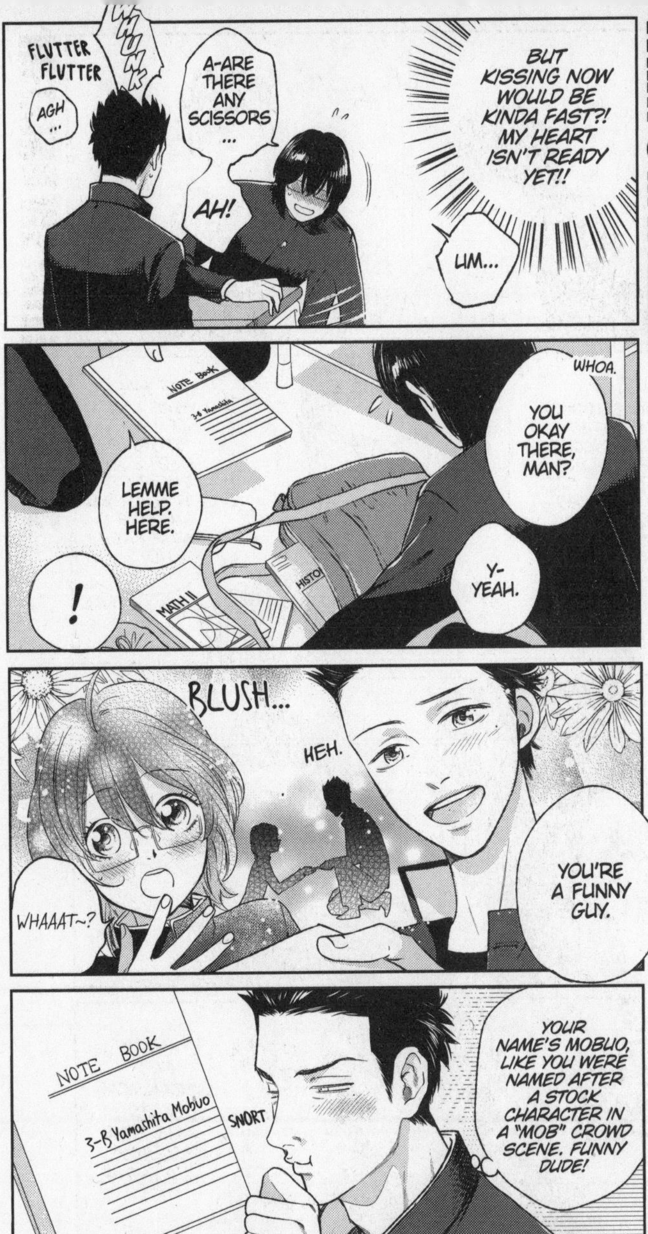
BUT KISSING NOW WOULD BE KINDA FAST?! MY HEART ISN'T READY YET!!
UM...
A-ARE THERE ANY SCISSORS ...
AH!
WHUNK
FLUTTER FLUTTER
AGH ...
WHOA.
YOU OKAY THERE, MAN?
Y- YEAH.
NOTE BOOK
3-B Yamashita
LEMME HELP. HERE.
!
MATH II
BLUSH...
HEH.
YOU'RE A FUNNY GUY.
WHAAAT~?
YOUR NAME'S MOBUO, LIKE YOU WERE NAMED AFTER A STOCK CHARACTER IN A "MOB" CROWD SCENE. FUNNY DUDE!
SNORT
NOTE BOOK
3-B Yamashita Mobuo

OH, I KNOW

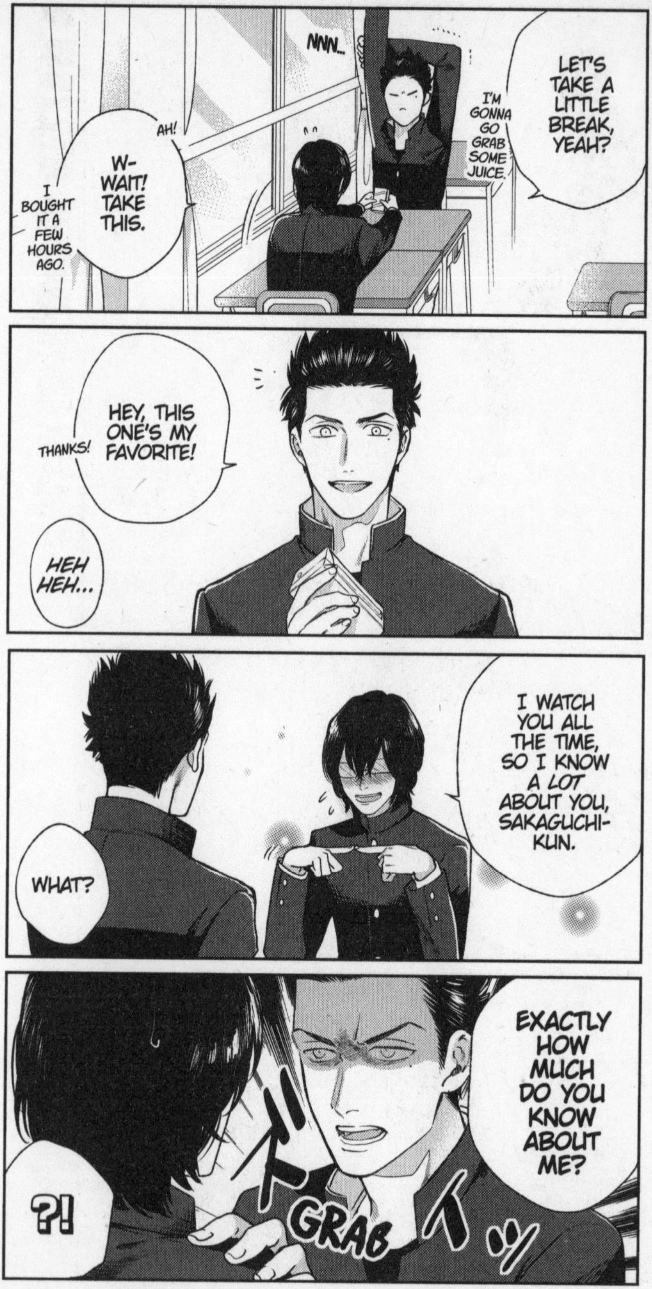
LET'S TAKE A LITTLE BREAK, YEAH?
I'M GONNA GO GRAB SOME JUICE.
NNN...
AH!
W-WAIT! TAKE THIS.
I BOUGHT IT A FEW HOURS AGO.
HEY, THIS ONE'S MY FAVORITE!
THANKS!
HEH HEH...
I WATCH YOU ALL THE TIME, SO I KNOW A *LOT* ABOUT YOU, SAKAGUCHI-KUN.
WHAT?
EXACTLY HOW MUCH DO YOU KNOW ABOUT ME?
GRAB
?!

A MATTER OF INTERPRETATION

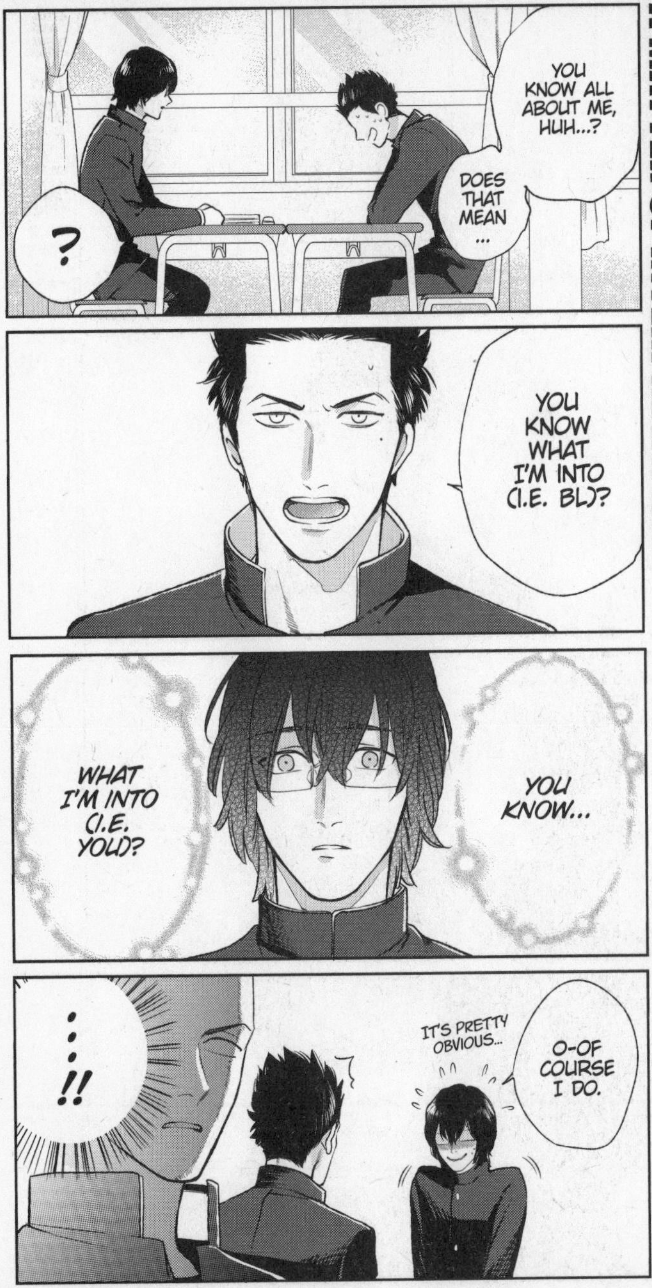
YOU KNOW ALL ABOUT ME, HUH...?
DOES THAT MEAN ...
?
YOU KNOW WHAT I'M INTO (I.E. BL)?
YOU KNOW...
WHAT I'M INTO (I.E. YOU)?
O-OF COURSE I DO.
IT'S PRETTY OBVIOUS...
...!!

JUST BETWEEN US☆

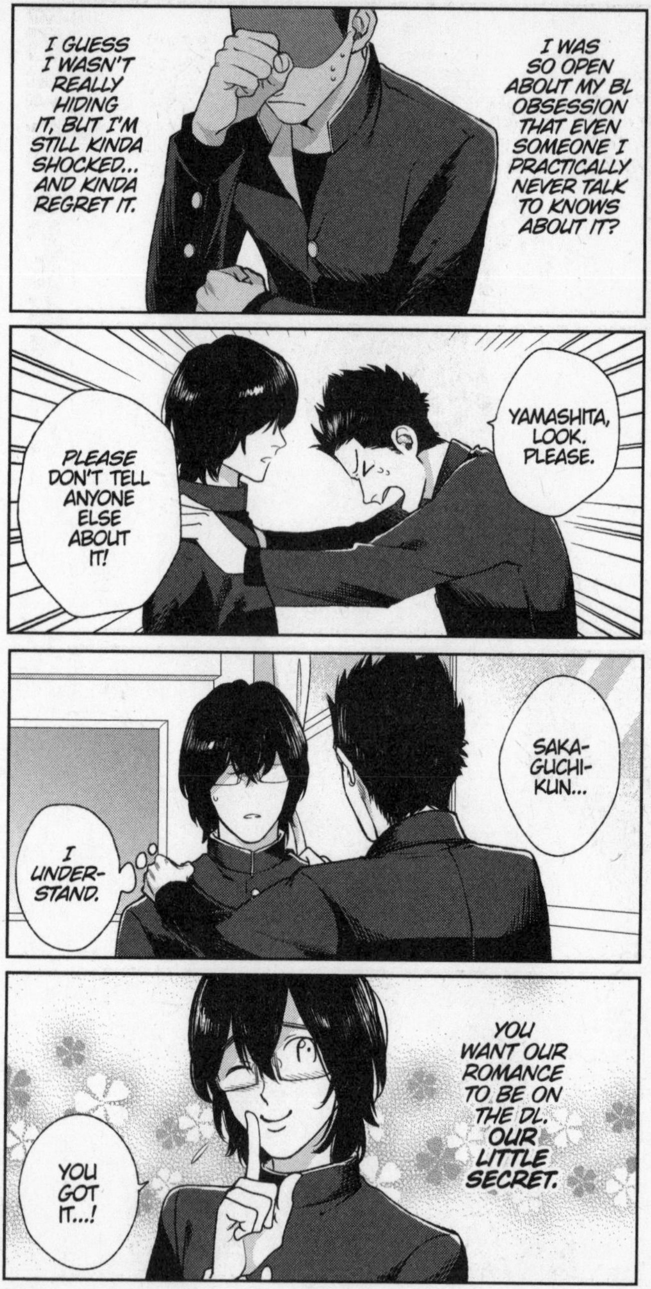
I WAS SO OPEN ABOUT MY BL OBSESSION THAT EVEN SOMEONE I PRACTICALLY NEVER TALK TO KNOWS ABOUT IT?
I GUESS I WASN'T REALLY HIDING IT, BUT I'M STILL KINDA SHOCKED... AND KINDA REGRET IT.
YAMASHITA, LOOK. PLEASE.
PLEASE DON'T TELL ANYONE ELSE ABOUT IT!
SAKA-GUCHI-KUN...
I UNDER-STAND.
YOU WANT OUR ROMANCE TO BE ON THE DL. OUR LITTLE SECRET.
YOU GOT IT...!

RIGHT UP HIS ALLEY

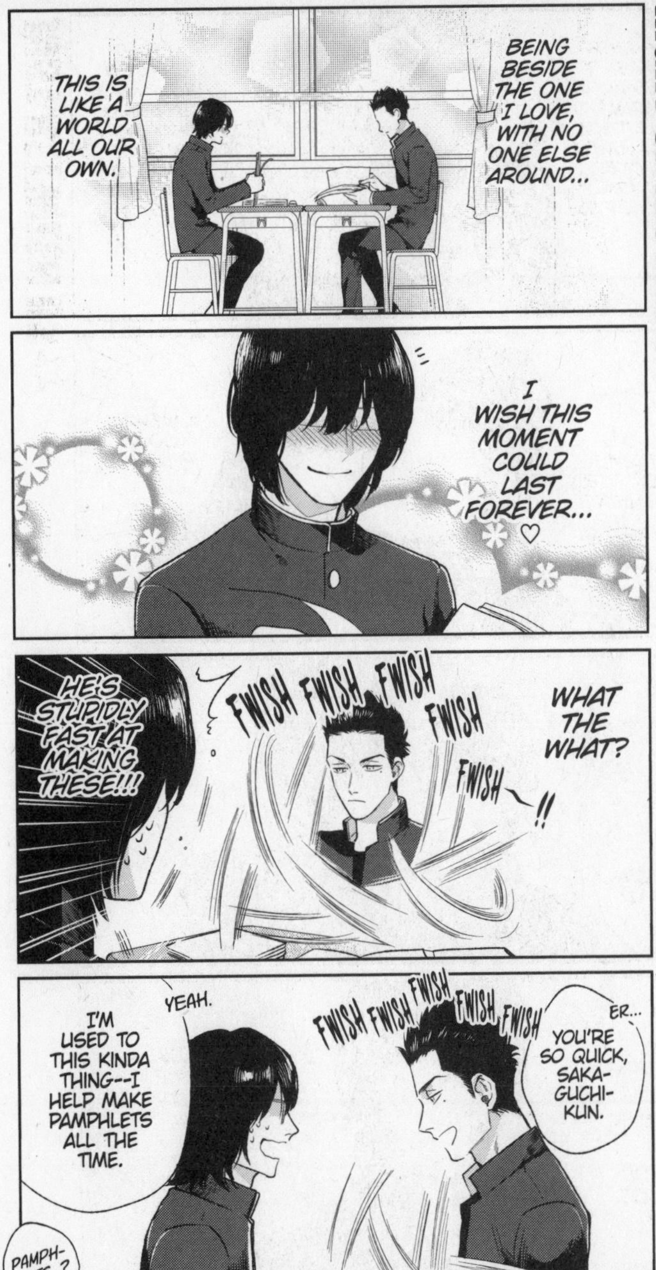
BEING BESIDE THE ONE I LOVE, WITH NO ONE ELSE AROUND...
THIS IS LIKE A WORLD ALL OUR OWN.
I WISH THIS MOMENT COULD LAST FOREVER... ♡
WHAT THE WHAT?
FWISH FWISH FWISH FWISH FWISH~!!
HE'S STUPIDLY FAST AT MAKING THESE!!!
ER... YOU'RE SO QUICK, SAKAGUCHI-KUN.
FWISH FWISH FWISH FWISH FWISH
YEAH.
I'M USED TO THIS KINDA THING--I HELP MAKE PAMPHLETS ALL THE TIME.
PAMPHLETS...?

OUT OF FOCUS

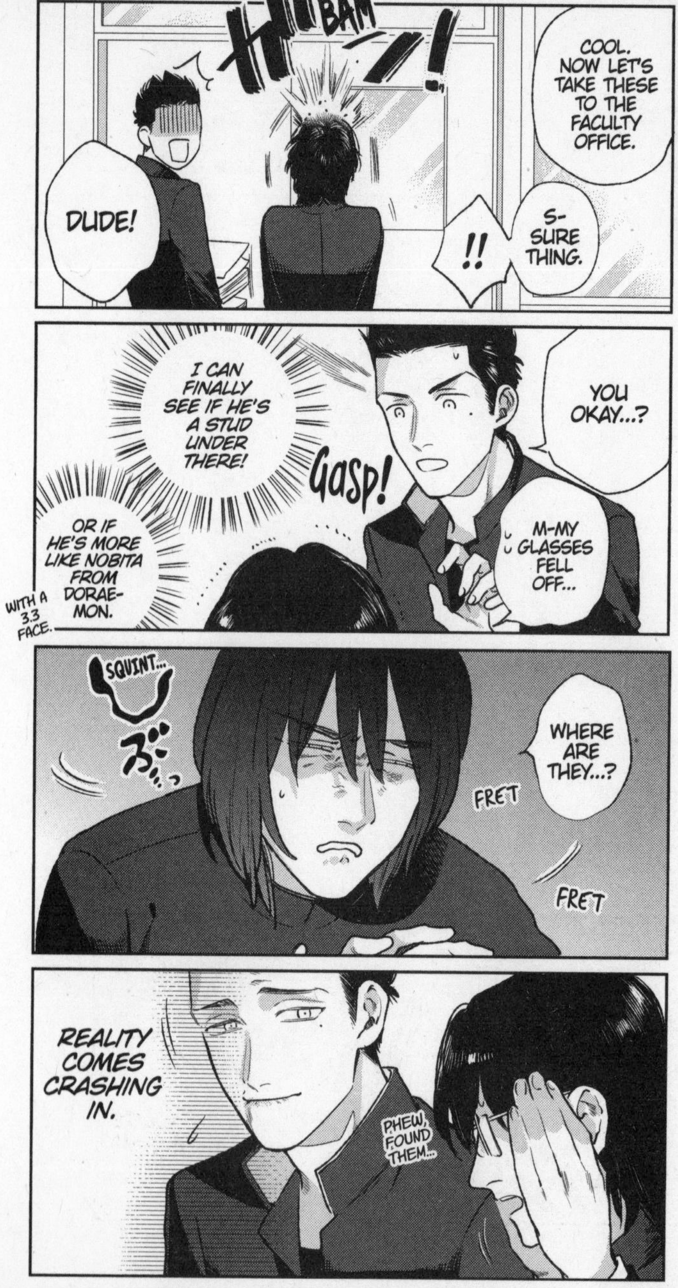
COOL. NOW LET'S TAKE THESE TO THE FACULTY OFFICE.
BAM
S-SURE THING.
!!
DUDE!
YOU OKAY...?
M-MY GLASSES FELL OFF...
Gasp!
I CAN FINALLY SEE IF HE'S A STUD UNDER THERE!
OR IF HE'S MORE LIKE NOBITA FROM DORAEMON.
WITH A 3.3 FACE.
WHERE ARE THEY...?
FRET
FRET
SQUINT...
ぶ...
PHEW, FOUND THEM...
REALITY COMES CRASHING IN.

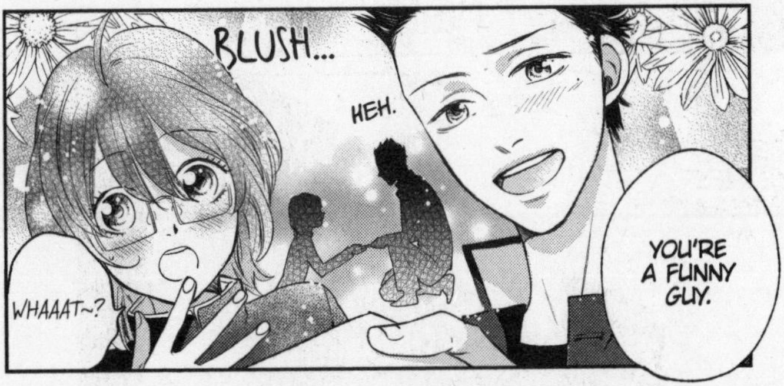
YOU'RE A FUNNY GUY.
HEH.
BLUSH...
WHAAAT~?

KFS

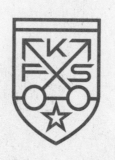

CHAPTER 27

Trip for Two Doujin-Sellers to Naniwa

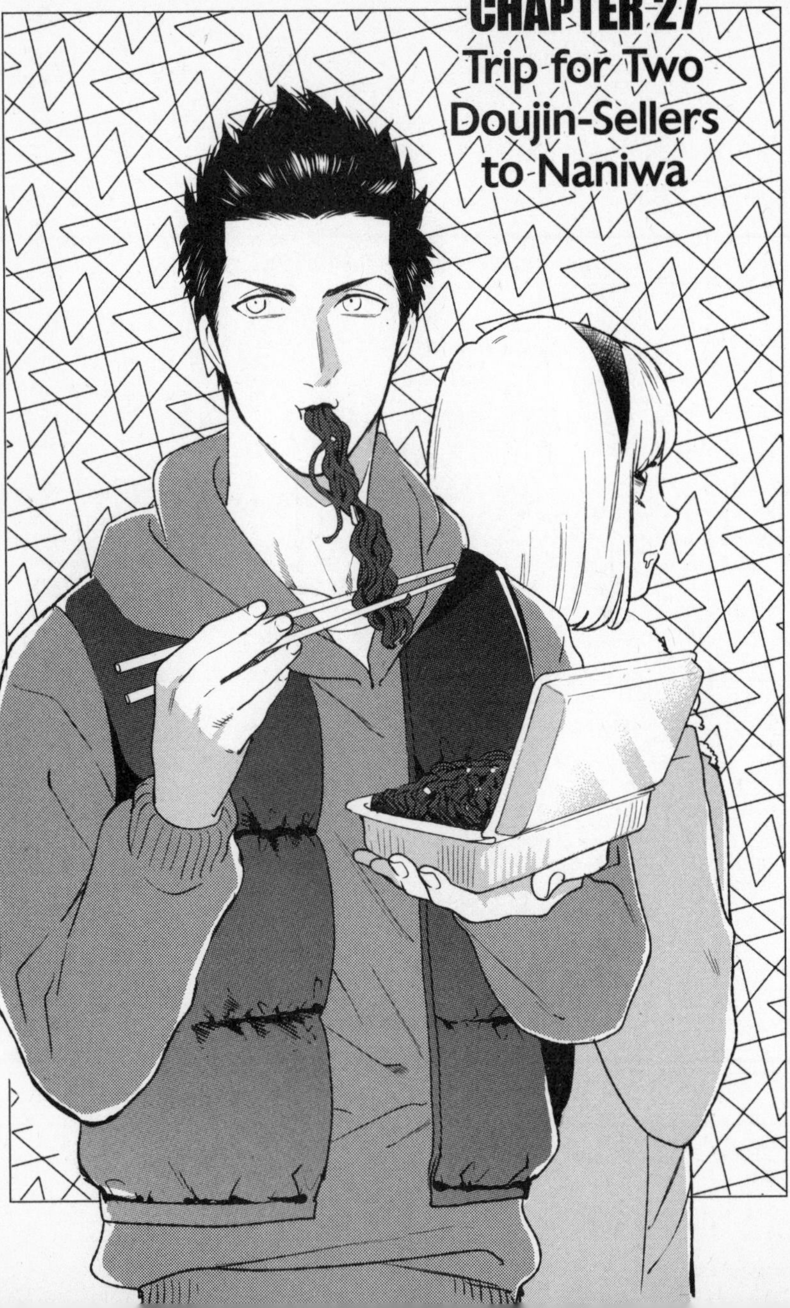

YOU REALLY THOUGHT THAT WOULD MAKE ME HAPPY?

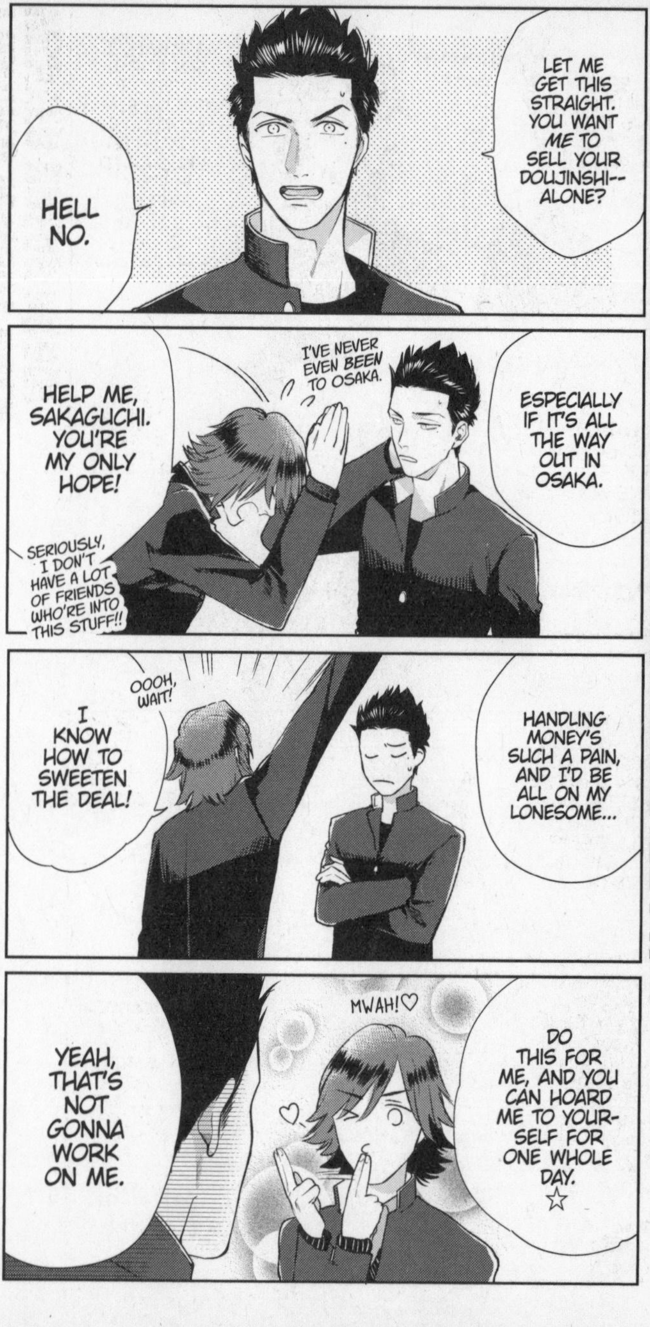
LET ME GET THIS STRAIGHT. YOU WANT ME TO SELL YOUR DOUJINSHI--ALONE?
HELL NO.
ESPECIALLY IF IT'S ALL THE WAY OUT IN OSAKA.
I'VE NEVER EVEN BEEN TO OSAKA.
HELP ME, SAKAGUCHI. YOU'RE MY ONLY HOPE!
SERIOUSLY, I DON'T HAVE A LOT OF FRIENDS WHO'RE INTO THIS STUFF!!
HANDLING MONEY'S SUCH A PAIN, AND I'D BE ALL ON MY LONESOME...
OOOH, WAIT!
I KNOW HOW TO SWEETEN THE DEAL!
DO THIS FOR ME, AND YOU CAN HOARD ME TO YOUR-SELF FOR ONE WHOLE DAY. ☆
MWAH!♡
YEAH, THAT'S NOT GONNA WORK ON ME.

I GAINED WEIGHT OVER WINTER BREAK AGAIN

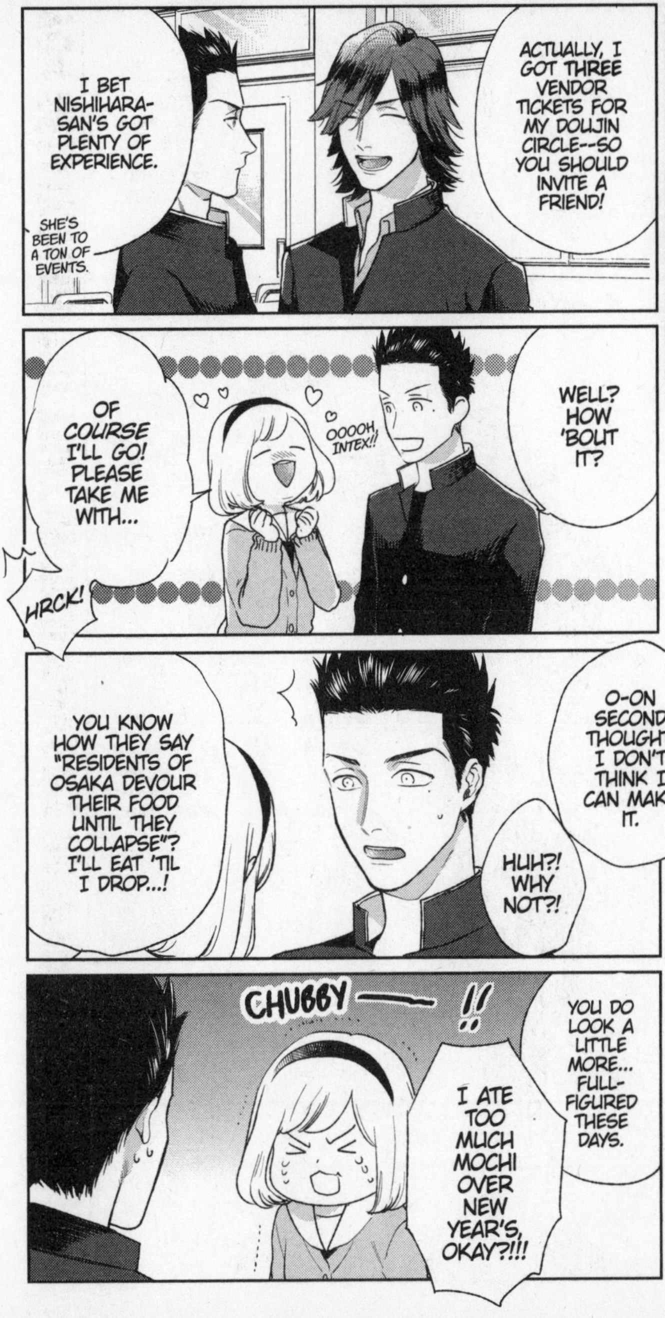
ACTUALLY, I GOT THREE VENDOR TICKETS FOR MY DOUJIN CIRCLE--SO YOU SHOULD INVITE A FRIEND!
I BET NISHIHARA-SAN'S GOT PLENTY OF EXPERIENCE.
SHE'S BEEN TO A TON OF EVENTS.
WELL? HOW 'BOUT IT?
OOOOH, INTEX!!
OF COURSE I'LL GO! PLEASE TAKE ME WITH...
HRCK!
O-ON SECOND THOUGHT, I DON'T THINK I CAN MAKE IT.
HUH?! WHY NOT?!
YOU KNOW HOW THEY SAY "RESIDENTS OF OSAKA DEVOUR THEIR FOOD UNTIL THEY COLLAPSE"? I'LL EAT 'TIL I DROP...!
CHUBBY——!!
YOU DO LOOK A LITTLE MORE... FULL-FIGURED THESE DAYS.
I ATE TOO MUCH MOCHI OVER NEW YEAR'S, OKAY?!!!

OPERATION: DIET

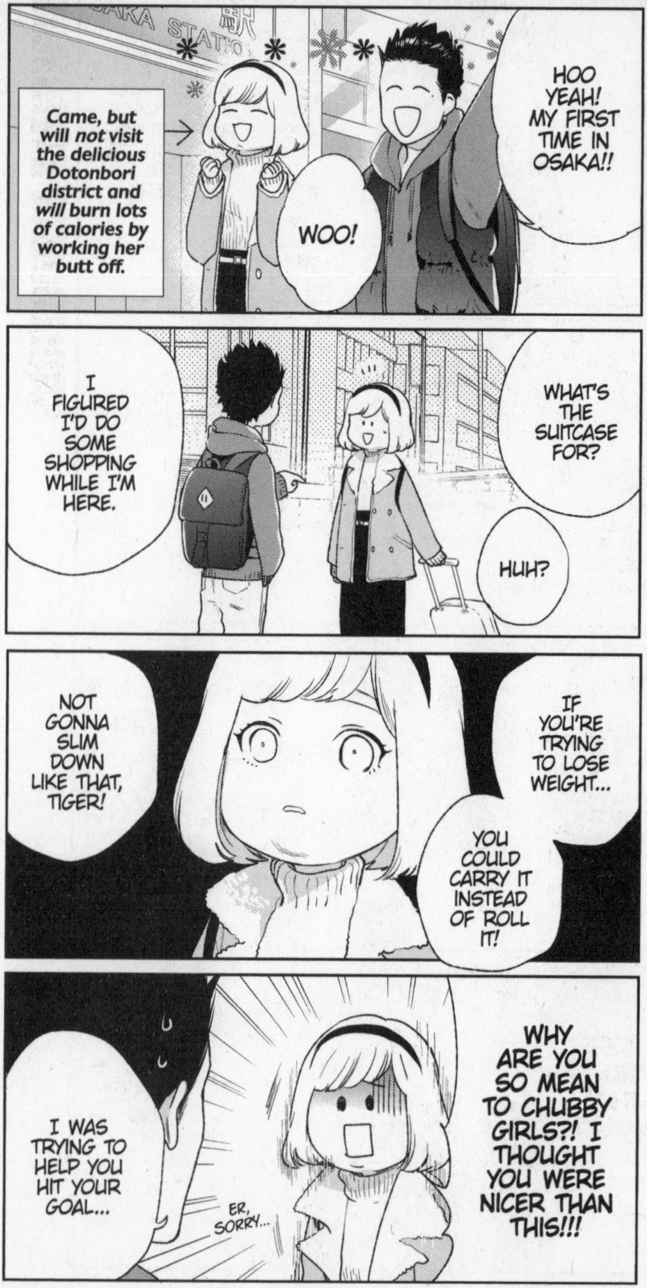
HOO YEAH! MY FIRST TIME IN OSAKA!!
WOO!
Came, but will *not* visit the delicious Dotonbori district and *will* burn lots of calories by working her butt off.
WHAT'S THE SUITCASE FOR?
HUH?
I FIGURED I'D DO SOME SHOPPING WHILE I'M HERE.
IF YOU'RE TRYING TO LOSE WEIGHT...
YOU COULD CARRY IT INSTEAD OF ROLL IT!
NOT GONNA SLIM DOWN LIKE THAT, TIGER!
WHY ARE YOU SO MEAN TO CHUBBY GIRLS?! I THOUGHT YOU WERE NICER THAN THIS!!!
ER, SORRY...
I WAS TRYING TO HELP YOU HIT YOUR GOAL...

SIDEWALK SEDUCTIONS

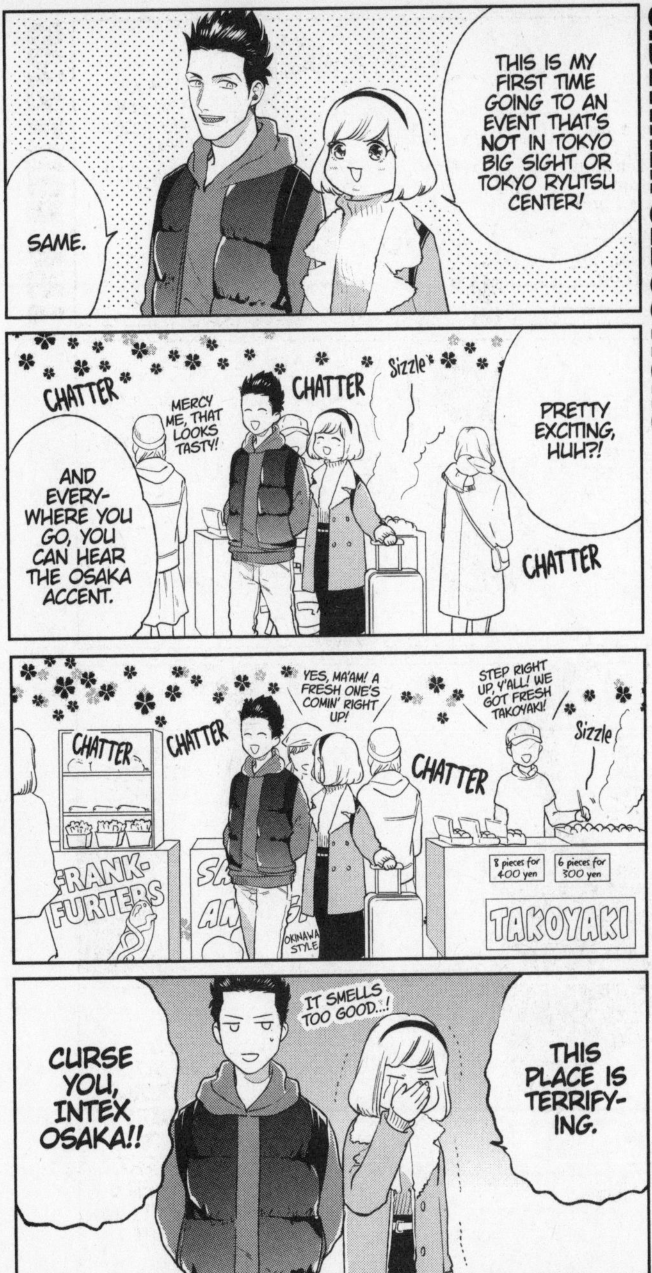
THIS IS MY FIRST TIME GOING TO AN EVENT THAT'S NOT IN TOKYO BIG SIGHT OR TOKYO RYUTSU CENTER!
SAME.
PRETTY EXCITING, HUH?!
CHATTER
Sizzle
CHATTER
MERCY ME, THAT LOOKS TASTY!
CHATTER
AND EVERY-WHERE YOU GO, YOU CAN HEAR THE OSAKA ACCENT.
STEP RIGHT UP, Y'ALL! WE GOT FRESH TAKOYAKI!
Sizzle
6 pieces for 300 yen
8 pieces for 400 yen
TAKOYAKI
CHATTER
YES, MA'AM! A FRESH ONE'S COMIN' RIGHT UP!
CHATTER
CHATTER
FRANK-FURTERS
OKINAWA STYLE
THIS PLACE IS TERRIFY-ING.
IT SMELLS TOO GOOD...!
CURSE YOU, INTEX OSAKA!!

INEXPLICABLY OVERCOME BY EMOTION

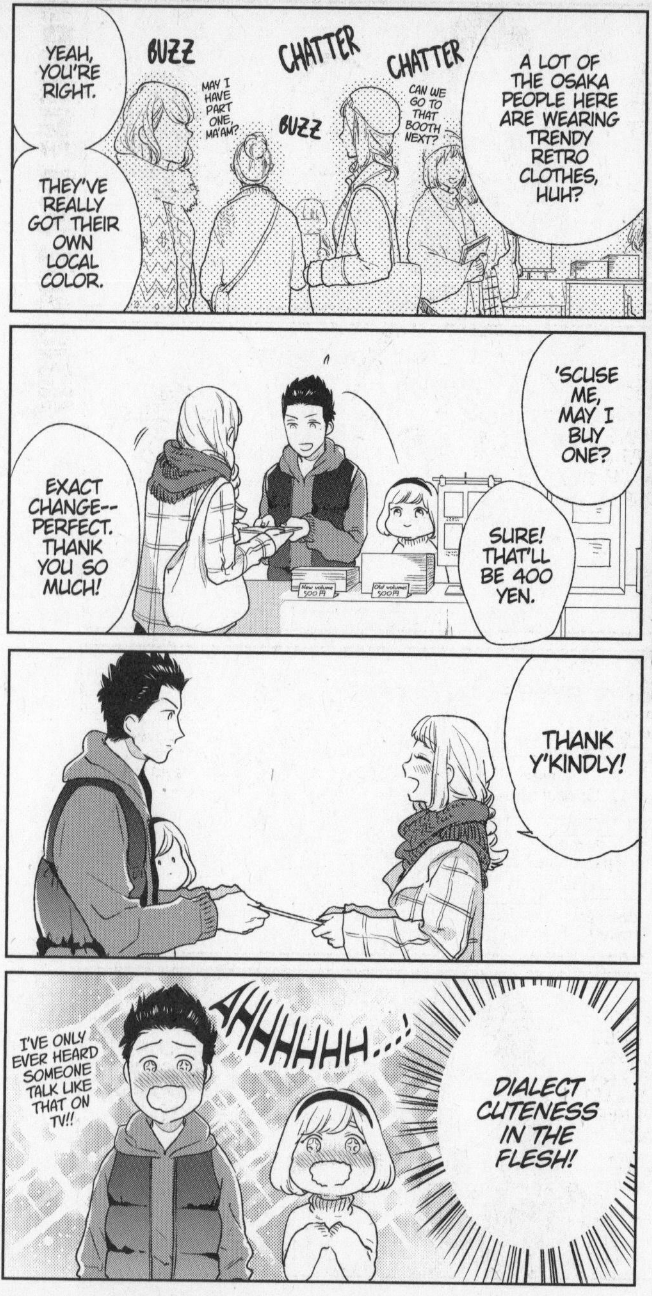
A LOT OF THE OSAKA PEOPLE HERE ARE WEARING TRENDY RETRO CLOTHES, HUH?
CHATTER
CAN WE GO TO THAT BOOTH NEXT?
CHATTER
BUZZ
MAY I HAVE PART ONE, MA'AM?
BUZZ
YEAH, YOU'RE RIGHT.
THEY'VE REALLY GOT THEIR OWN LOCAL COLOR.
'SCUSE ME, MAY I BUY ONE?
SURE! THAT'LL BE 400 YEN.
Old volumes 500円
New volume 500円
EXACT CHANGE--PERFECT. THANK YOU SO MUCH!
THANK Y'KINDLY!
DIALECT CUTENESS IN THE FLESH!
AHHHHHH...!
I'VE ONLY EVER HEARD SOMEONE TALK LIKE THAT ON TV!!

PASTIME FOR THE RICH

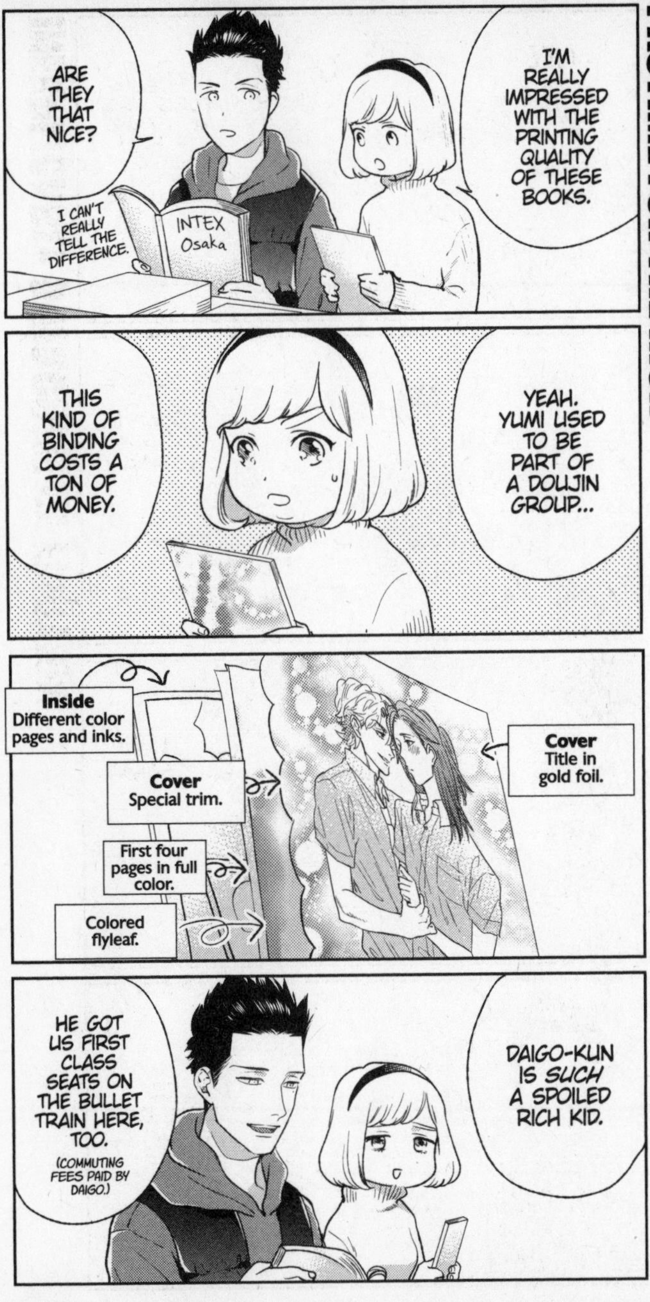
I'M REALLY IMPRESSED WITH THE PRINTING QUALITY OF THESE BOOKS.
ARE THEY THAT NICE?
INTEX Osaka
I CAN'T REALLY TELL THE DIFFERENCE.
YEAH. YUMI USED TO BE PART OF A DOUJIN GROUP...
THIS KIND OF BINDING COSTS A TON OF MONEY.
Cover Title in gold foil.
Inside Different color pages and inks.
Cover Special trim.
First four pages in full color.
Colored flyleaf.
DAIGO-KUN IS SUCH A SPOILED RICH KID.
HE GOT US FIRST CLASS SEATS ON THE BULLET TRAIN HERE, TOO.
(COMMUTING FEES PAID BY DAIGO.)

ONE OF THOSE OTAKU

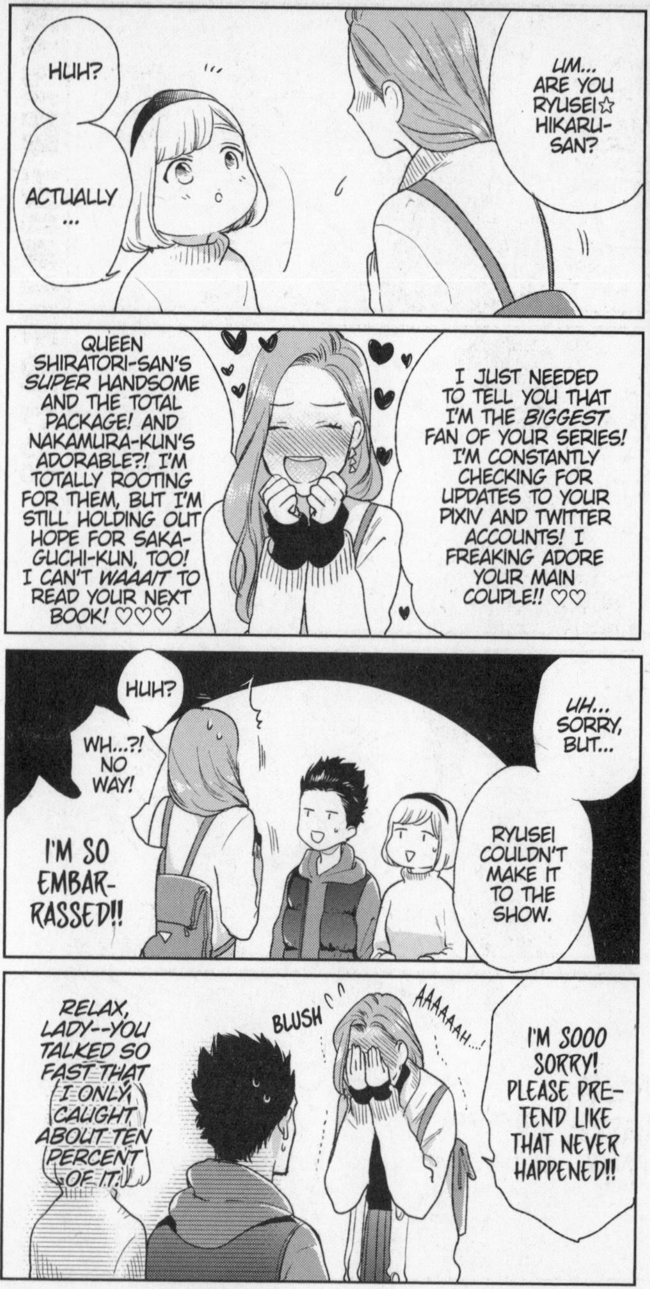
UM... ARE YOU RYUSEI☆ HIKARU-SAN?
HUH?
ACTUALLY ...
I JUST NEEDED TO TELL YOU THAT I'M THE BIGGEST FAN OF YOUR SERIES! I'M CONSTANTLY CHECKING FOR UPDATES TO YOUR PIXIV AND TWITTER ACCOUNTS! I FREAKING ADORE YOUR MAIN COUPLE!! ♡♡
QUEEN SHIRATORI-SAN'S SUPER HANDSOME AND THE TOTAL PACKAGE! AND NAKAMURA-KUN'S ADORABLE?! I'M TOTALLY ROOTING FOR THEM, BUT I'M STILL HOLDING OUT HOPE FOR SAKA-GUCHI-KUN, TOO! I CAN'T WAAAIT TO READ YOUR NEXT BOOK! ♡♡♡
UH... SORRY, BUT...
RYUSEI COULDN'T MAKE IT TO THE SHOW.
HUH?
WH...?! NO WAY!
I'M SO EMBAR-RASSED!!
I'M SOOO SORRY! PLEASE PRE-TEND LIKE THAT NEVER HAPPENED!!
AAAAAAH...!
BLUSH
RELAX, LADY--YOU TALKED SO FAST THAT I ONLY CAUGHT ABOUT TEN PERCENT OF IT.

MY PLAN FROM THE GET-GO

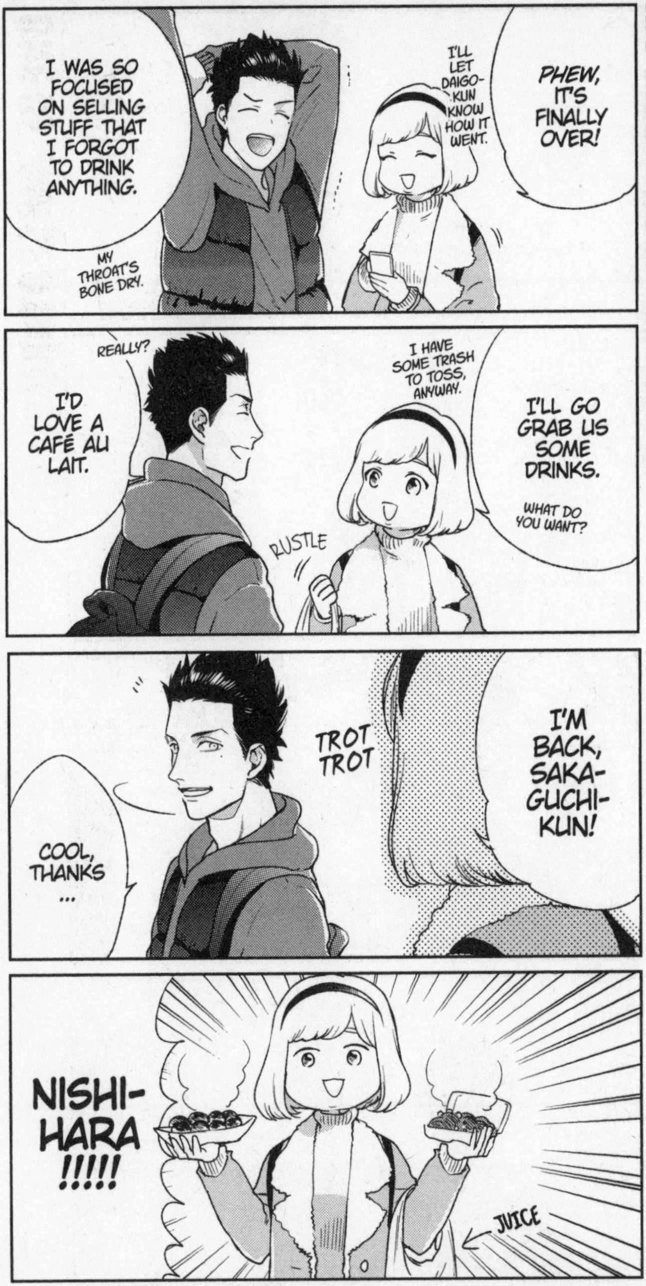
PHEW, IT'S FINALLY OVER!
I'LL LET DAIGO-KUN KNOW HOW IT WENT.
I WAS SO FOCUSED ON SELLING STUFF THAT I FORGOT TO DRINK ANYTHING.
MY THROAT'S BONE DRY.
I'LL GO GRAB US SOME DRINKS.
WHAT DO YOU WANT?
I HAVE SOME TRASH TO TOSS, ANYWAY.
RUSTLE
I'D LOVE A CAFÉ AU LAIT.
REALLY?
I'M BACK, SAKAGUCHI-KUN!
TROT TROT
COOL, THANKS ...
JUICE
NISHI-HARA!!!!!

A TOWN FULL OF MERCHANTS

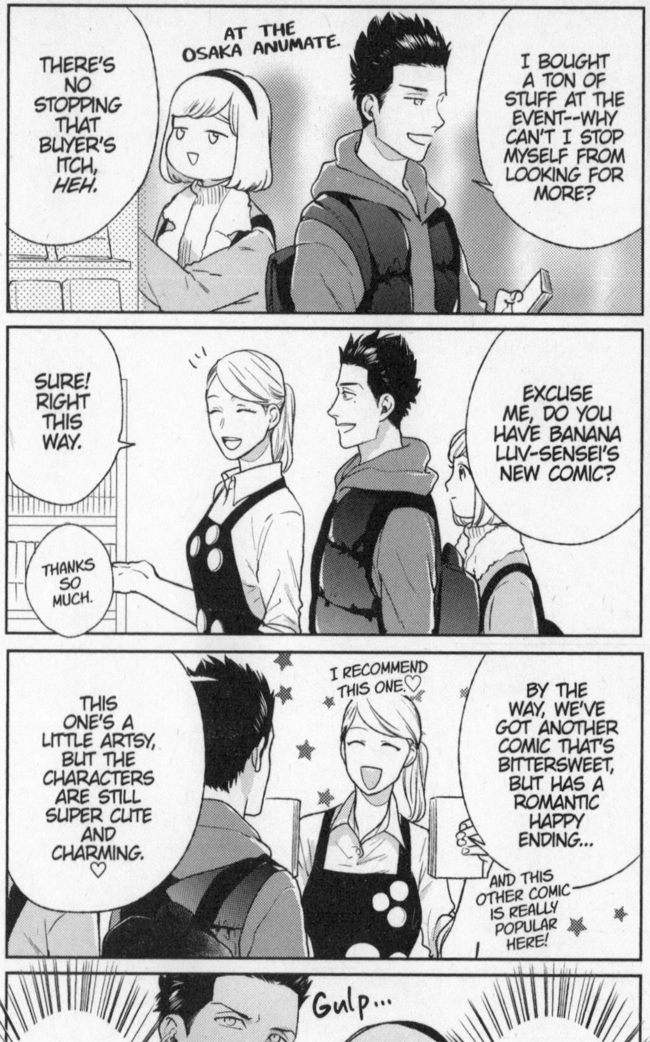
I BOUGHT A TON OF STUFF AT THE EVENT--WHY CAN'T I STOP MYSELF FROM LOOKING FOR MORE?
AT THE OSAKA ANUMATE.
THERE'S NO STOPPING THAT BUYER'S ITCH, HEH.
EXCUSE ME, DO YOU HAVE BANANA LUV-SENSEI'S NEW COMIC?
SURE! RIGHT THIS WAY.
THANKS SO MUCH.
BY THE WAY, WE'VE GOT ANOTHER COMIC THAT'S BITTERSWEET, BUT HAS A ROMANTIC HAPPY ENDING...
I RECOMMEND THIS ONE.♡
THIS ONE'S A LITTLE ARTSY, BUT THE CHARACTERS ARE STILL SUPER CUTE AND CHARMING.♡
AND THIS OTHER COMIC IS REALLY POPULAR HERE!
Gulp...
WHOA... THESE OSAKA CLERKS ARE NEXT-LEVEL.
FOR EVERY ONE REQUEST, SHE'S GOT TEN RECS!

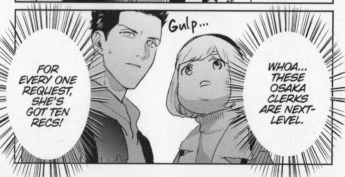

Inside
Different color
pages and inks.

Cover
Special trim.

First four
pages in full
color.

Colored
flyleaf.

Cover
Title in
gold foil.

KFS

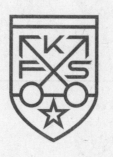

CHAPTER 28
Me, Versitops, and Gender Benders

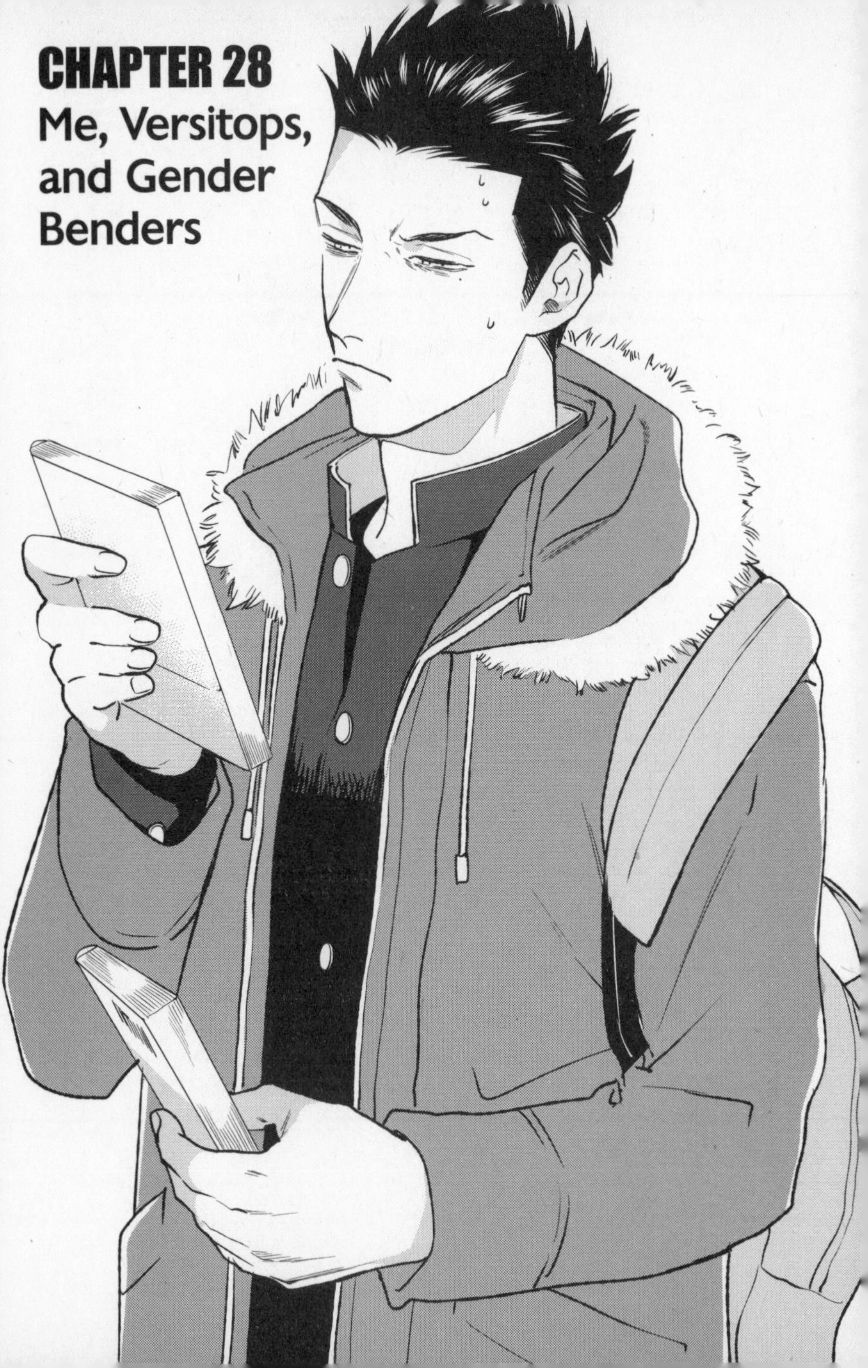

THROWING A CURVEBALL

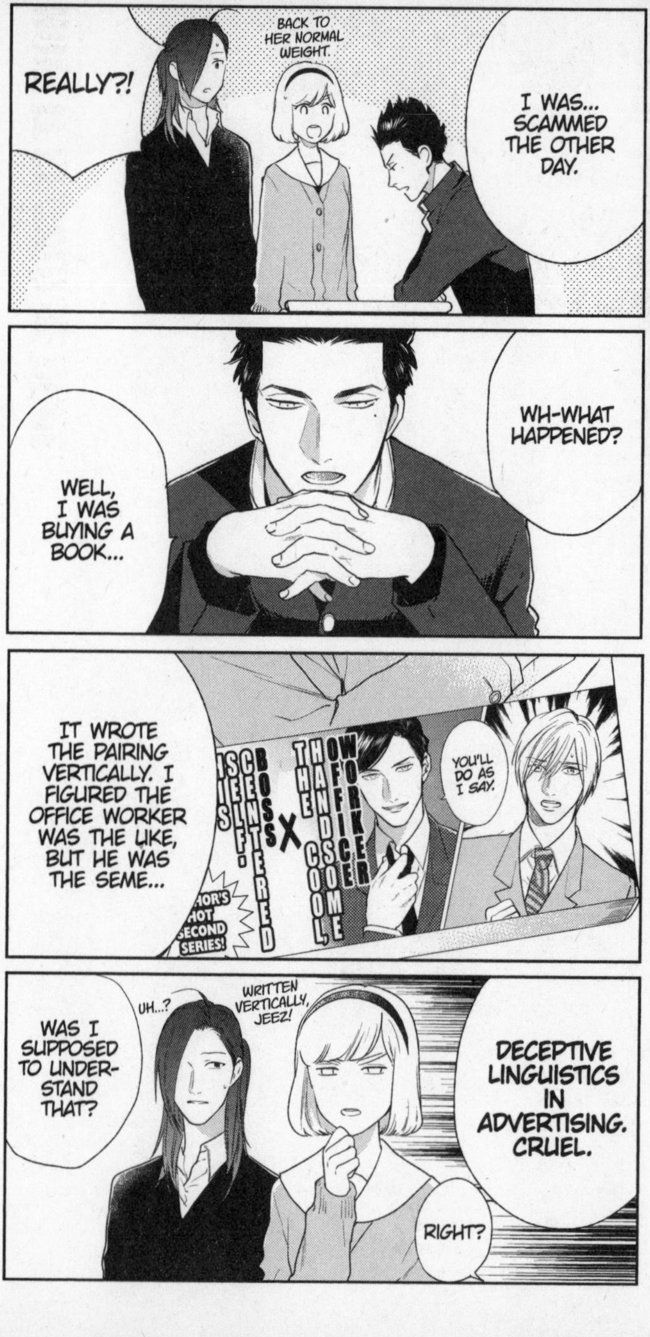
I WAS... SCAMMED THE OTHER DAY.
BACK TO HER NORMAL WEIGHT.
REALLY?!
WH-WHAT HAPPENED?
WELL, I WAS BUYING A BOOK...
YOU'LL DO AS I SAY.
HIS SELF-CENTERED BOSS X THE COOL, HANDSOME OFFICE WORKER
HOR'S HOT SECOND SERIES!
IT WROTE THE PAIRING VERTICALLY. I FIGURED THE OFFICE WORKER WAS THE UKE, BUT HE WAS THE SEME...
DECEPTIVE LINGUISTICS IN ADVERTISING. CRUEL.
RIGHT?
WRITTEN VERTICALLY, JEEZ!
UH...?
WAS I SUPPOSED TO UNDER-STAND THAT?

HOW IT SHOULD BE DONE

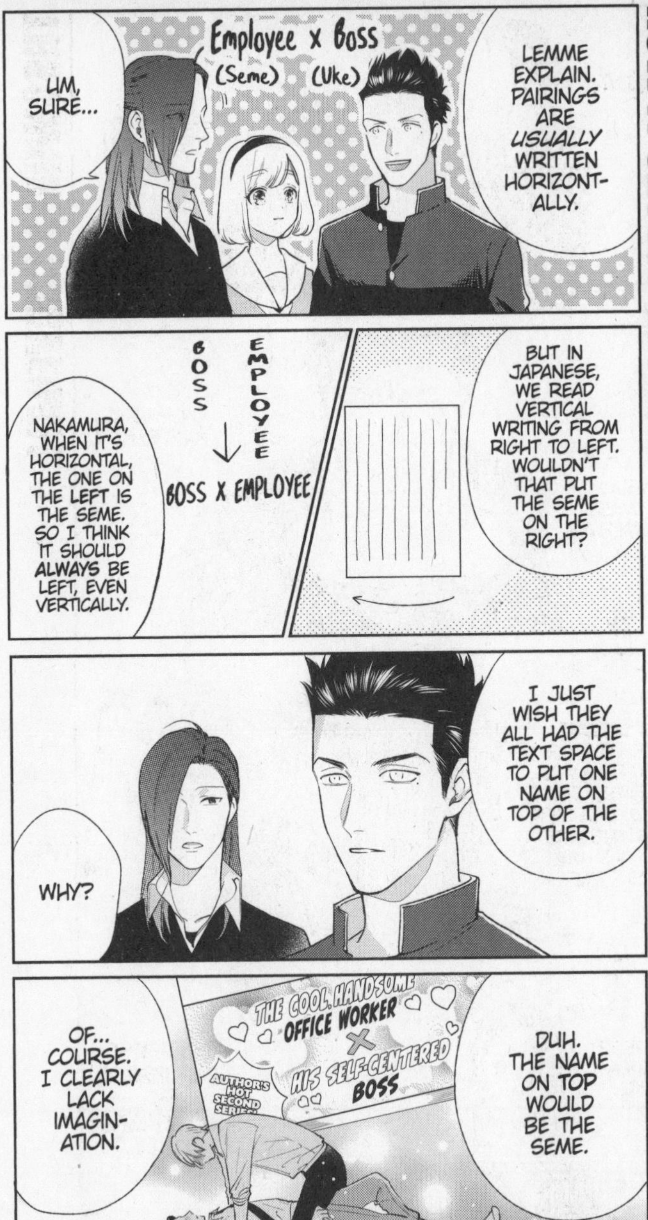
LEMME EXPLAIN. PAIRINGS ARE *USUALLY* WRITTEN HORIZONT-ALLY.
Employee x Boss
(Seme) (Uke)
UM, SURE...
BUT IN JAPANESE, WE READ VERTICAL WRITING FROM RIGHT TO LEFT. WOULDN'T THAT PUT THE SEME ON THE RIGHT?
EMPLOYEE
BOSS
BOSS X EMPLOYEE
NAKAMURA, WHEN IT'S HORIZONTAL, THE ONE ON THE LEFT IS THE SEME. SO I THINK IT SHOULD ALWAYS BE LEFT, EVEN VERTICALLY.
I JUST WISH THEY ALL HAD THE TEXT SPACE TO PUT ONE NAME ON TOP OF THE OTHER.
WHY?
DUH. THE NAME ON TOP WOULD BE THE SEME.
THE COOL, HANDSOME OFFICE WORKER
×
HIS SELF-CENTERED BOSS
AUTHOR'S HOT SECOND SERIES
OF... COURSE. I CLEARLY LACK IMAGIN-ATION.

THE GAMBLE OF BUYING A BOOK FOR ITS COVER

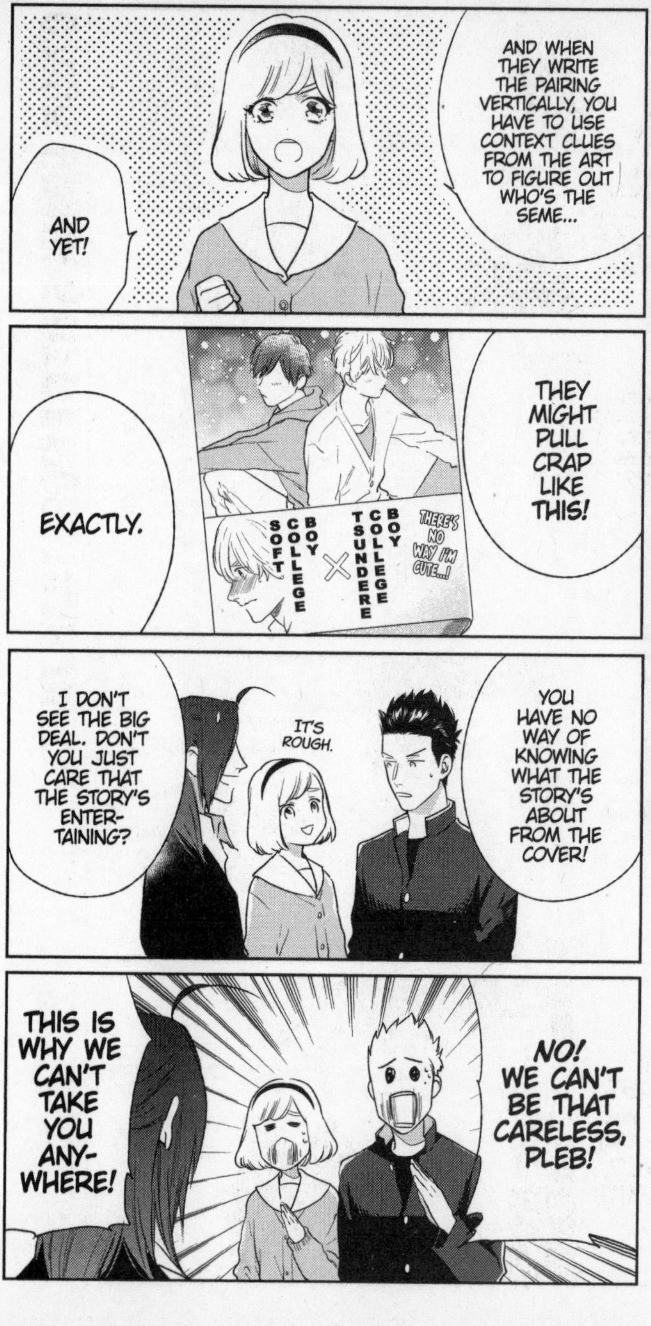
AND WHEN THEY WRITE THE PAIRING VERTICALLY, YOU HAVE TO USE CONTEXT CLUES FROM THE ART TO FIGURE OUT WHO'S THE SEME...
AND YET!
THEY MIGHT PULL CRAP LIKE THIS!
THERE'S NO WAY I'M CUTE...!
TSUNDERE COLLEGE BOY × SOFT COLLEGE BOY
EXACTLY.
YOU HAVE NO WAY OF KNOWING WHAT THE STORY'S ABOUT FROM THE COVER!
IT'S ROUGH.
I DON'T SEE THE BIG DEAL. DON'T YOU JUST CARE THAT THE STORY'S ENTER-TAINING?
NO! WE CAN'T BE THAT CARELESS, PLEB!
THIS IS WHY WE CAN'T TAKE YOU ANY-WHERE!

C'MON, GIMME A LITTLE MORE THAN THAT

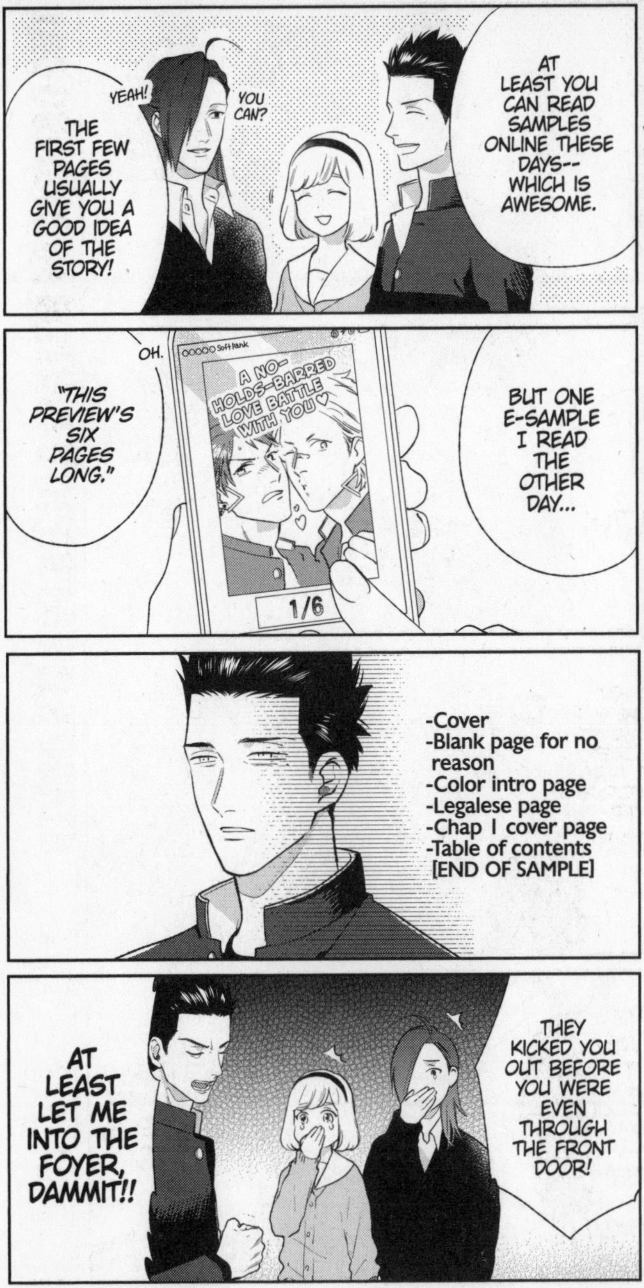
AT LEAST YOU CAN READ SAMPLES ONLINE THESE DAYS-- WHICH IS AWESOME.
YOU CAN?
YEAH!
THE FIRST FEW PAGES USUALLY GIVE YOU A GOOD IDEA OF THE STORY!
BUT ONE E-SAMPLE I READ THE OTHER DAY...
A NO-HOLDS-BARRED LOVE BATTLE WITH YOU♥
1/6
OH.
"THIS PREVIEW'S SIX PAGES LONG."
-Cover
-Blank page for no reason
-Color intro page
-Legalese page
-Chap 1 cover page
-Table of contents
[END OF SAMPLE]
THEY KICKED YOU OUT BEFORE YOU WERE EVEN THROUGH THE FRONT DOOR!
AT LEAST LET ME INTO THE FOYER, DAMMIT!!

THAT PERFECT FIT

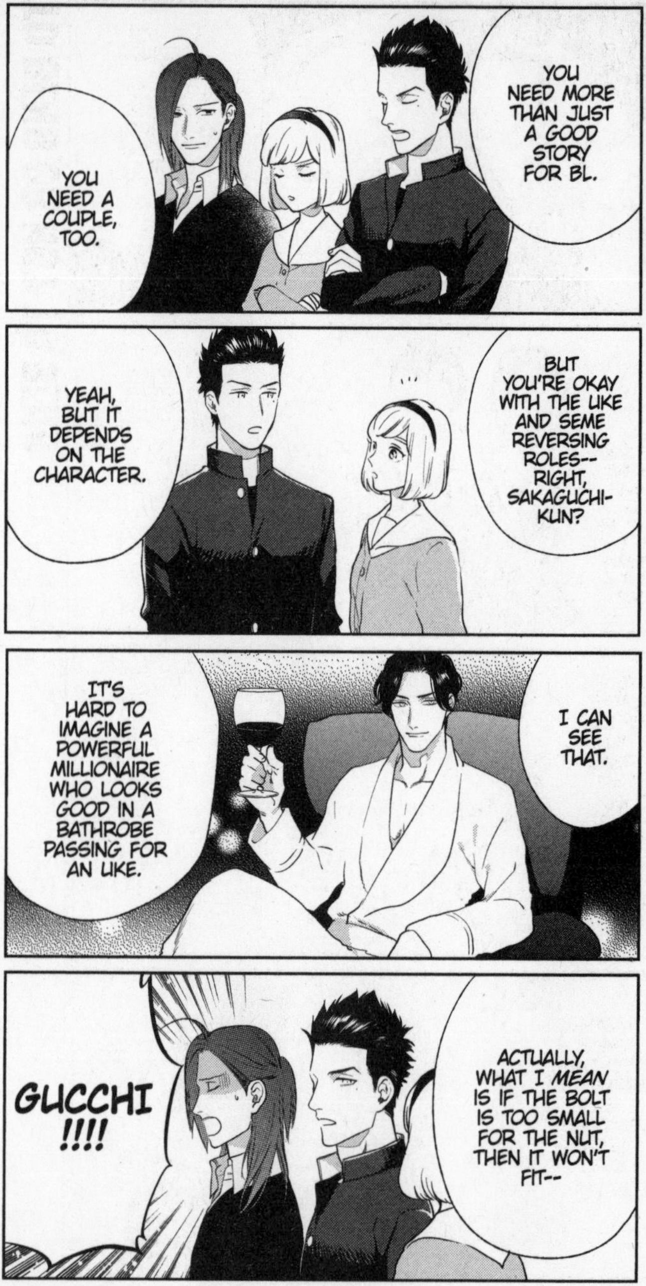
YOU NEED MORE THAN JUST A GOOD STORY FOR BL.
YOU NEED A COUPLE, TOO.
BUT YOU'RE OKAY WITH THE UKE AND SEME REVERSING ROLES--RIGHT, SAKAGUCHI-KUN?
YEAH, BUT IT DEPENDS ON THE CHARACTER.
I CAN SEE THAT.
IT'S HARD TO IMAGINE A POWERFUL MILLIONAIRE WHO LOOKS GOOD IN A BATHROBE PASSING FOR AN UKE.
ACTUALLY, WHAT I *MEAN* IS IF THE BOLT IS TOO SMALL FOR THE NUT, THEN IT WON'T FIT--
GUCCHI !!!!

TO BEND OR NOT TO BEND

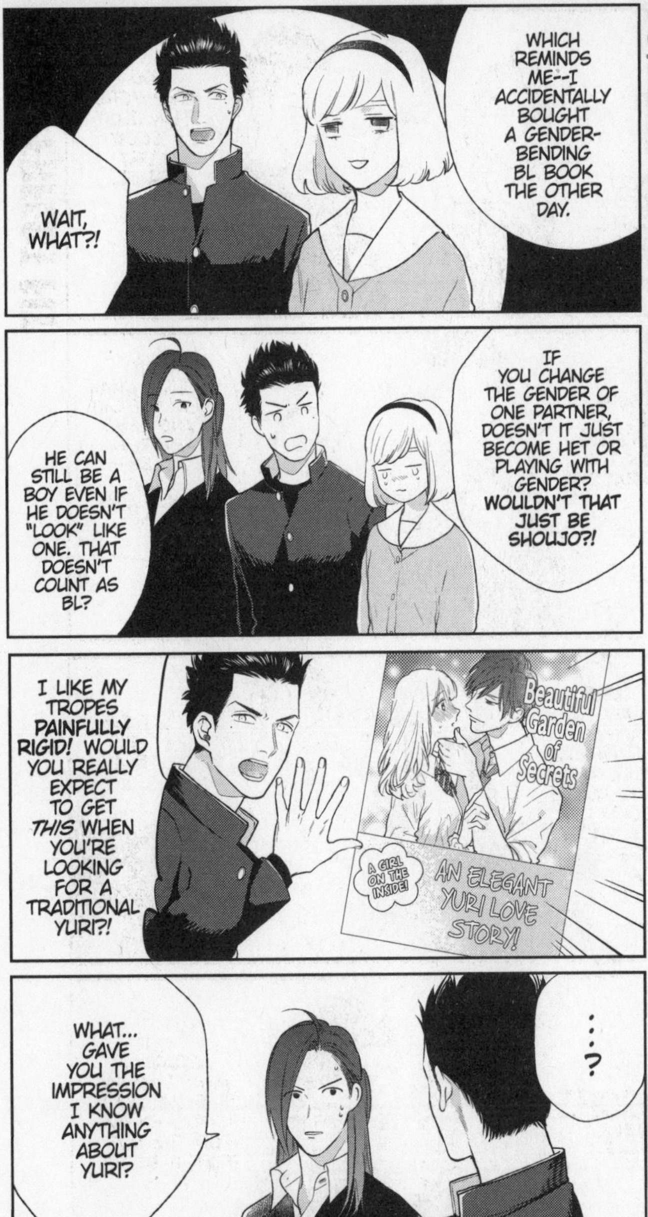
WHICH REMINDS ME--I ACCIDENTALLY BOUGHT A GENDER-BENDING BL BOOK THE OTHER DAY.
WAIT, WHAT?!
IF YOU CHANGE THE GENDER OF ONE PARTNER, DOESN'T IT JUST BECOME HET OR PLAYING WITH GENDER? WOULDN'T THAT JUST BE SHOUJO?!
HE CAN STILL BE A BOY EVEN IF HE DOESN'T "LOOK" LIKE ONE. THAT DOESN'T COUNT AS BL?
Beautiful Garden of Secrets
AN ELEGANT YURI LOVE STORY!
A GIRL ON THE INSIDE!
I LIKE MY TROPES PAINFULLY RIGID! WOULD YOU REALLY EXPECT TO GET *THIS* WHEN YOU'RE LOOKING FOR A TRADITIONAL YURI?!
...?
WHAT... GAVE YOU THE IMPRESSION I KNOW ANYTHING ABOUT YURI?

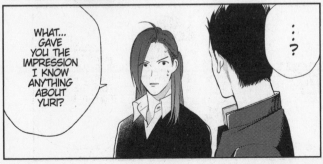

ADDICT

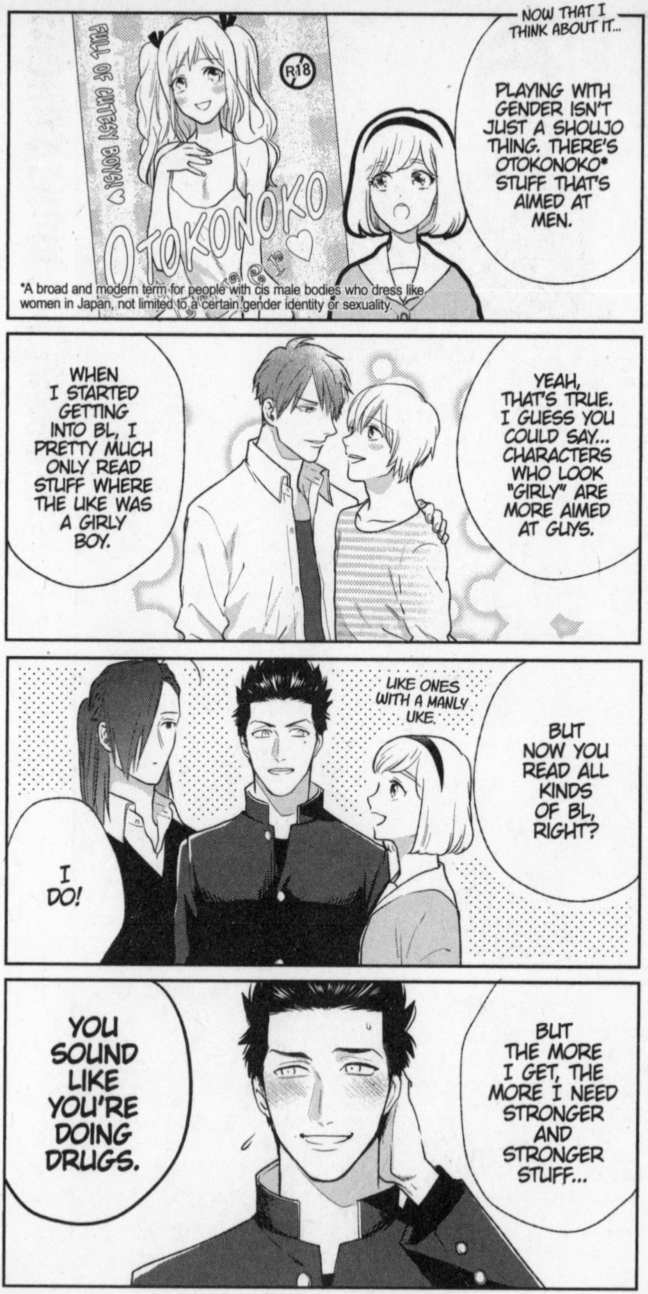
NOW THAT I THINK ABOUT IT...
PLAYING WITH GENDER ISN'T JUST A SHOUJO THING. THERE'S OTOKONOKO* STUFF THAT'S AIMED AT MEN.
R18
FULL OF CUTESY BOYS!♥
OTOKONOKO
*A broad and modern term for people with cis male bodies who dress like women in Japan, not limited to a certain gender identity or sexuality.
YEAH, THAT'S TRUE. I GUESS YOU COULD SAY... CHARACTERS WHO LOOK "GIRLY" ARE MORE AIMED AT GUYS.
WHEN I STARTED GETTING INTO BL, I PRETTY MUCH ONLY READ STUFF WHERE THE UKE WAS A GIRLY BOY.
BUT NOW YOU READ ALL KINDS OF BL, RIGHT?
I DO!
LIKE ONES WITH A MANLY UKE.
BUT THE MORE I GET, THE MORE I NEED STRONGER AND STRONGER STUFF...
YOU SOUND LIKE YOU'RE DOING DRUGS.

WORDS FROM THE IGNORANT

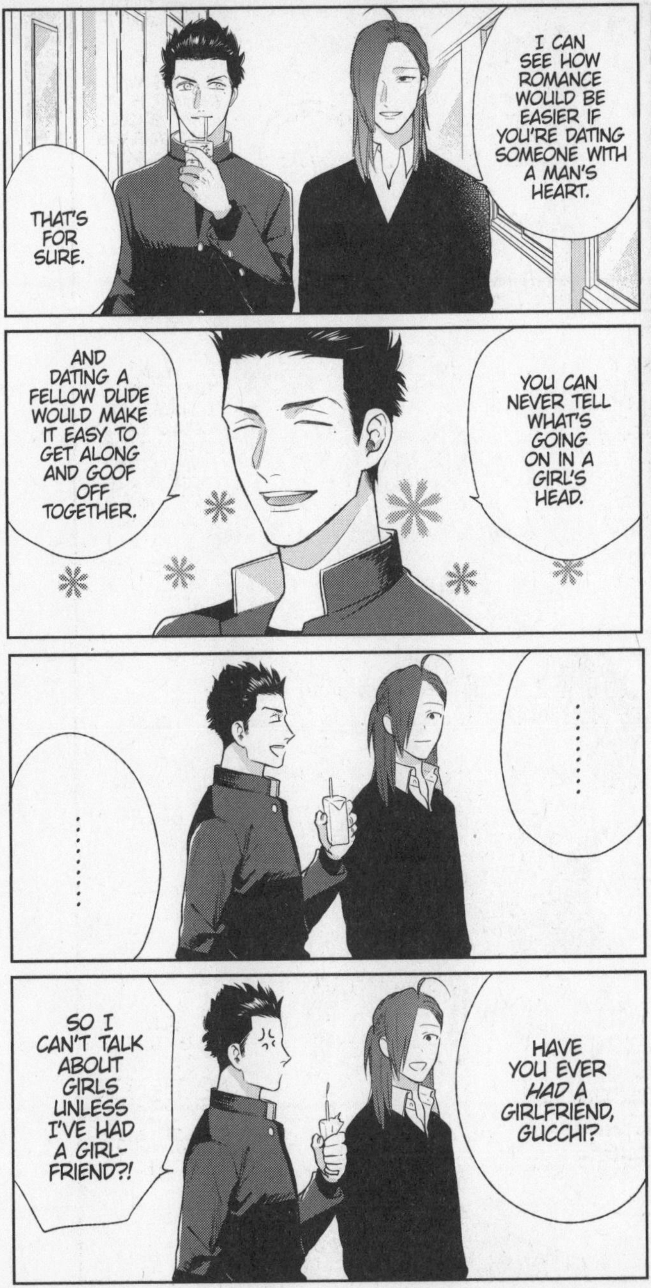
I CAN SEE HOW ROMANCE WOULD BE EASIER IF YOU'RE DATING SOMEONE WITH A MAN'S HEART.
THAT'S FOR SURE.
YOU CAN NEVER TELL WHAT'S GOING ON IN A GIRL'S HEAD.
AND DATING A FELLOW DUDE WOULD MAKE IT EASY TO GET ALONG AND GOOF OFF TOGETHER.
......
......
HAVE YOU EVER *HAD* A GIRLFRIEND, GUCCHI?
SO I CAN'T TALK ABOUT GIRLS UNLESS I'VE HAD A GIRL-FRIEND?!

DATING

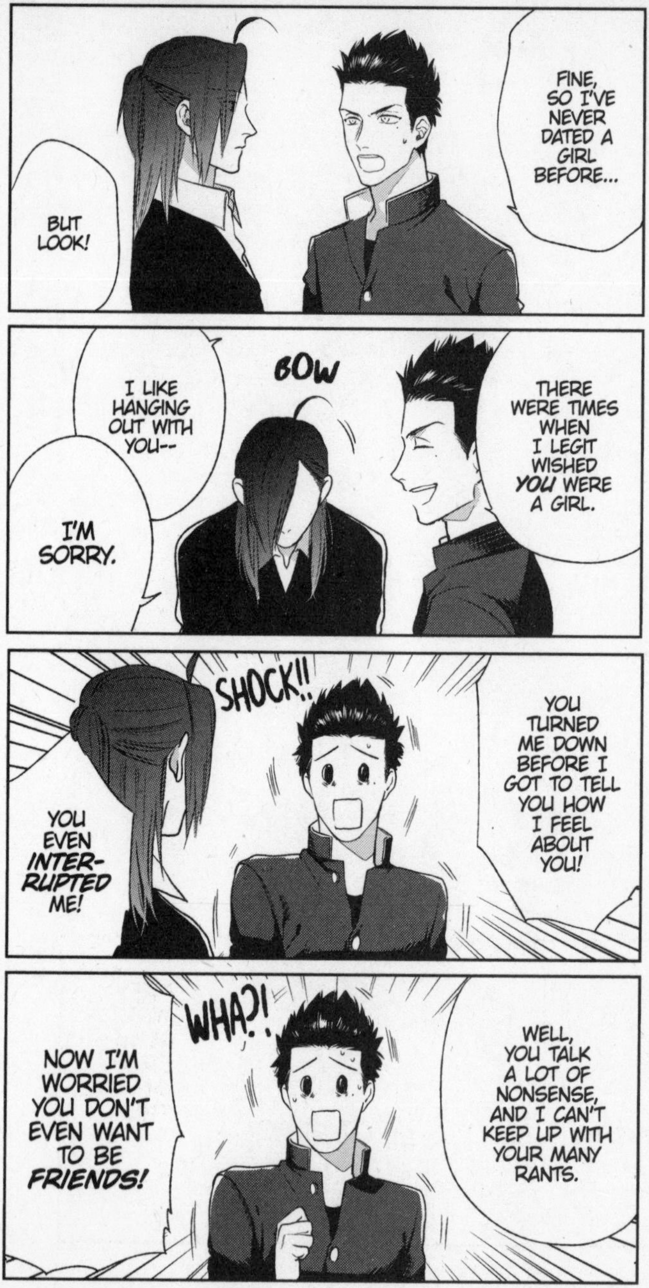
FINE, SO I'VE NEVER DATED A GIRL BEFORE...
BUT LOOK!
THERE WERE TIMES WHEN I LEGIT WISHED *YOU* WERE A GIRL.
BOW
I LIKE HANGING OUT WITH YOU--
I'M SORRY.
YOU TURNED ME DOWN BEFORE I GOT TO TELL YOU HOW I FEEL ABOUT YOU!
SHOCK!!
YOU EVEN *INTER-RUPTED* ME!
WELL, YOU TALK A LOT OF NONSENSE, AND I CAN'T KEEP UP WITH YOUR MANY RANTS.
WHA?!
NOW I'M WORRIED YOU DON'T EVEN WANT TO BE *FRIENDS!*

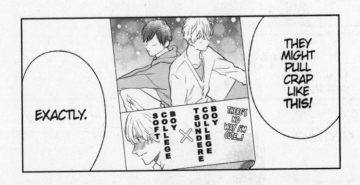

THEY MIGHT PULL CRAP LIKE THIS!
THERE'S NO WAY I'M CUTE...!
SOFT COLLEGE BOY × TSUNDERE COLLEGE BOY
EXACTLY.

KFS

CHAPTER 29
Operation White Day!

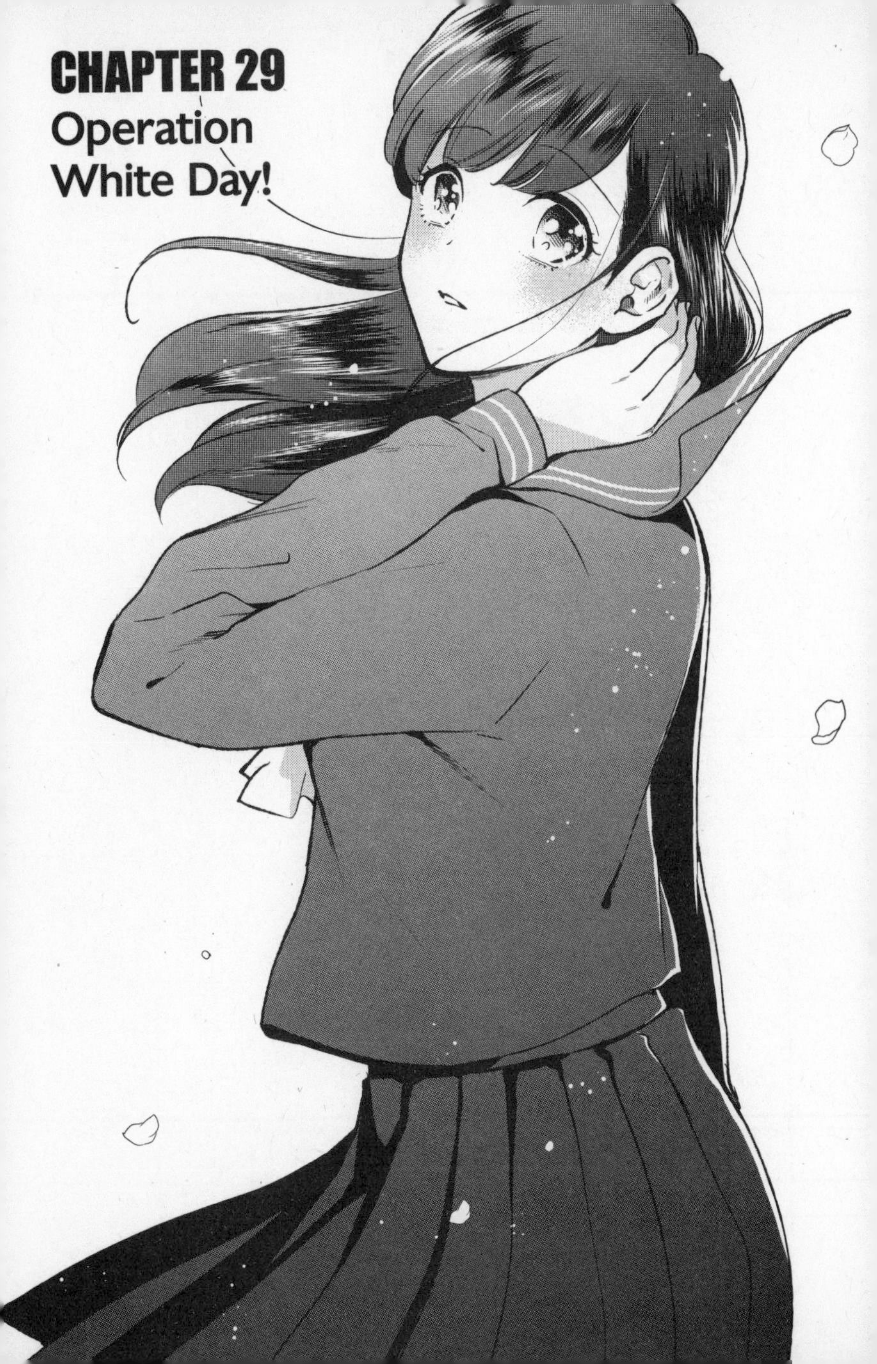

DON'T RUB IT IN

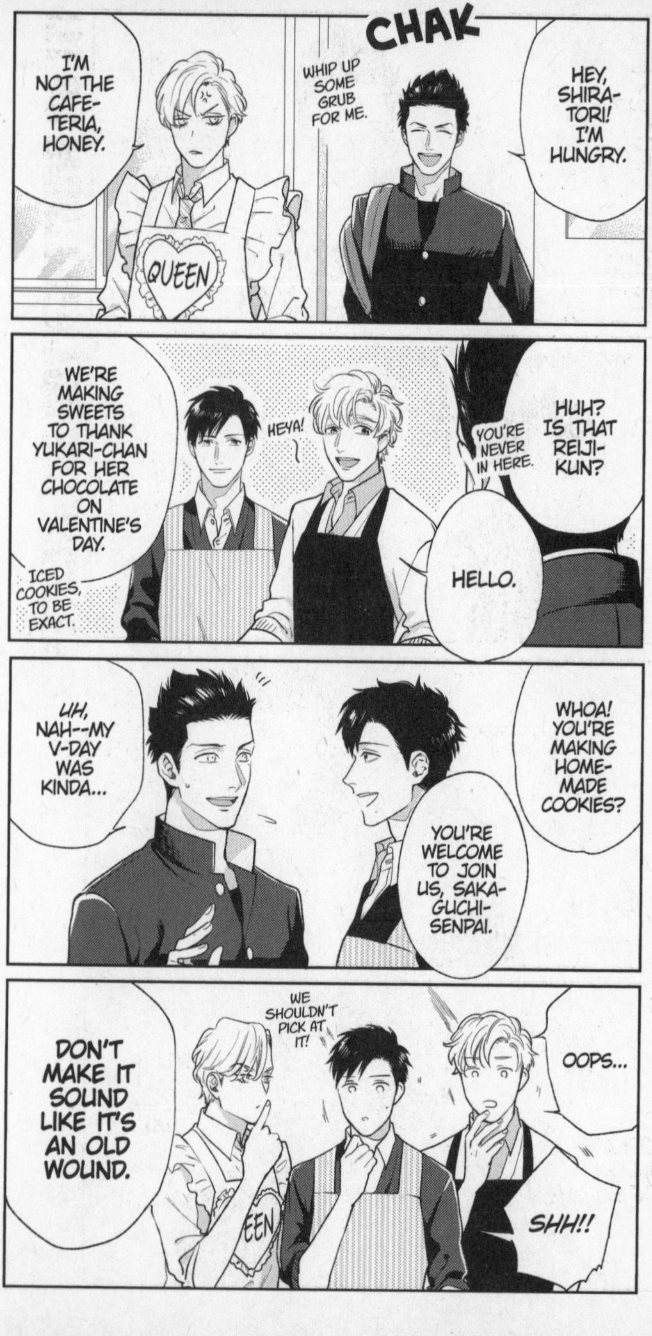
CHAK
HEY, SHIRATORI! I'M HUNGRY.
WHIP UP SOME GRUB FOR ME.
I'M NOT THE CAFETERIA, HONEY.
QUEEN
HUH? IS THAT REIJI-KUN?
YOU'RE NEVER IN HERE.
HELLO.
HEYA!
WE'RE MAKING SWEETS TO THANK YUKARI-CHAN FOR HER CHOCOLATE ON VALENTINE'S DAY.
ICED COOKIES, TO BE EXACT.
WHOA! YOU'RE MAKING HOMEMADE COOKIES?
YOU'RE WELCOME TO JOIN US, SAKAGUCHI-SENPAI.
UH, NAH--MY V-DAY WAS KINDA...
OOPS...
SHH!!
WE SHOULDN'T PICK AT IT!
DON'T MAKE IT SOUND LIKE IT'S AN OLD WOUND.

I'LL DO WHATEVER YOU SAY, MASTER♡

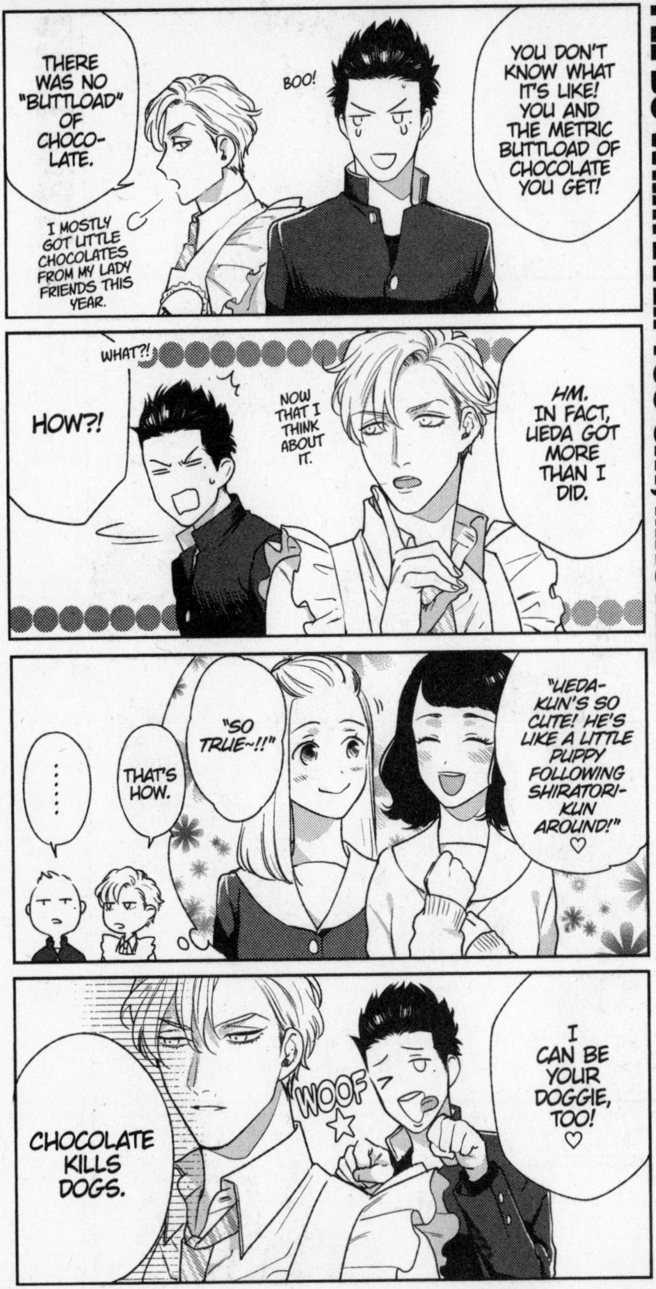
YOU DON'T KNOW WHAT IT'S LIKE! YOU AND THE METRIC BUTTLOAD OF CHOCOLATE YOU GET!
BOO!
THERE WAS NO "BUTTLOAD" OF CHOCO-LATE.
I MOSTLY GOT LITTLE CHOCOLATES FROM MY LADY FRIENDS THIS YEAR.
HM. IN FACT, UEDA GOT MORE THAN I DID.
NOW THAT I THINK ABOUT IT.
WHAT?!
HOW?!
"UEDA-KUN'S SO CUTE! HE'S LIKE A LITTLE PUPPY FOLLOWING SHIRATORI-KUN AROUND!" ♡
"SO TRUE~!!"
THAT'S HOW.
......
I CAN BE YOUR DOGGIE, TOO! ♡
WOOF ☆
CHOCOLATE KILLS DOGS.

A DIFFERENCE IN QUALITY

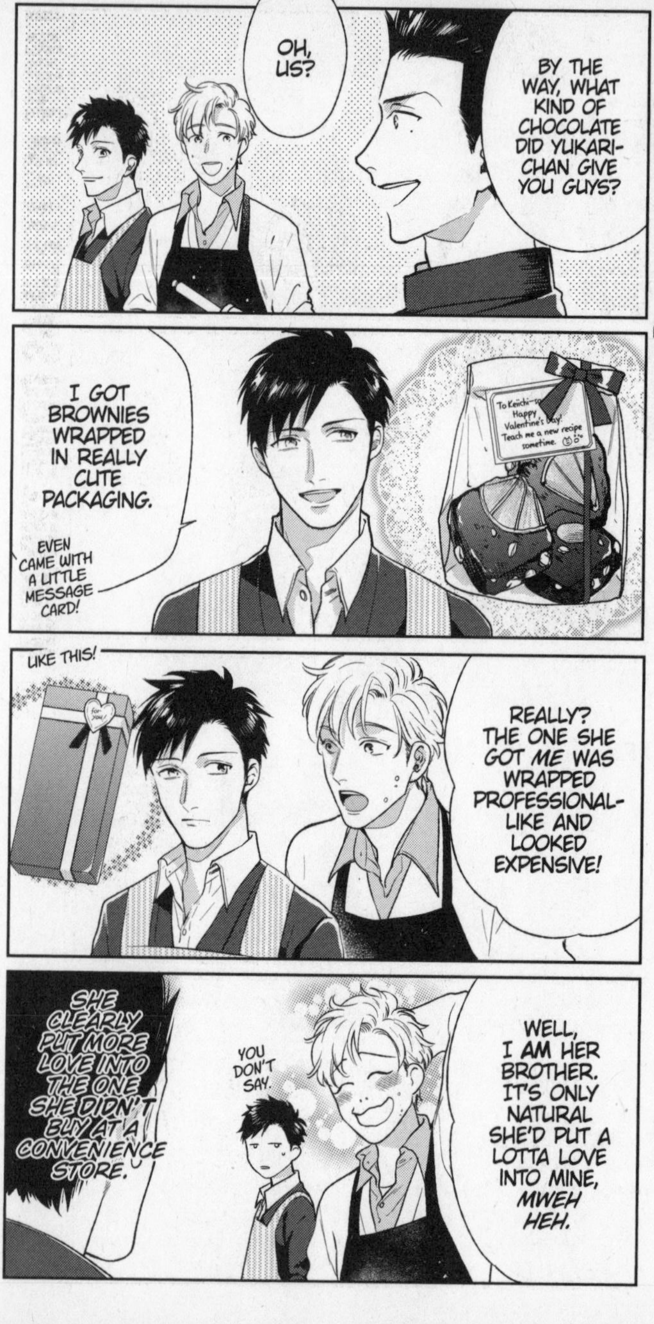
BY THE WAY, WHAT KIND OF CHOCOLATE DID YUKARI-CHAN GIVE YOU GUYS?
OH, US?
I GOT BROWNIES WRAPPED IN REALLY CUTE PACKAGING.
EVEN CAME WITH A LITTLE MESSAGE CARD!
To Keiichi-sa
Happy Valentine's Day!
Teach me a new recipe sometime.
REALLY? THE ONE SHE GOT ME WAS WRAPPED PROFESSIONAL-LIKE AND LOOKED EXPENSIVE!
LIKE THIS!
for you
WELL, I AM HER BROTHER. IT'S ONLY NATURAL SHE'D PUT A LOTTA LOVE INTO MINE, MWEH HEH.
YOU DON'T SAY.
SHE CLEARLY PUT MORE LOVE INTO THE ONE SHE DIDN'T BUY AT A CONVENIENCE STORE.

I HOPE MY FEELINGS COME THROUGH

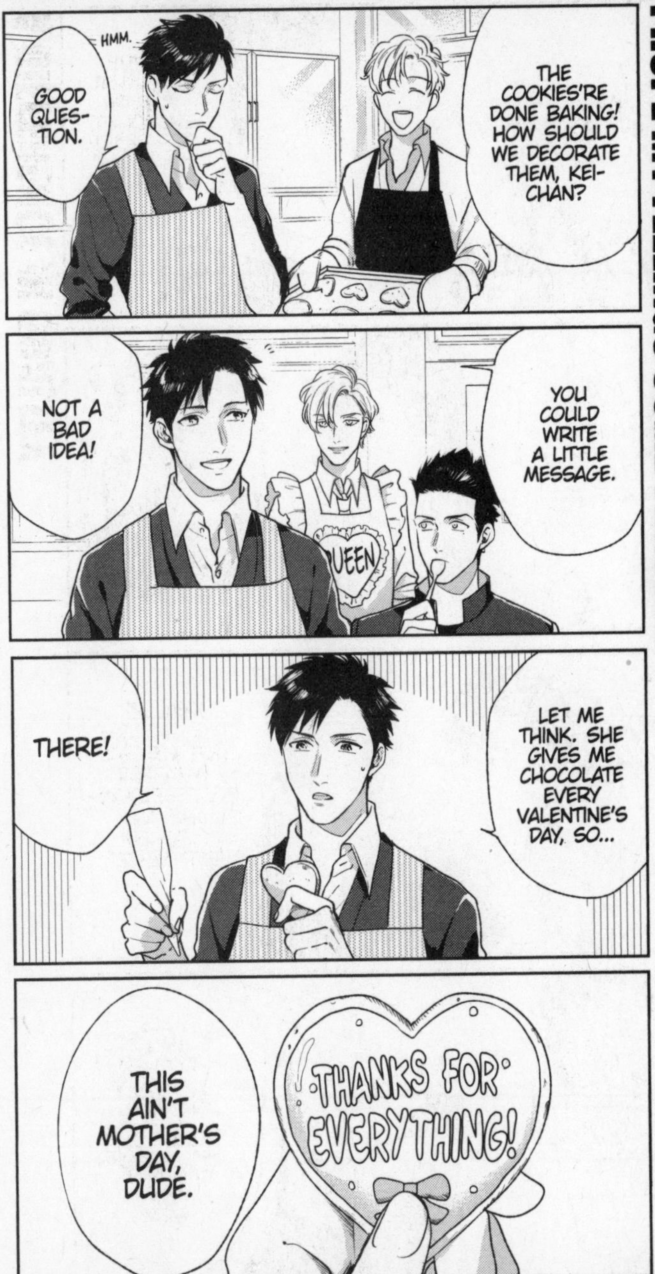
THE COOKIES'RE DONE BAKING! HOW SHOULD WE DECORATE THEM, KEI-CHAN?
HMM.
GOOD QUES-TION.
YOU COULD WRITE A LITTLE MESSAGE.
NOT A BAD IDEA!
QUEEN
LET ME THINK. SHE GIVES ME CHOCOLATE EVERY VALENTINE'S DAY, SO...
THERE!
THANKS FOR EVERYTHING!
THIS AIN'T MOTHER'S DAY, DUDE.

MY BROTHER IS MY ROMANTIC RIVAL!

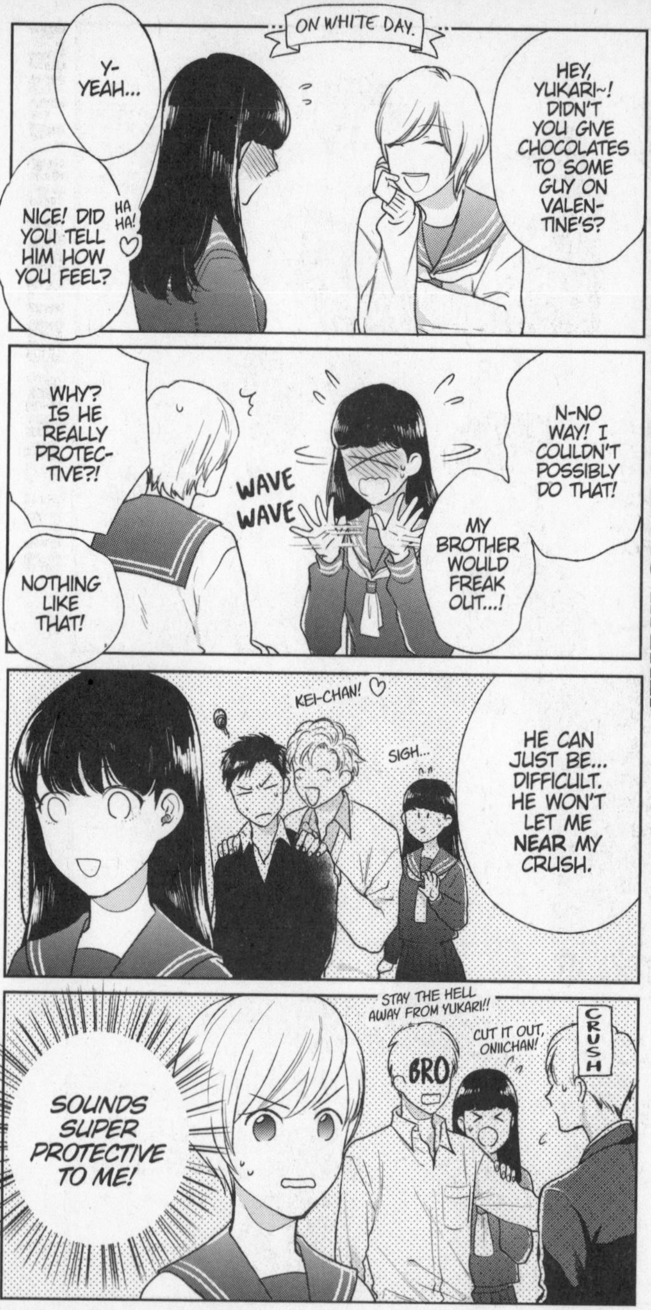
ON WHITE DAY.
HEY, YUKARI~! DIDN'T YOU GIVE CHOCOLATES TO SOME GUY ON VALENTINE'S?
Y-YEAH...
HA HA! ♡
NICE! DID YOU TELL HIM HOW YOU FEEL?
N-NO WAY! I COULDN'T POSSIBLY DO THAT!
MY BROTHER WOULD FREAK OUT...!
WAVE WAVE
WHY? IS HE REALLY PROTEC-TIVE?!
NOTHING LIKE THAT!
HE CAN JUST BE... DIFFICULT. HE WON'T LET ME NEAR MY CRUSH.
SIGH...
KEI-CHAN! ♡
CRUSH
CUT IT OUT, ONIICHAN!
STAY THE HELL AWAY FROM YUKARI!!
BRO
SOUNDS SUPER PROTECTIVE TO ME!

HAPPY, NO MATTER WHAT IT IS

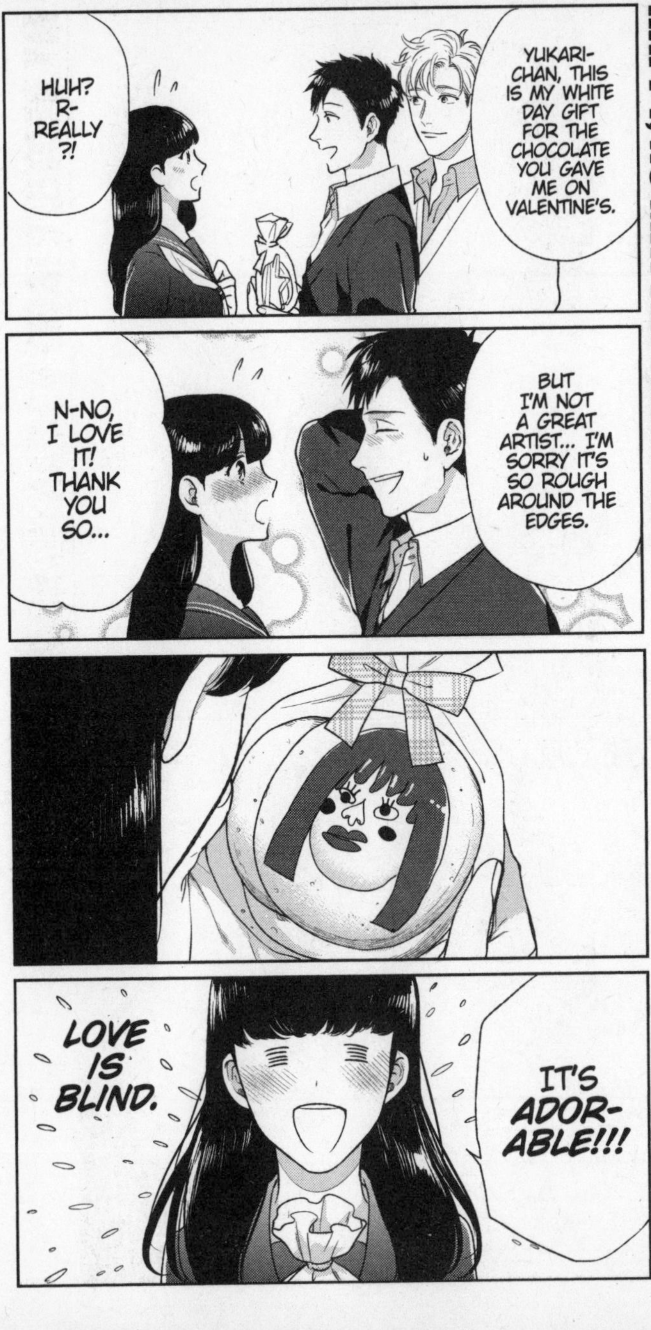
YUKARI-CHAN, THIS IS MY WHITE DAY GIFT FOR THE CHOCOLATE YOU GAVE ME ON VALENTINE'S.
HUH? R-REALLY?!
BUT I'M NOT A GREAT ARTIST... I'M SORRY IT'S SO ROUGH AROUND THE EDGES.
N-NO, I LOVE IT! THANK YOU SO...
IT'S ADORABLE!!!
LOVE IS BLIND.

MIND YOUR SPACE

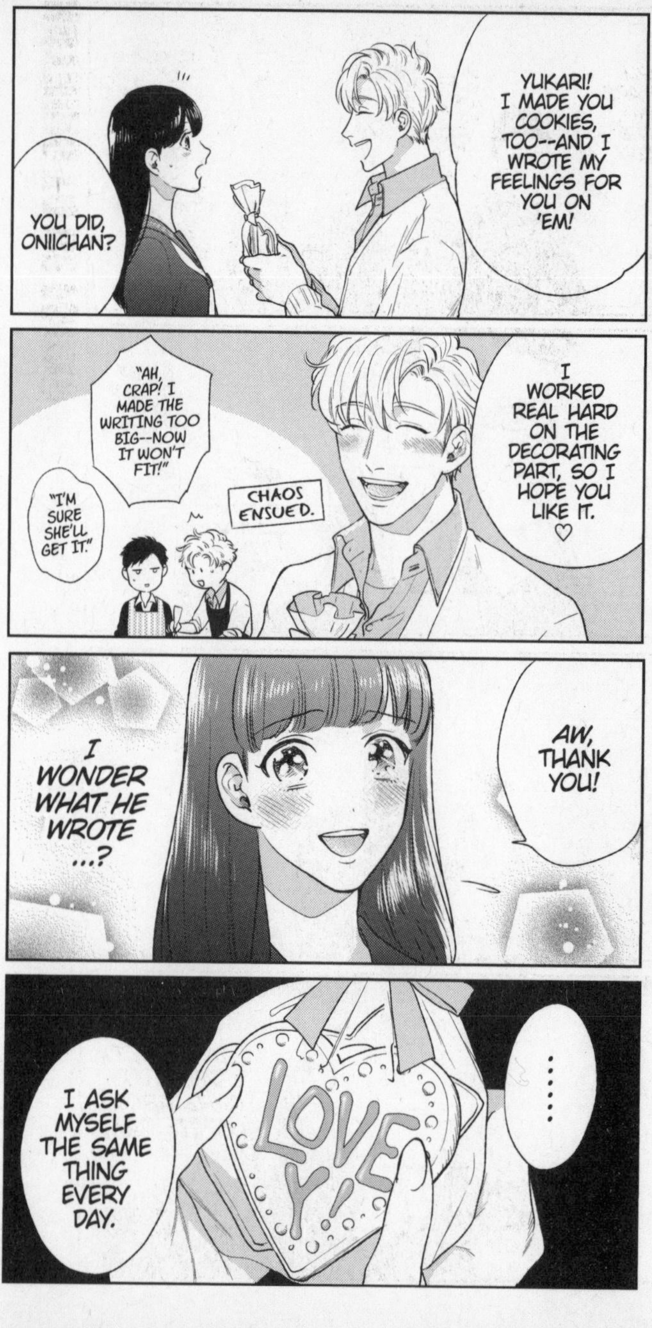

YUKARI! I MADE YOU COOKIES, TOO--AND I WROTE MY FEELINGS FOR YOU ON 'EM!
YOU DID, ONIICHAN?
I WORKED REAL HARD ON THE DECORATING PART, SO I HOPE YOU LIKE IT. ♡
CHAOS ENSUED.
"AH, CRAP! I MADE THE WRITING TOO BIG--NOW IT WON'T FIT!"
"I'M SURE SHE'LL GET IT."
AW, THANK YOU!
I WONDER WHAT HE WROTE ...?
......
LOVE Y!
I ASK MYSELF THE SAME THING EVERY DAY.

NOTHING TO BE FOUND

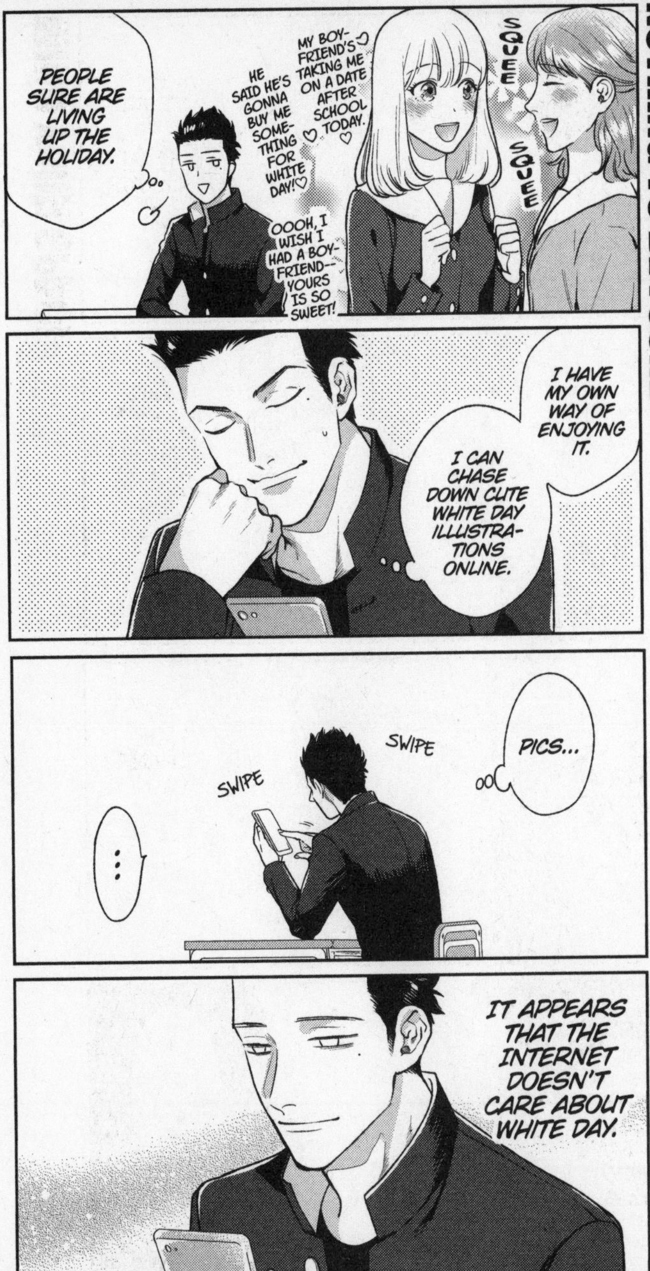
SQUEE
SQUEE
MY BOY-FRIEND'S TAKING ME ON A DATE AFTER SCHOOL TODAY.
HE SAID HE'S GONNA BUY ME SOME-THING FOR WHITE DAY!
OOOH, I WISH I HAD A BOY-FRIEND-- YOURS IS SO SWEET!
PEOPLE SURE ARE LIVING UP THE HOLIDAY.
I HAVE MY OWN WAY OF ENJOYING IT.
I CAN CHASE DOWN CUTE WHITE DAY ILLUSTRA-TIONS ONLINE.
PICS...
SWIPE
SWIPE
...
IT APPEARS THAT THE INTERNET DOESN'T CARE ABOUT WHITE DAY.

GUCCHI CAN NEVER WIN

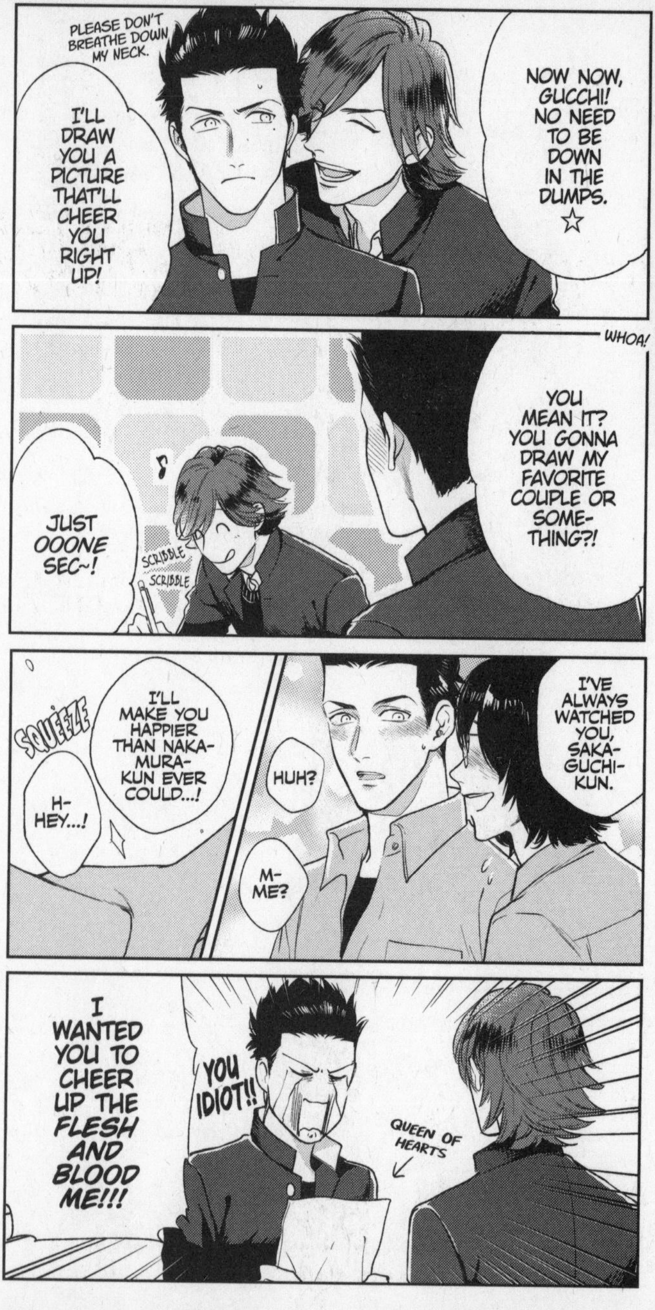
NOW NOW, GUCCHI! NO NEED TO BE DOWN IN THE DUMPS. ☆
PLEASE DON'T BREATHE DOWN MY NECK.
I'LL DRAW YOU A PICTURE THAT'LL CHEER YOU RIGHT UP!
WHOA!
YOU MEAN IT? YOU GONNA DRAW MY FAVORITE COUPLE OR SOME-THING?!
JUST OOONE SEC~!
SCRIBBLE SCRIBBLE
I'VE ALWAYS WATCHED YOU, SAKA-GUCHI-KUN.
HUH?
M-ME?
I'LL MAKE YOU HAPPIER THAN NAKA-MURA-KUN EVER COULD...!
SQUEEZE
H-HEY...!
QUEEN OF HEARTS
YOU IDIOT!!
I WANTED YOU TO CHEER UP THE FLESH AND BLOOD ME!!!

KFS

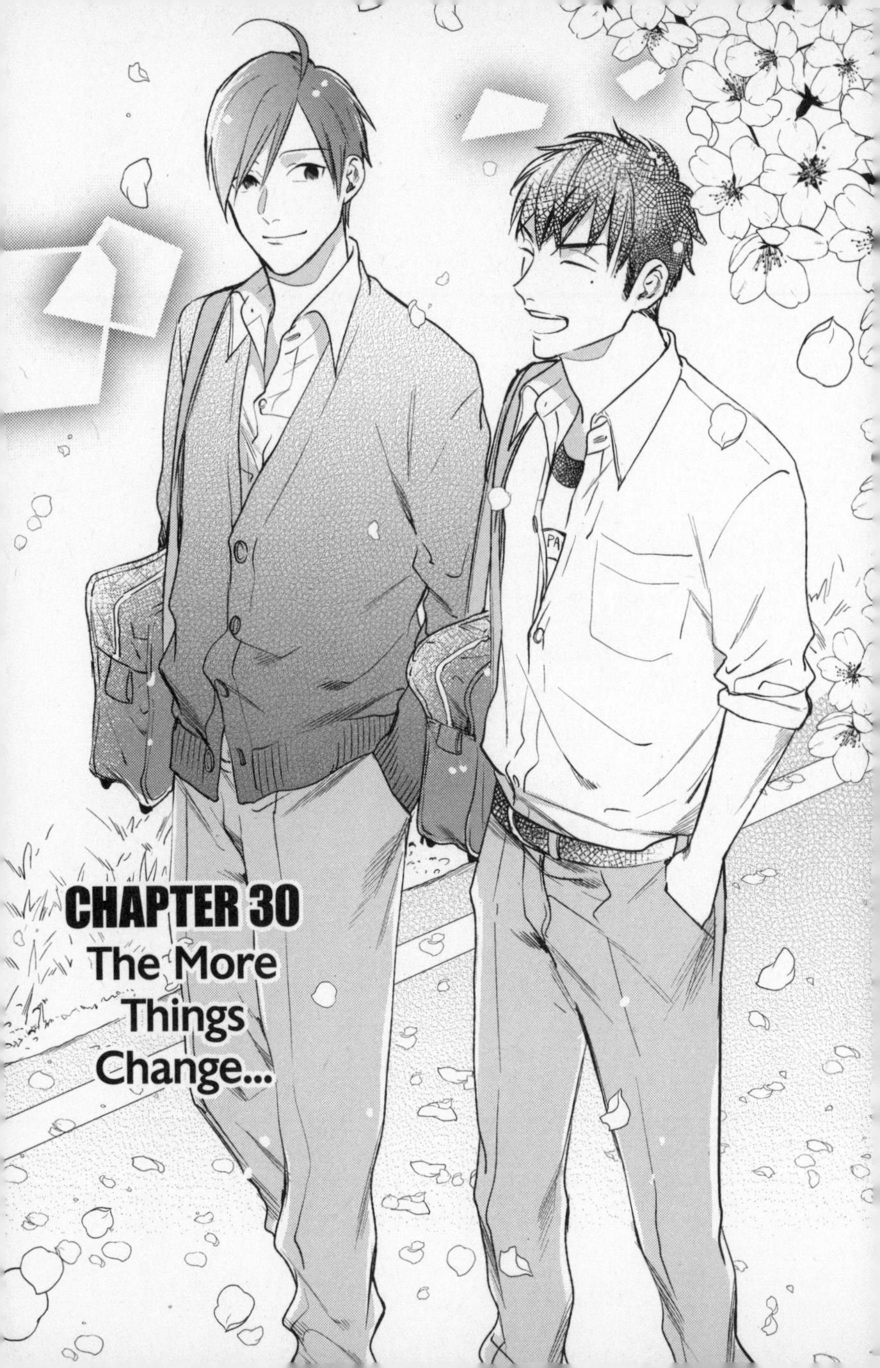
CHAPTER 30
The More Things Change...

FOREVER SPRING

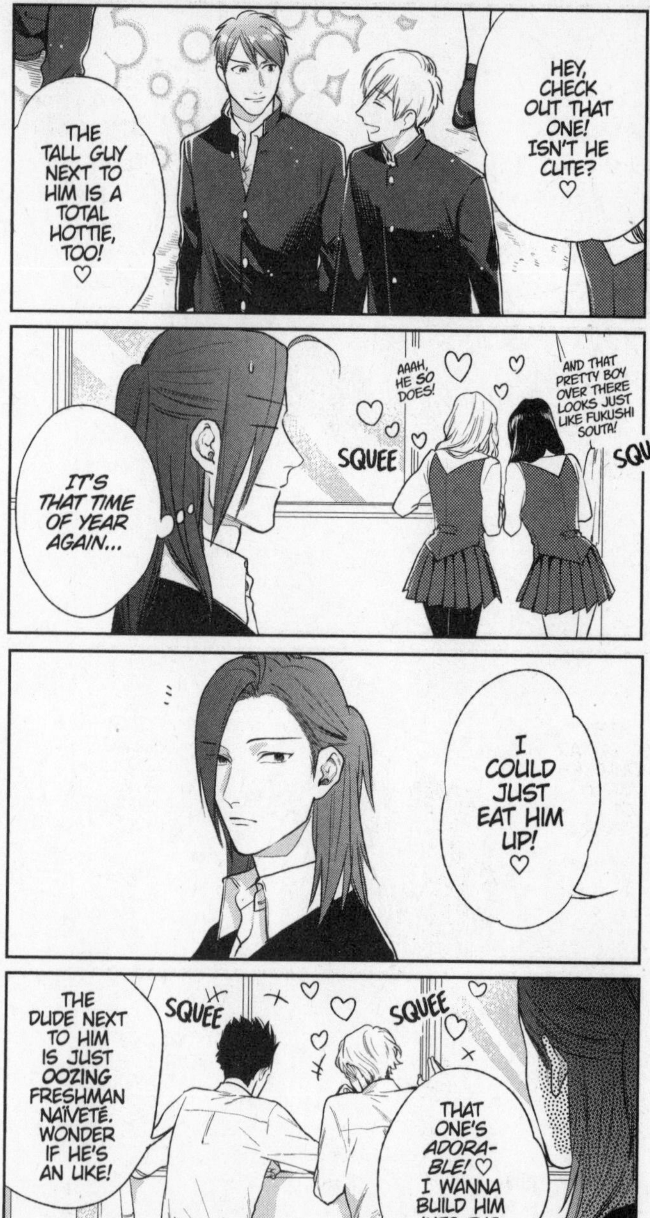
HEY, CHECK OUT THAT ONE! ISN'T HE CUTE? ♡
THE TALL GUY NEXT TO HIM IS A TOTAL HOTTIE, TOO! ♡
SQUEE
AND THAT PRETTY BOY OVER THERE LOOKS JUST LIKE FUKUSHI SOUTA!
AAAH, HE SO DOES!
SQUEE
IT'S THAT TIME OF YEAR AGAIN...
I COULD JUST EAT HIM UP! ♡
THAT ONE'S ADORABLE! ♡ I WANNA BUILD HIM INTO THE PERFECT MAN!
SQUEE
SQUEE
THE DUDE NEXT TO HIM IS JUST OOZING FRESHMAN NAÏVETÉ. WONDER IF HE'S AN UKE!

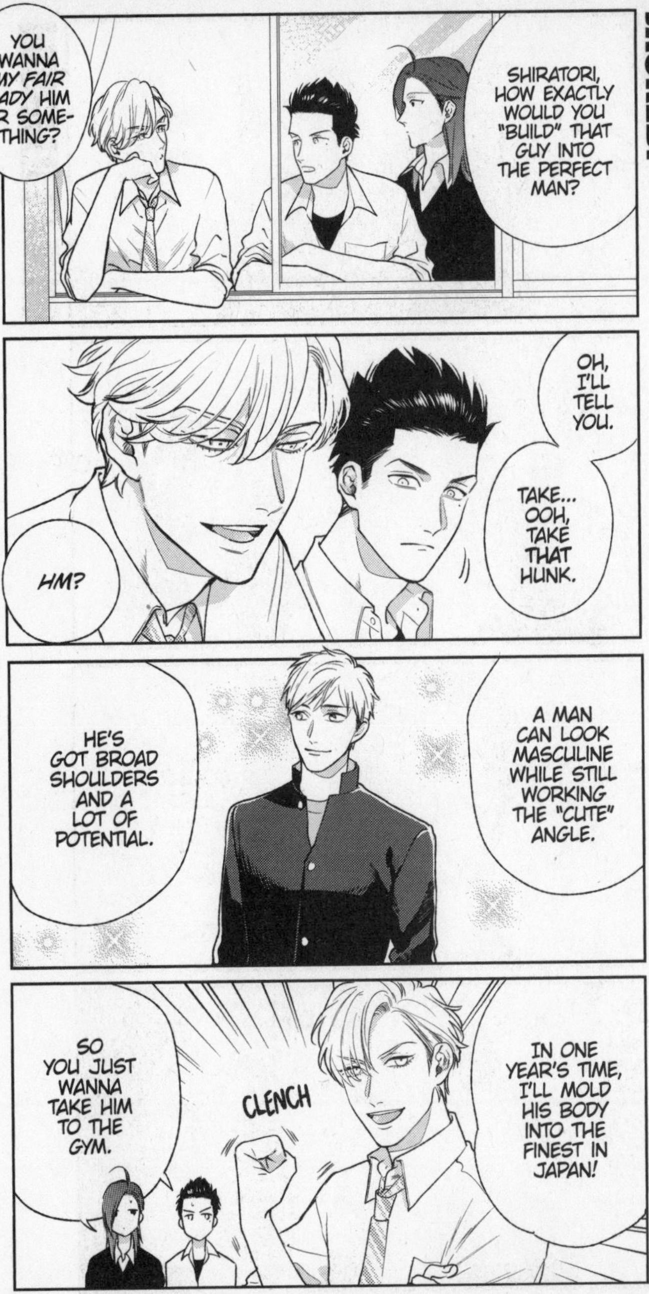
SHIRATORI, HOW EXACTLY WOULD YOU "BUILD" THAT GUY INTO THE PERFECT MAN?
YOU WANNA *MY FAIR LADY* HIM OR SOME-THING?
OH, I'LL TELL YOU.
TAKE... OOH, TAKE THAT HUNK.
HM?
A MAN CAN LOOK MASCULINE WHILE STILL WORKING THE "CUTE" ANGLE.
HE'S GOT BROAD SHOULDERS AND A LOT OF POTENTIAL.
IN ONE YEAR'S TIME, I'LL MOLD HIS BODY INTO THE FINEST IN JAPAN!
CLENCH
SO YOU JUST WANNA TAKE HIM TO THE GYM.

ROOM FOR GROWTH

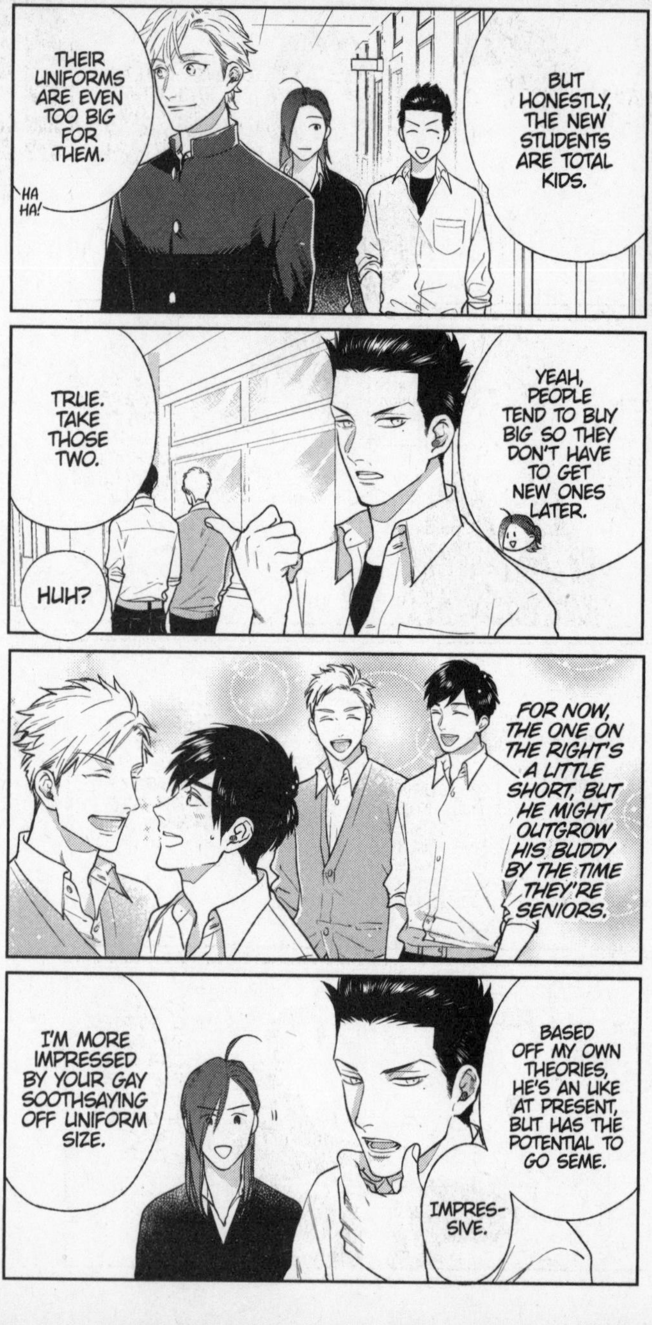
BUT HONESTLY, THE NEW STUDENTS ARE TOTAL KIDS.
THEIR UNIFORMS ARE EVEN TOO BIG FOR THEM.
HA HA!
YEAH, PEOPLE TEND TO BUY BIG SO THEY DON'T HAVE TO GET NEW ONES LATER.
TRUE. TAKE THOSE TWO.
HUH?
FOR NOW, THE ONE ON THE RIGHT'S A LITTLE SHORT, BUT HE MIGHT OUTGROW HIS BUDDY BY THE TIME THEY'RE SENIORS.
BASED OFF MY OWN THEORIES, HE'S AN UKE AT PRESENT, BUT HAS THE POTENTIAL TO GO SEME.
IMPRES-SIVE.
I'M MORE IMPRESSED BY YOUR GAY SOOTHSAYING OFF UNIFORM SIZE.

EVERY INCH MATTERS

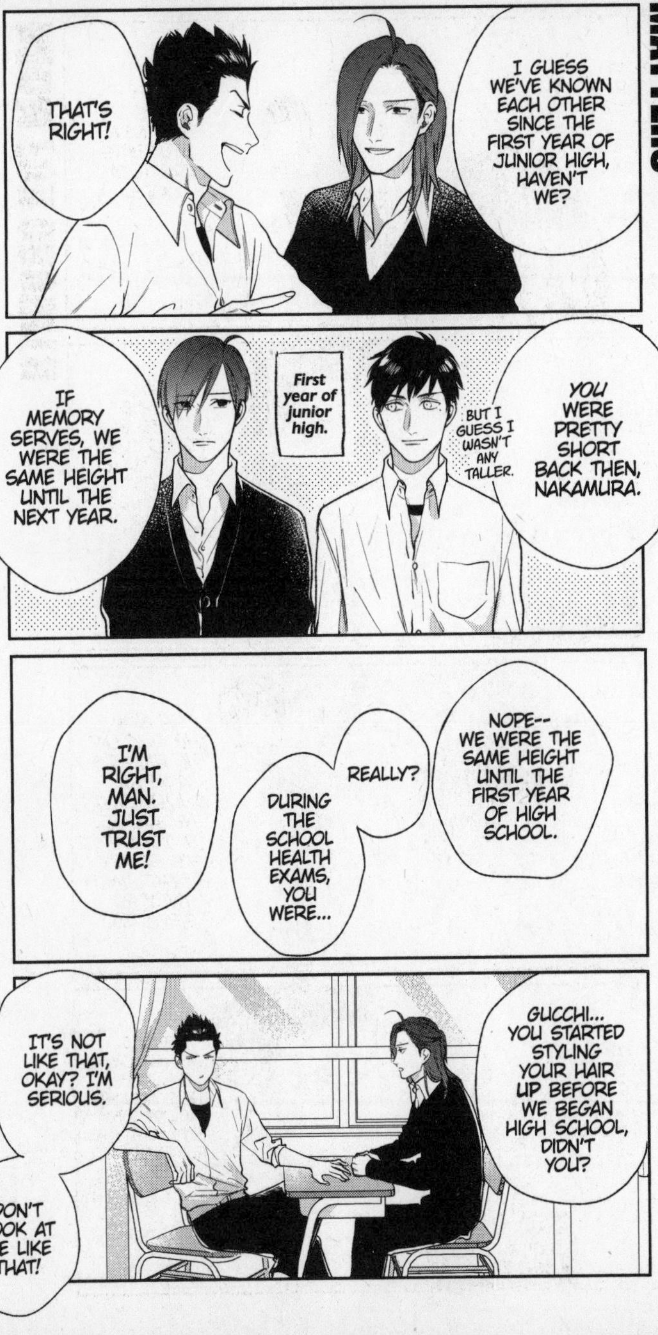
I GUESS WE'VE KNOWN EACH OTHER SINCE THE FIRST YEAR OF JUNIOR HIGH, HAVEN'T WE?
THAT'S RIGHT!
First year of junior high.
YOU WERE PRETTY SHORT BACK THEN, NAKAMURA.
BUT I GUESS I WASN'T ANY TALLER.
IF MEMORY SERVES, WE WERE THE SAME HEIGHT UNTIL THE NEXT YEAR.
NOPE-- WE WERE THE SAME HEIGHT UNTIL THE FIRST YEAR OF HIGH SCHOOL.
REALLY?
DURING THE SCHOOL HEALTH EXAMS, YOU WERE...
I'M RIGHT, MAN. JUST TRUST ME!
GUCCHI... YOU STARTED STYLING YOUR HAIR UP BEFORE WE BEGAN HIGH SCHOOL, DIDN'T YOU?
IT'S NOT LIKE THAT, OKAY? I'M SERIOUS.
DON'T LOOK AT ME LIKE THAT!

CHANCE ENCOUNTER

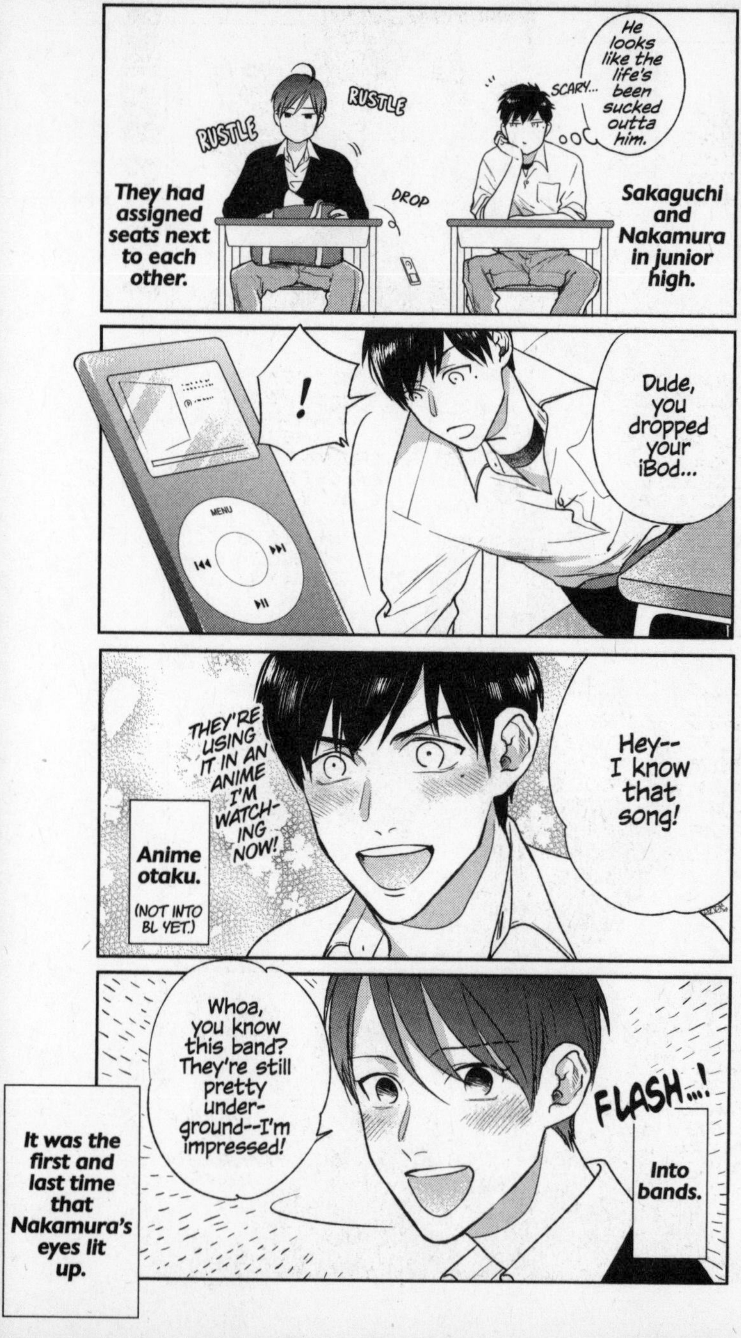
Sakaguchi and Nakamura in junior high.
He looks like the life's been sucked outta him.
SCARY...
RUSTLE
RUSTLE
DROP
They had assigned seats next to each other.
Dude, you dropped your iBod...
!
MENU
Hey-- I know that song!
THEY'RE USING IT IN AN ANIME I'M WATCHING NOW!
Anime otaku.
(NOT INTO BL YET.)
Into bands.
FLASH...!
Whoa, you know this band? They're still pretty under-ground--I'm impressed!
It was the first and last time that Nakamura's eyes lit up.

BOILING PATHOS

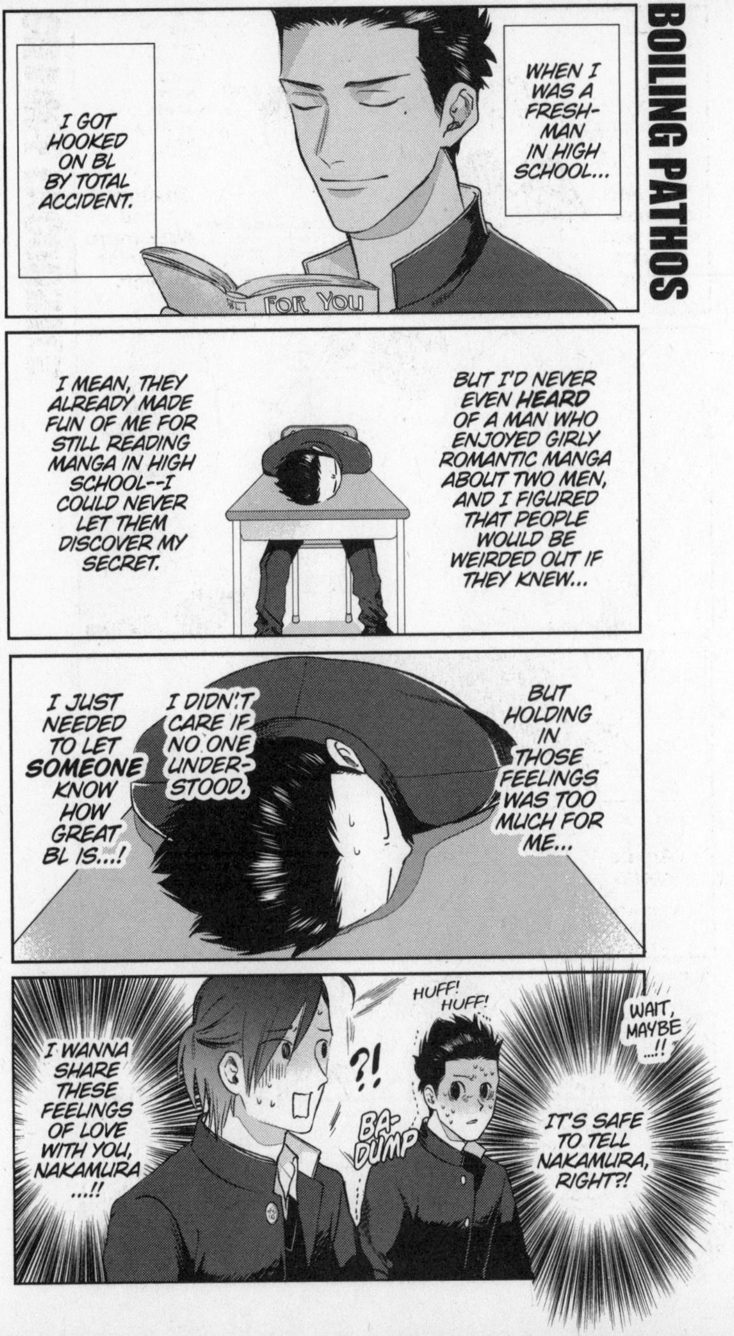
WHEN I WAS A FRESHMAN IN HIGH SCHOOL...
I GOT HOOKED ON BL BY TOTAL ACCIDENT.
FOR YOU
BUT I'D NEVER EVEN **HEARD** OF A MAN WHO ENJOYED GIRLY ROMANTIC MANGA ABOUT TWO MEN, AND I FIGURED THAT PEOPLE WOULD BE WEIRDED OUT IF THEY KNEW...
I MEAN, THEY ALREADY MADE FUN OF ME FOR STILL READING MANGA IN HIGH SCHOOL--I COULD NEVER LET THEM DISCOVER MY SECRET.
BUT HOLDING IN THOSE FEELINGS WAS TOO MUCH FOR ME...
I DIDN'T CARE IF NO ONE UNDERSTOOD.
I JUST NEEDED TO LET **SOMEONE** KNOW HOW GREAT BL IS...!
WAIT, MAYBE ...!!
IT'S SAFE TO TELL NAKAMURA, RIGHT?!
HUFF! HUFF!
BA-DUMP
?!
I WANNA SHARE THESE FEELINGS OF LOVE WITH YOU, NAKAMURA ...!!

DANGER LOOMING

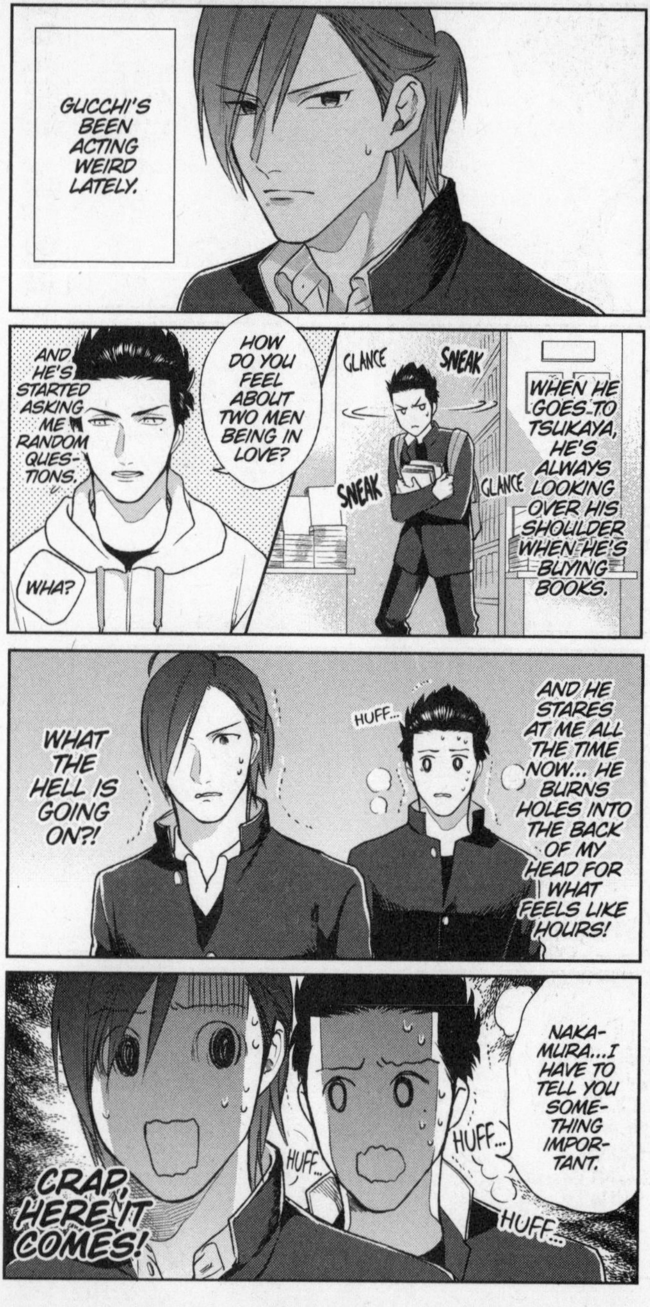
GUCCHI'S BEEN ACTING WEIRD LATELY.
WHEN HE GOES TO TSUKAYA, HE'S ALWAYS LOOKING OVER HIS SHOULDER WHEN HE'S BUYING BOOKS.
SNEAK
GLANCE
GLANCE
SNEAK
AND HE'S STARTED ASKING ME RANDOM QUES-TIONS.
HOW DO YOU FEEL ABOUT TWO MEN BEING IN LOVE?
WHA?
AND HE STARES AT ME ALL THE TIME NOW... HE BURNS HOLES INTO THE BACK OF MY HEAD FOR WHAT FEELS LIKE HOURS!
HUFF...
WHAT THE HELL IS GOING ON?!
NAKA-MURA...I HAVE TO TELL YOU SOME-THING IMPOR-TANT.
HUFF...
HUFF...
HUFF...
CRAP, HERE IT COMES!

TO EACH HIS OWN

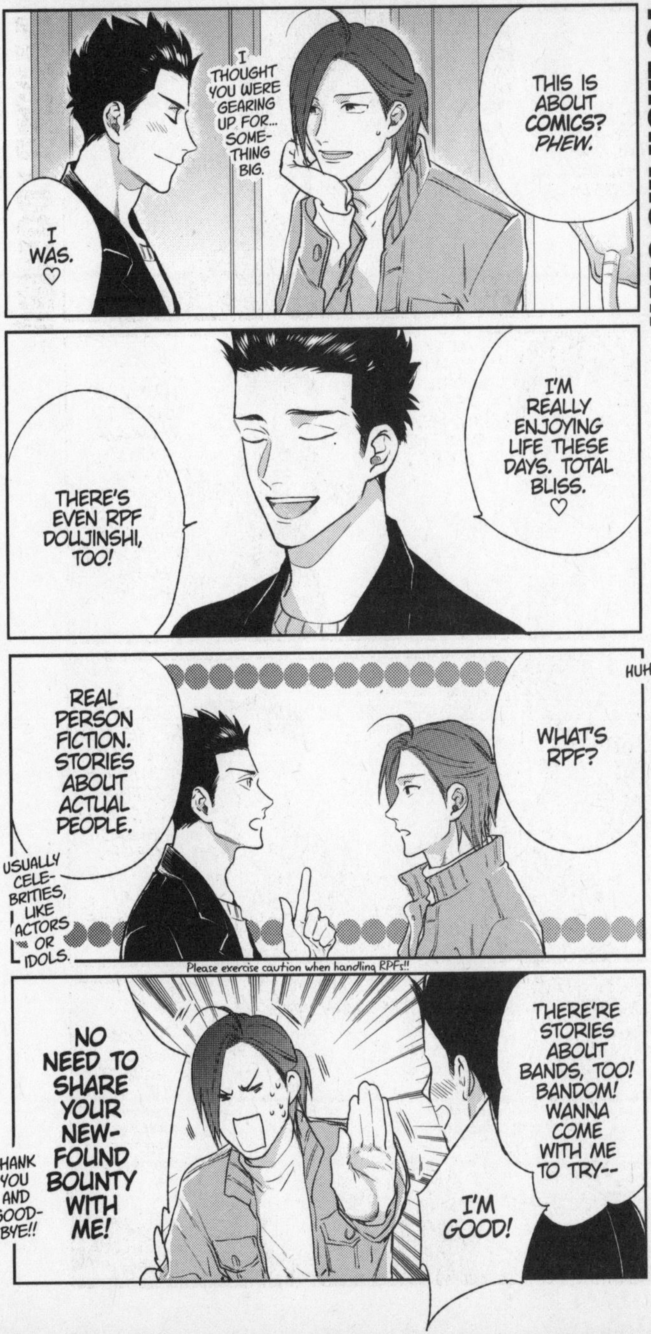
THIS IS ABOUT COMICS? PHEW.
I THOUGHT YOU WERE GEARING UP FOR... SOMETHING BIG.
I WAS. ♡
I'M REALLY ENJOYING LIFE THESE DAYS. TOTAL BLISS. ♡
THERE'S EVEN RPF DOUJINSHI, TOO!
HUH?
WHAT'S RPF?
REAL PERSON FICTION. STORIES ABOUT ACTUAL PEOPLE.
USUALLY CELEBRITIES, LIKE ACTORS OR IDOLS.
Please exercise caution when handling RPFs!!
THERE'RE STORIES ABOUT BANDS, TOO! BANDOM! WANNA COME WITH ME TO TRY--
I'M GOOD!
NO NEED TO SHARE YOUR NEWFOUND BOUNTY WITH ME!
THANK YOU AND GOODBYE!!

BEHIND-THE-SCENES DEALINGS

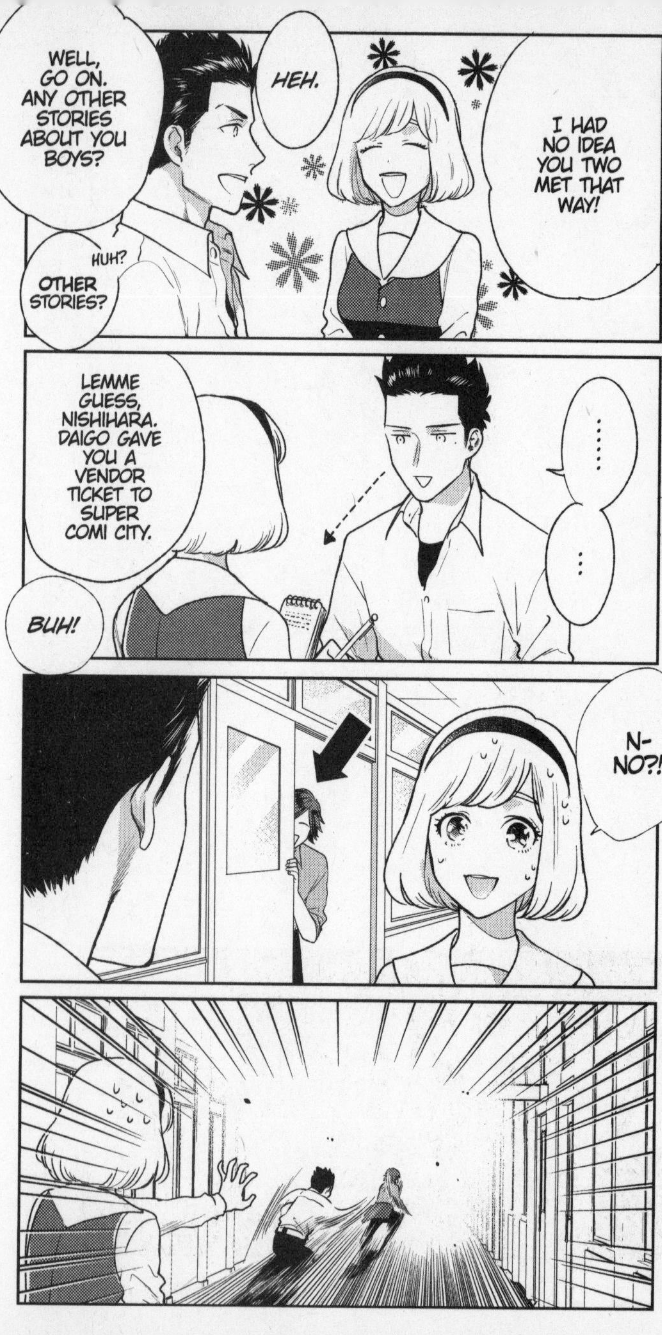

I HAD NO IDEA YOU TWO MET THAT WAY!
HEH.
WELL, GO ON. ANY OTHER STORIES ABOUT YOU BOYS?
HUH? OTHER STORIES?
......
...
LEMME GUESS, NISHIHARA. DAIGO GAVE YOU A VENDOR TICKET TO SUPER COMI CITY.
BUH!
N-NO?!

KFS

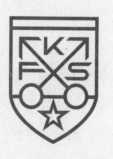

CHAPTER 31
Gucchi at Work!

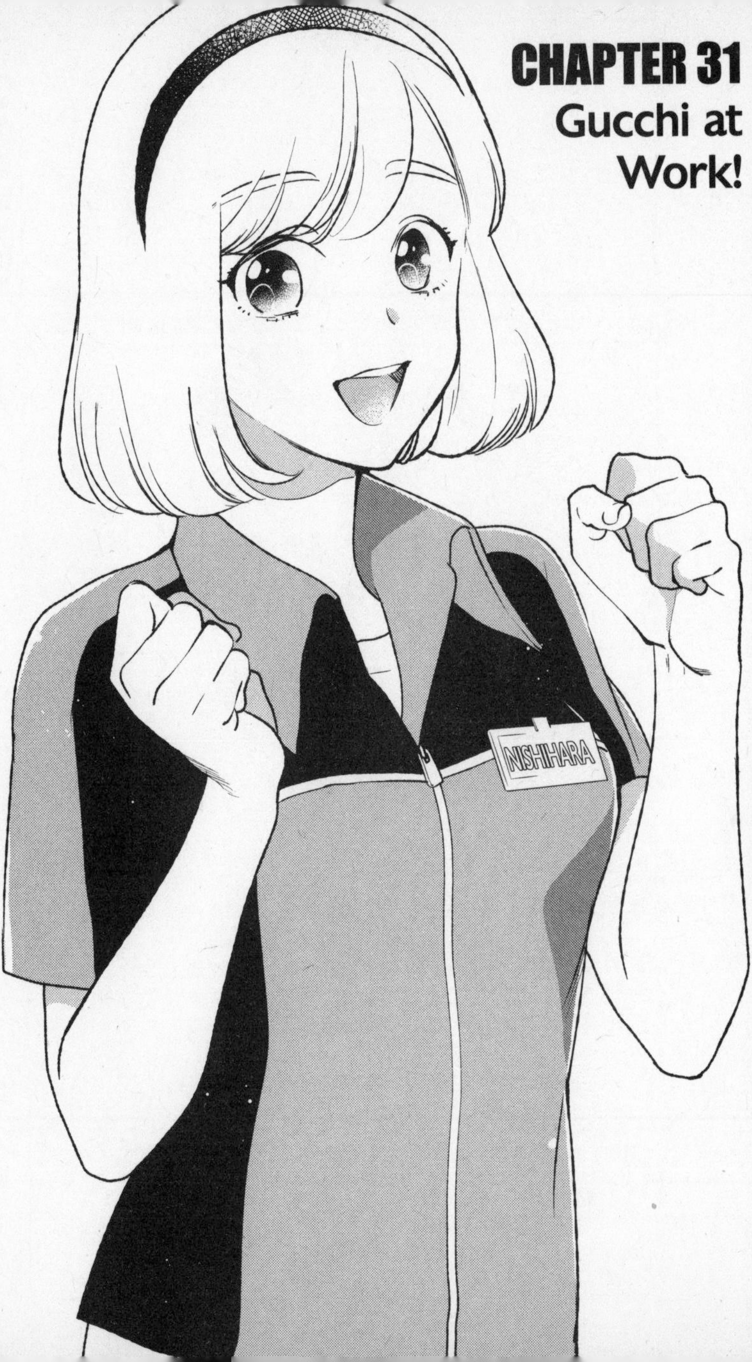
NISHIHARA

GETTING A JOB

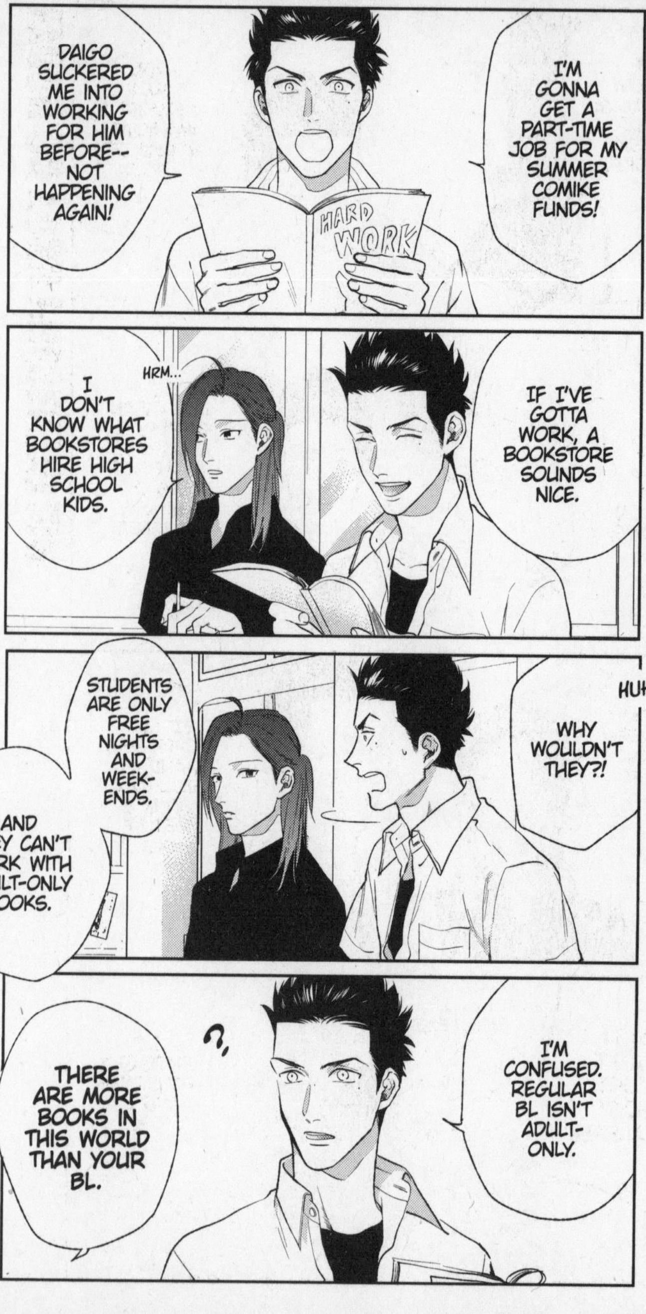

I'M GONNA GET A PART-TIME JOB FOR MY SUMMER COMIKE FUNDS!
DAIGO SUCKERED ME INTO WORKING FOR HIM BEFORE--NOT HAPPENING AGAIN!
HARD WORK
IF I'VE GOTTA WORK, A BOOKSTORE SOUNDS NICE.
HRM...
I DON'T KNOW WHAT BOOKSTORES HIRE HIGH SCHOOL KIDS.
HUH?
WHY WOULDN'T THEY?!
STUDENTS ARE ONLY FREE NIGHTS AND WEEK-ENDS.
AND THEY CAN'T WORK WITH ADULT-ONLY BOOKS.
I'M CONFUSED. REGULAR BL ISN'T ADULT-ONLY.
?
THERE ARE MORE BOOKS IN THIS WORLD THAN YOUR BL.

WORK ON YOUR PRESENTATION

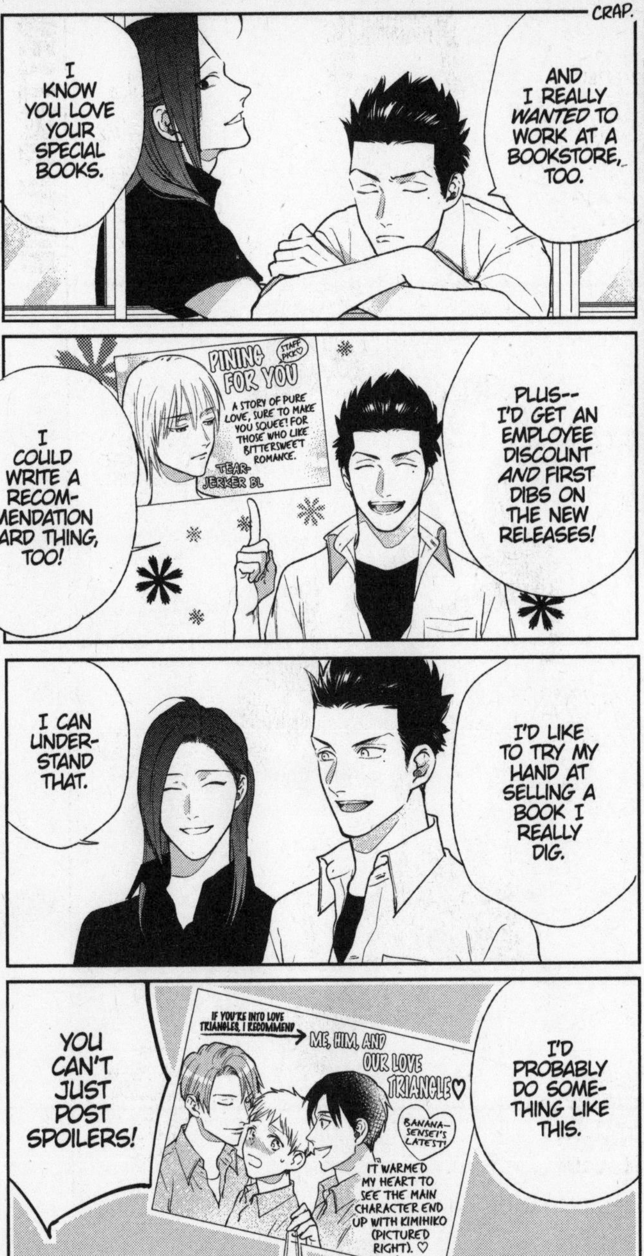
CRAP.
AND I REALLY *WANTED* TO WORK AT A BOOKSTORE, TOO.
I KNOW YOU LOVE YOUR SPECIAL BOOKS.
PLUS-- I'D GET AN EMPLOYEE DISCOUNT *AND* FIRST DIBS ON THE NEW RELEASES!
STAFF PICK♡
PINING FOR YOU
A STORY OF PURE LOVE, SURE TO MAKE YOU SQUEE! FOR THOSE WHO LIKE BITTERSWEET ROMANCE.
TEAR-JERKER BL
I COULD WRITE A RECOMMENDATION CARD THING, TOO!
I'D LIKE TO TRY MY HAND AT SELLING A BOOK I REALLY DIG.
I CAN UNDERSTAND THAT.
I'D PROBABLY DO SOMETHING LIKE THIS.
IF YOU'RE INTO LOVE TRIANGLES, I RECOMMEND
ME, HIM, AND OUR LOVE TRIANGLE♡
BANANA-SENSEI'S LATEST!
IT WARMED MY HEART TO SEE THE MAIN CHARACTER END UP WITH KIMIHIKO (PICTURED RIGHT). ♡
YOU CAN'T JUST POST SPOILERS!

NO SUCH THING AS TOO MANY

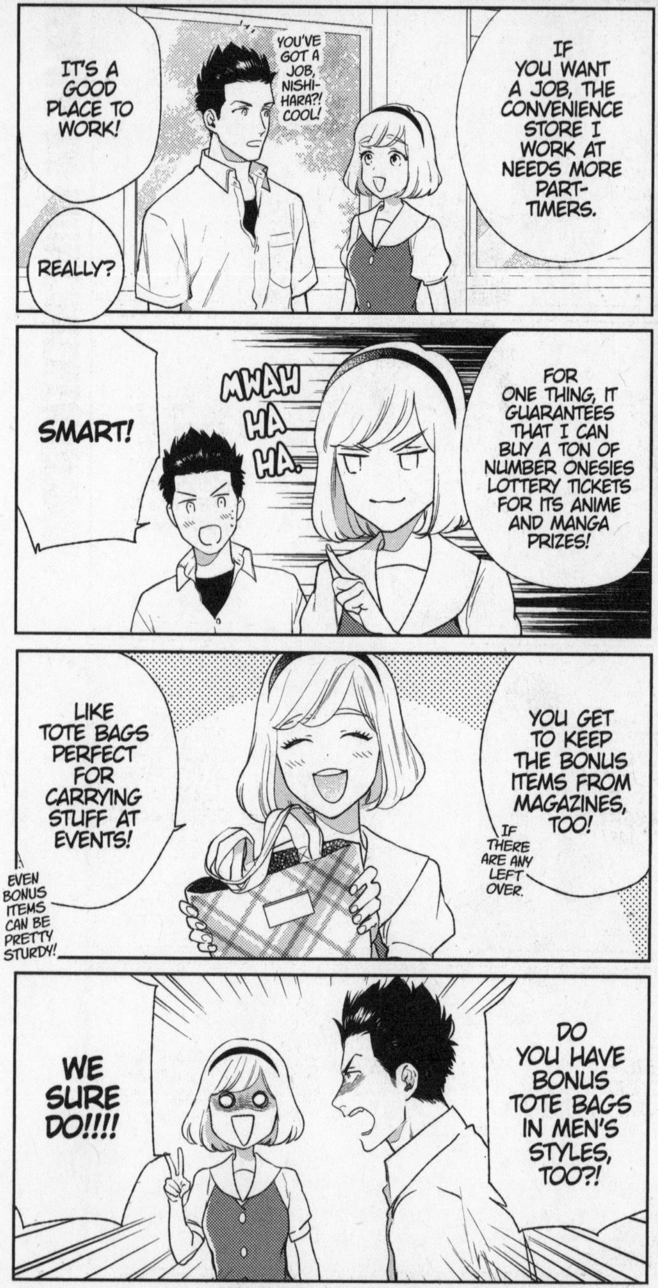
IF YOU WANT A JOB, THE CONVENIENCE STORE I WORK AT NEEDS MORE PART-TIMERS.
YOU'VE GOT A JOB, NISHI-HARA?! COOL!
IT'S A GOOD PLACE TO WORK!
REALLY?
FOR ONE THING, IT GUARANTEES THAT I CAN BUY A TON OF NUMBER ONESIES LOTTERY TICKETS FOR ITS ANIME AND MANGA PRIZES!
MWAH HA HA.
SMART!
YOU GET TO KEEP THE BONUS ITEMS FROM MAGAZINES, TOO!
IF THERE ARE ANY LEFT OVER.
LIKE TOTE BAGS PERFECT FOR CARRYING STUFF AT EVENTS!
EVEN BONUS ITEMS CAN BE PRETTY STURDY!
DO YOU HAVE BONUS TOTE BAGS IN MEN'S STYLES, TOO?!
WE SURE DO!!!!

RECALLING TRAUMA FROM A CERTAIN INCIDENT WITH A PAPER BAG.

ALL-OR-NOTHING MENTALITY

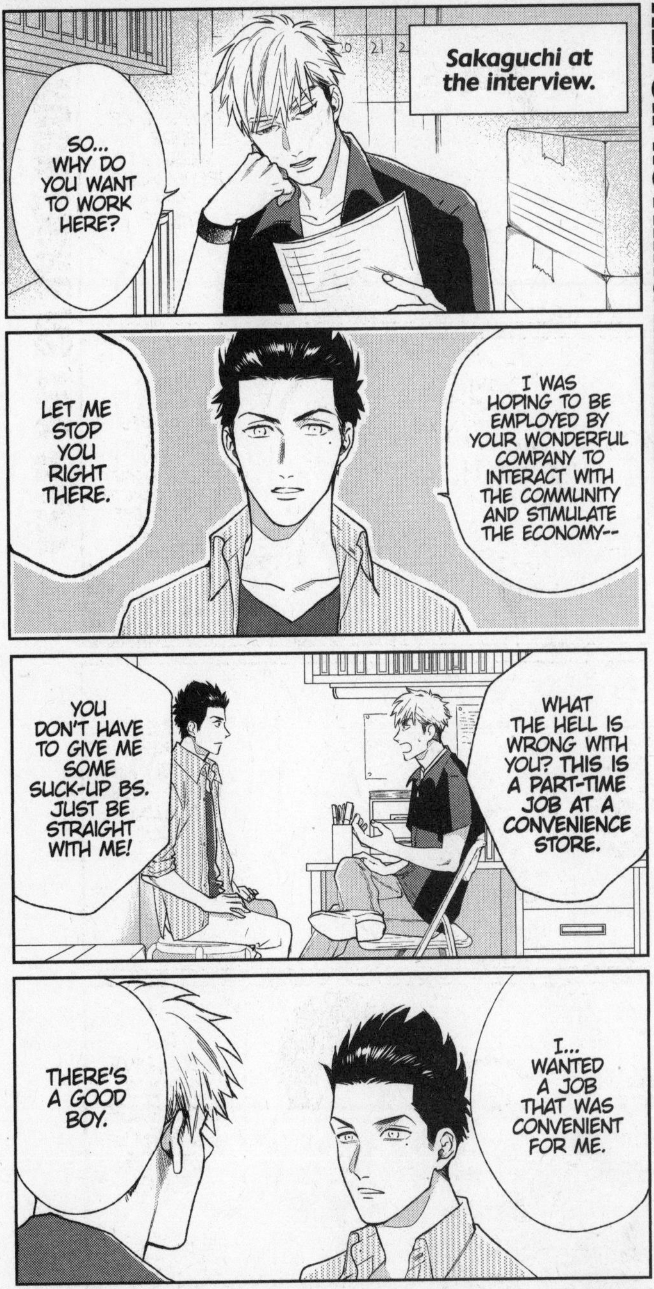
Sakaguchi at the interview.
SO... WHY DO YOU WANT TO WORK HERE?
I WAS HOPING TO BE EMPLOYED BY YOUR WONDERFUL COMPANY TO INTERACT WITH THE COMMUNITY AND STIMULATE THE ECONOMY--
LET ME STOP YOU RIGHT THERE.
WHAT THE HELL IS WRONG WITH YOU? THIS IS A PART-TIME JOB AT A CONVENIENCE STORE.
YOU DON'T HAVE TO GIVE ME SOME SUCK-UP BS. JUST BE STRAIGHT WITH ME!
I... WANTED A JOB THAT WAS CONVENIENT FOR ME.
THERE'S A GOOD BOY.

MNEMONICS

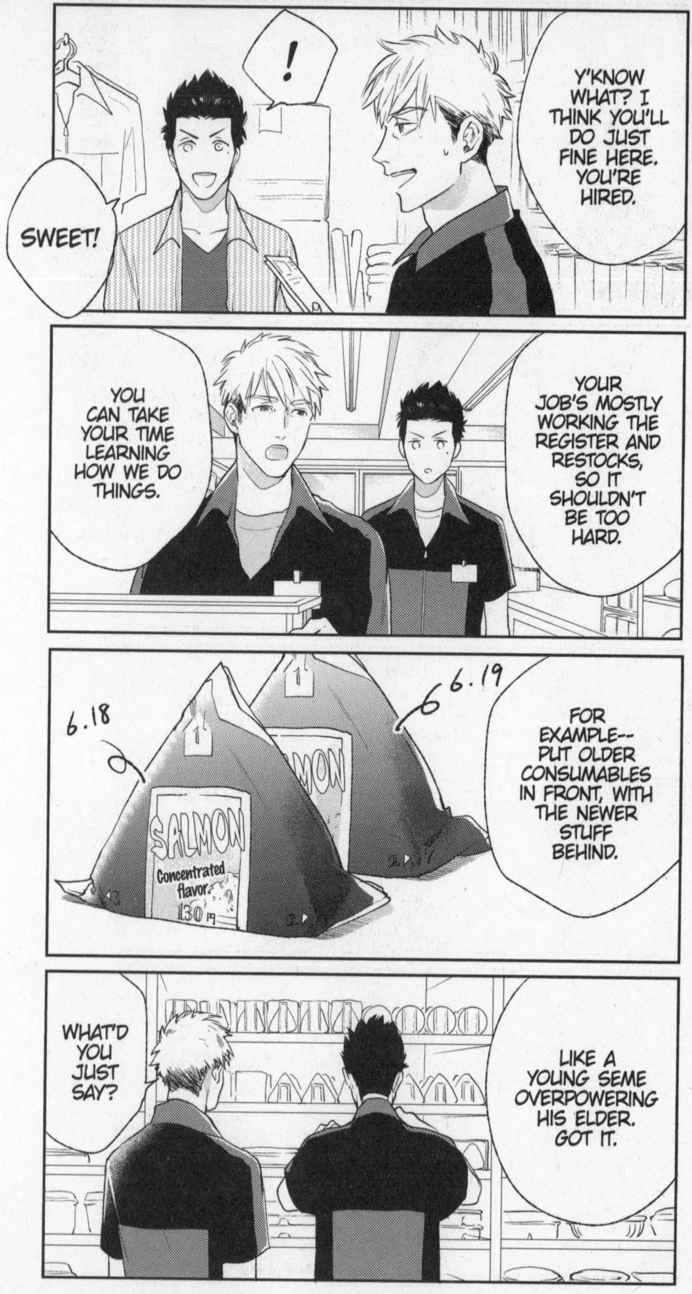

Y'KNOW WHAT? I THINK YOU'LL DO JUST FINE HERE. YOU'RE HIRED.
!
SWEET!
YOUR JOB'S MOSTLY WORKING THE REGISTER AND RESTOCKS, SO IT SHOULDN'T BE TOO HARD.
YOU CAN TAKE YOUR TIME LEARNING HOW WE DO THINGS.
6.19
FOR EXAMPLE-- PUT OLDER CONSUMABLES IN FRONT, WITH THE NEWER STUFF BEHIND.
6.18
SALMON
Concentrated flavor
130円
LIKE A YOUNG SEME OVERPOWERING HIS ELDER. GOT IT.
WHAT'D YOU JUST SAY?

PROMOTING HIS OTP

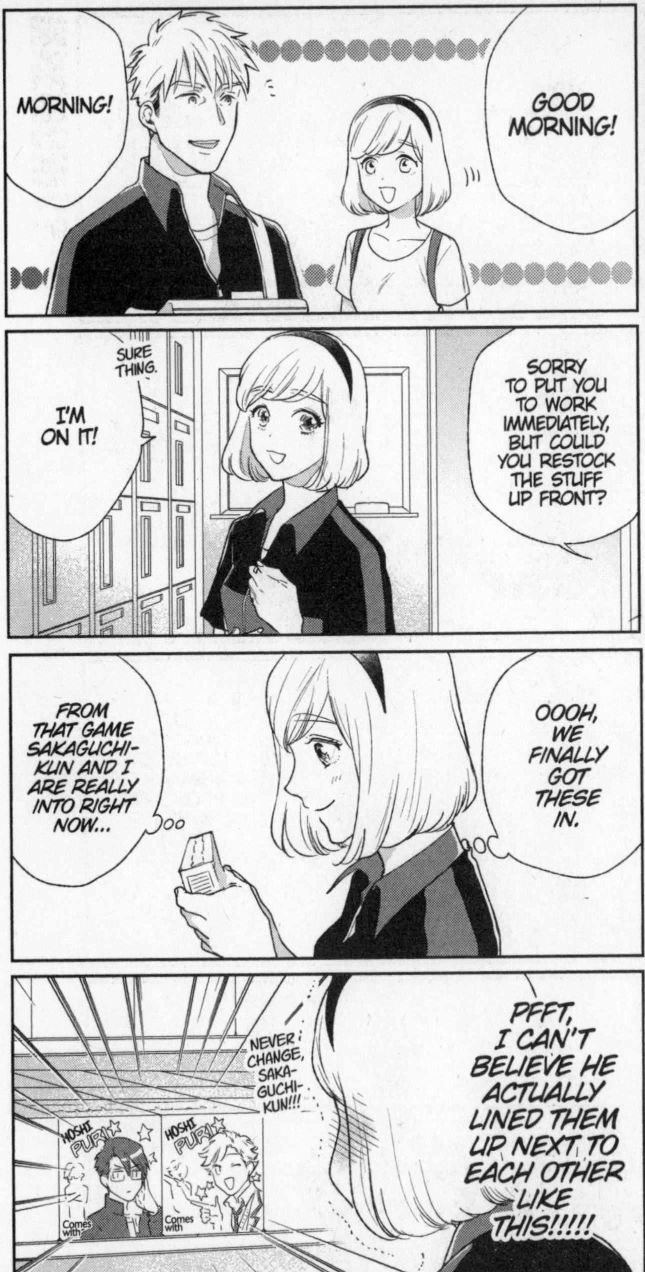
GOOD MORNING!
MORNING!
SORRY TO PUT YOU TO WORK IMMEDIATELY, BUT COULD YOU RESTOCK THE STUFF UP FRONT?
SURE THING.
I'M ON IT!
OOOH, WE FINALLY GOT THESE IN.
FROM THAT GAME SAKAGUCHI-KUN AND I ARE REALLY INTO RIGHT NOW...
PFFT, I CAN'T BELIEVE HE ACTUALLY LINED THEM UP NEXT TO EACH OTHER LIKE THIS!!!!!
NEVER CHANGE, SAKAGUCHI-KUN!!!
HOSHI PURI
Comes with
HOSHI PURI
Comes with

PARADOX

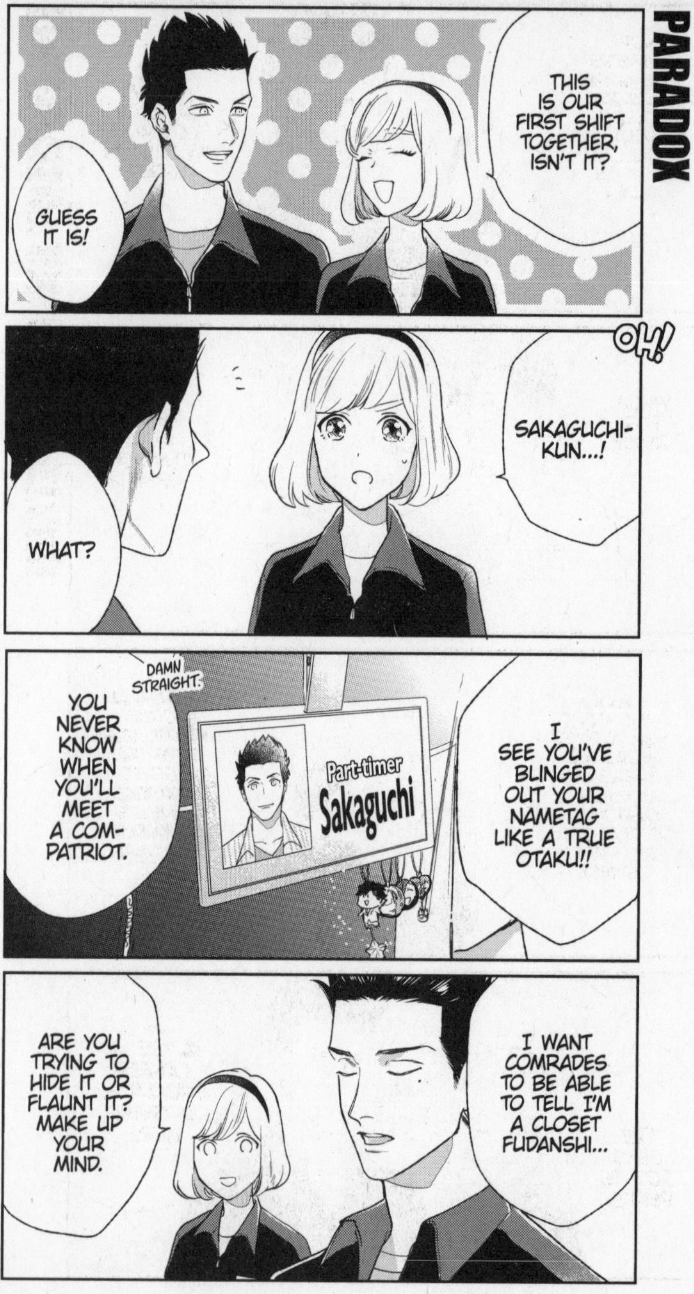
THIS IS OUR FIRST SHIFT TOGETHER, ISN'T IT?
GUESS IT IS!
OH!
SAKAGUCHI-KUN...!
WHAT?
I SEE YOU'VE BLINGED OUT YOUR NAMETAG LIKE A TRUE OTAKU!!
Part-timer Sakaguchi
YOU NEVER KNOW WHEN YOU'LL MEET A COM-PATRIOT.
DAMN STRAIGHT.
I WANT COMRADES TO BE ABLE TO TELL I'M A CLOSET FUDANSHI...
ARE YOU TRYING TO HIDE IT OR FLAUNT IT? MAKE UP YOUR MIND.

THE PERFECT JOB FOR AN OTAKU

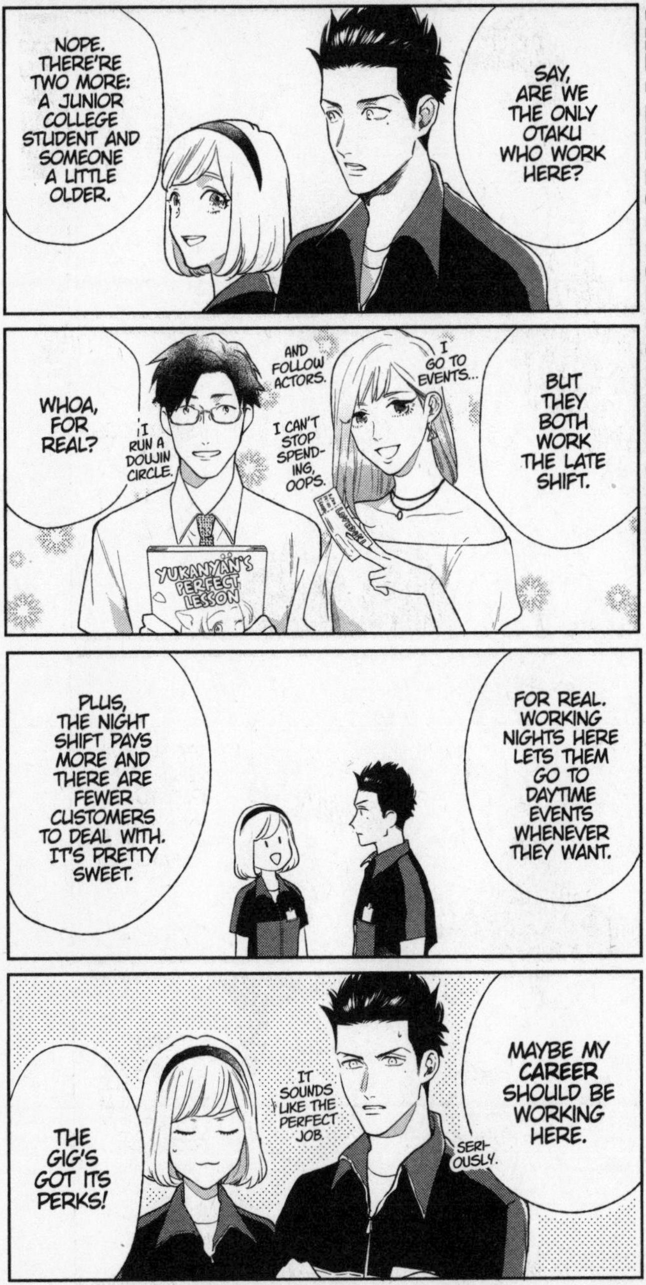
SAY, ARE WE THE ONLY OTAKU WHO WORK HERE?
NOPE. THERE'RE TWO MORE: A JUNIOR COLLEGE STUDENT AND SOMEONE A LITTLE OLDER.
BUT THEY BOTH WORK THE LATE SHIFT.
I GO TO EVENTS...
AND FOLLOW ACTORS.
I CAN'T STOP SPEND-ING, OOPS.
I RUN A DOUJIN CIRCLE.
YUKANYÄN'S PERFECT LESSON
WHOA, FOR REAL?
FOR REAL. WORKING NIGHTS HERE LETS THEM GO TO DAYTIME EVENTS WHENEVER THEY WANT.
PLUS, THE NIGHT SHIFT PAYS MORE AND THERE ARE FEWER CUSTOMERS TO DEAL WITH. IT'S PRETTY SWEET.
MAYBE MY CAREER SHOULD BE WORKING HERE.
SERI-OUSLY.
IT SOUNDS LIKE THE PERFECT JOB.
THE GIG'S GOT ITS PERKS!

MY HAND MOVED ON ITS OWN

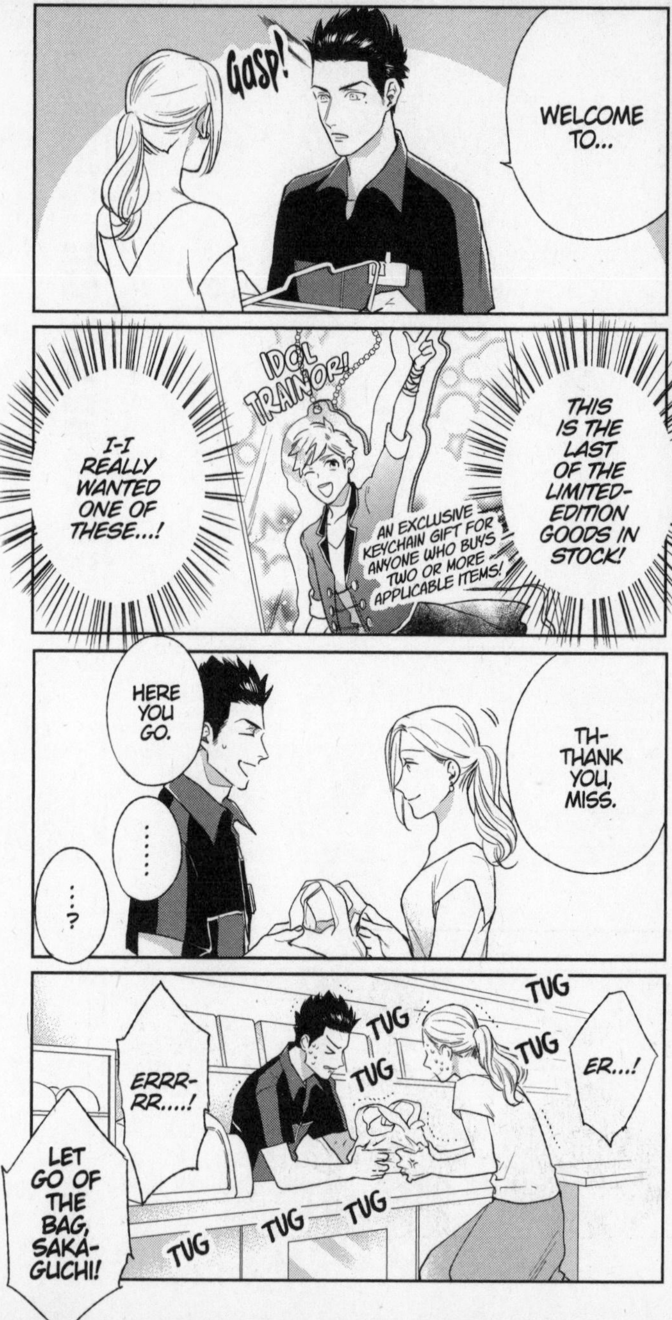
WELCOME TO...
Gasp!
THIS IS THE LAST OF THE LIMITED-EDITION GOODS IN STOCK!
IDOL TRAINOR!
AN EXCLUSIVE KEYCHAIN GIFT FOR ANYONE WHO BUYS TWO OR MORE APPLICABLE ITEMS!
I-I REALLY WANTED ONE OF THESE...!
TH-THANK YOU, MISS.
HERE YOU GO.
......
...?
TUG
ER...!
TUG
TUG
TUG
ERRRR-RR....!
TUG
TUG
TUG
LET GO OF THE BAG, SAKAGUCHI!

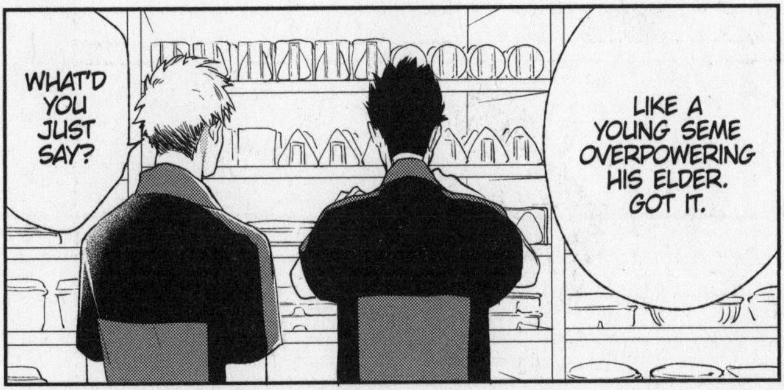
LIKE A YOUNG SEME OVERPOWERING HIS ELDER. GOT IT.
WHAT'D YOU JUST SAY?

KFS

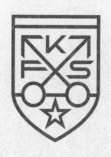

CHAPTER 32

Gucchi at Work! Part 2

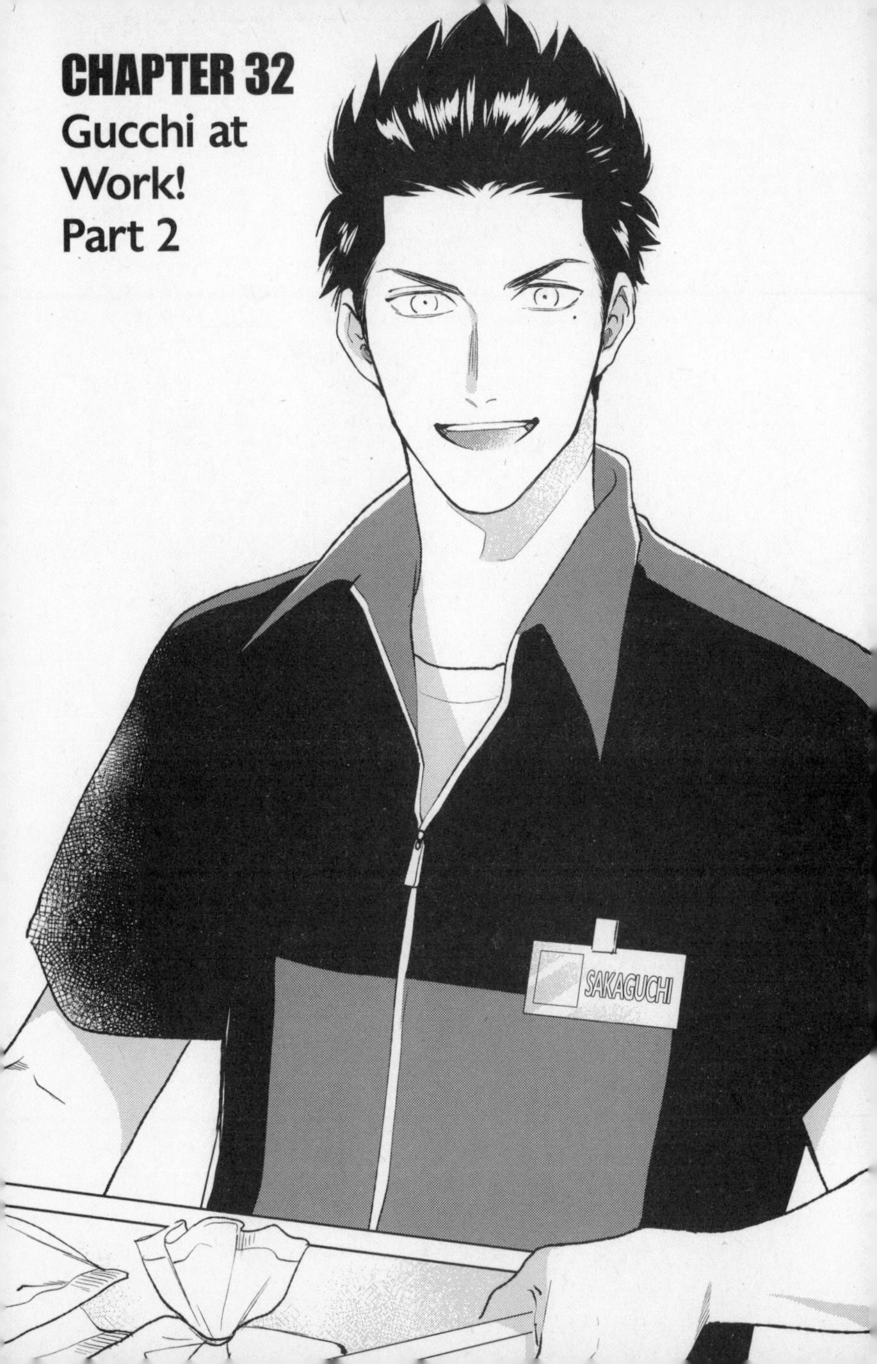
SAKAGUCHI

A SUCKER FOR BL

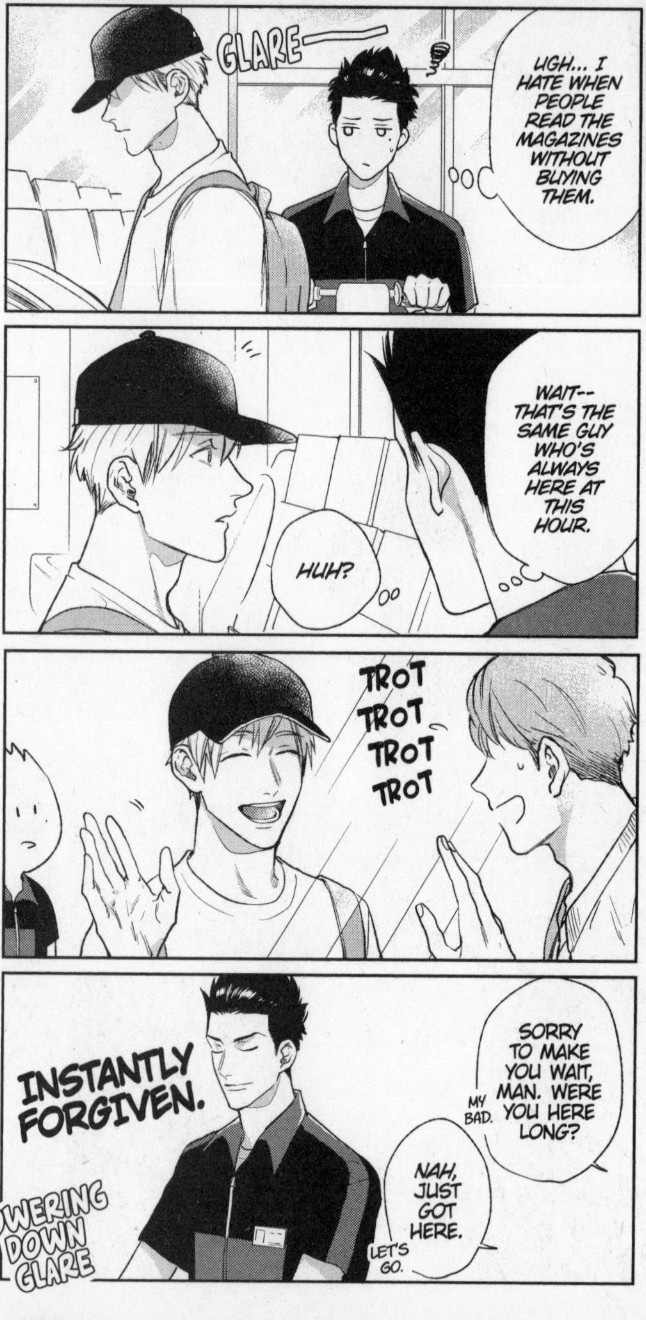
UGH... I HATE WHEN PEOPLE READ THE MAGAZINES WITHOUT BUYING THEM.
GLARE——
WAIT-- THAT'S THE SAME GUY WHO'S ALWAYS HERE AT THIS HOUR.
HUH?
TROT TROT TROT TROT
SORRY TO MAKE YOU WAIT, MAN. WERE YOU HERE LONG?
MY BAD.
NAH, JUST GOT HERE.
LET'S GO.
INSTANTLY FORGIVEN.
POWERING DOWN GLARE

HEART-POUNDING

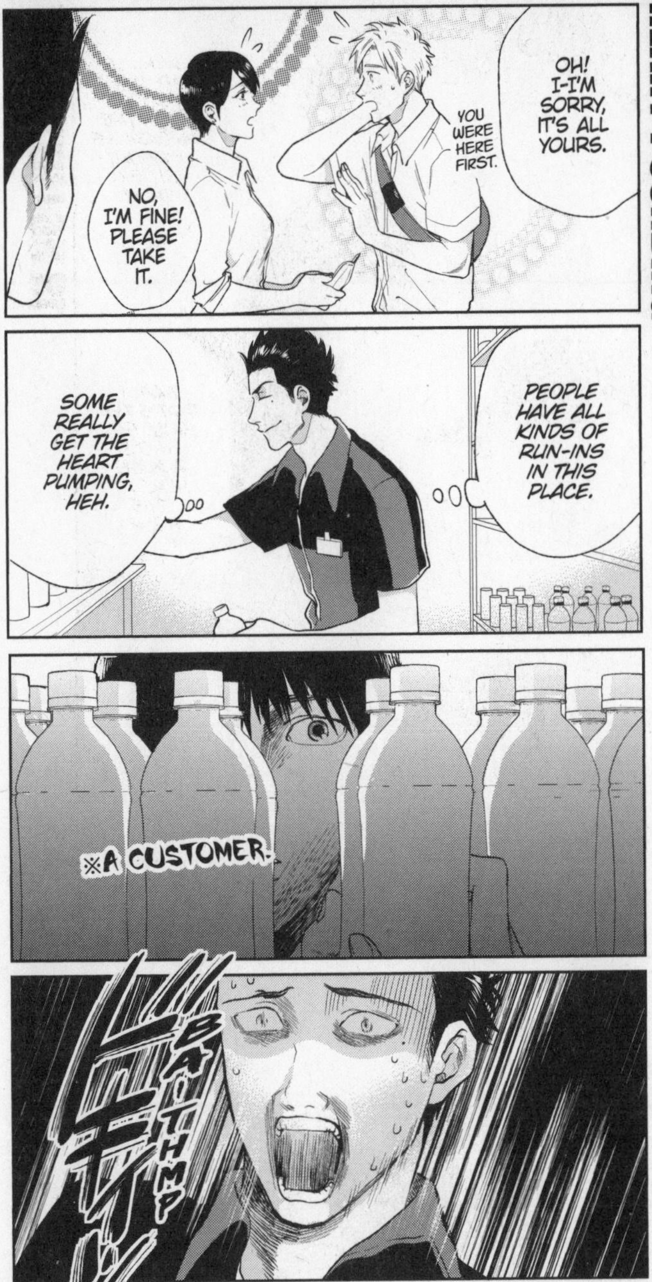
OH! I-I'M SORRY, IT'S ALL YOURS.
YOU WERE HERE FIRST.
NO, I'M FINE! PLEASE TAKE IT.
PEOPLE HAVE ALL KINDS OF RUN-INS IN THIS PLACE.
SOME REALLY GET THE HEART PUMPING, HEH.
※A CUSTOMER.
BA-THMP

HOW'D THAT GET IN THERE?

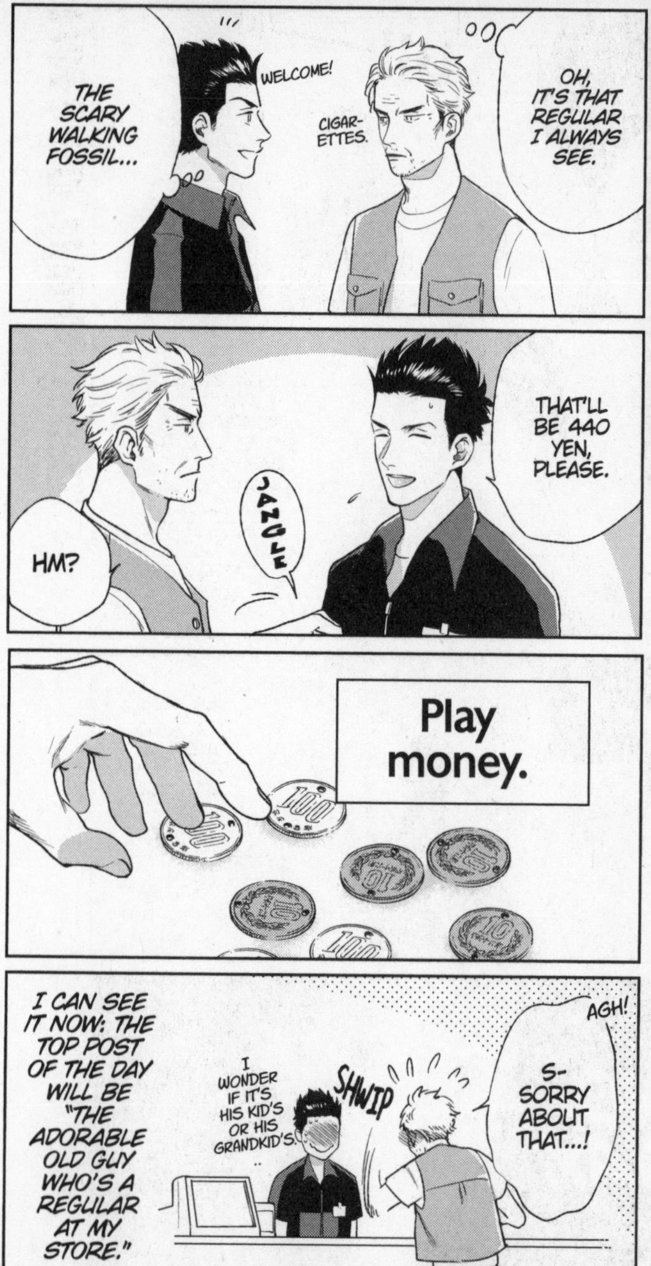
OH, IT'S THAT REGULAR I ALWAYS SEE.
CIGAR-ETTES.
WELCOME!
THE SCARY WALKING FOSSIL...
THAT'LL BE 440 YEN, PLEASE.
JANGLE
HM?
Play money.
AGH!
S-SORRY ABOUT THAT...!
SHWIP
I WONDER IF IT'S HIS KID'S OR HIS GRANDKID'S..
I CAN SEE IT NOW: THE TOP POST OF THE DAY WILL BE "THE ADORABLE OLD GUY WHO'S A REGULAR AT MY STORE."

I AM CALM, I AM COLLECTED

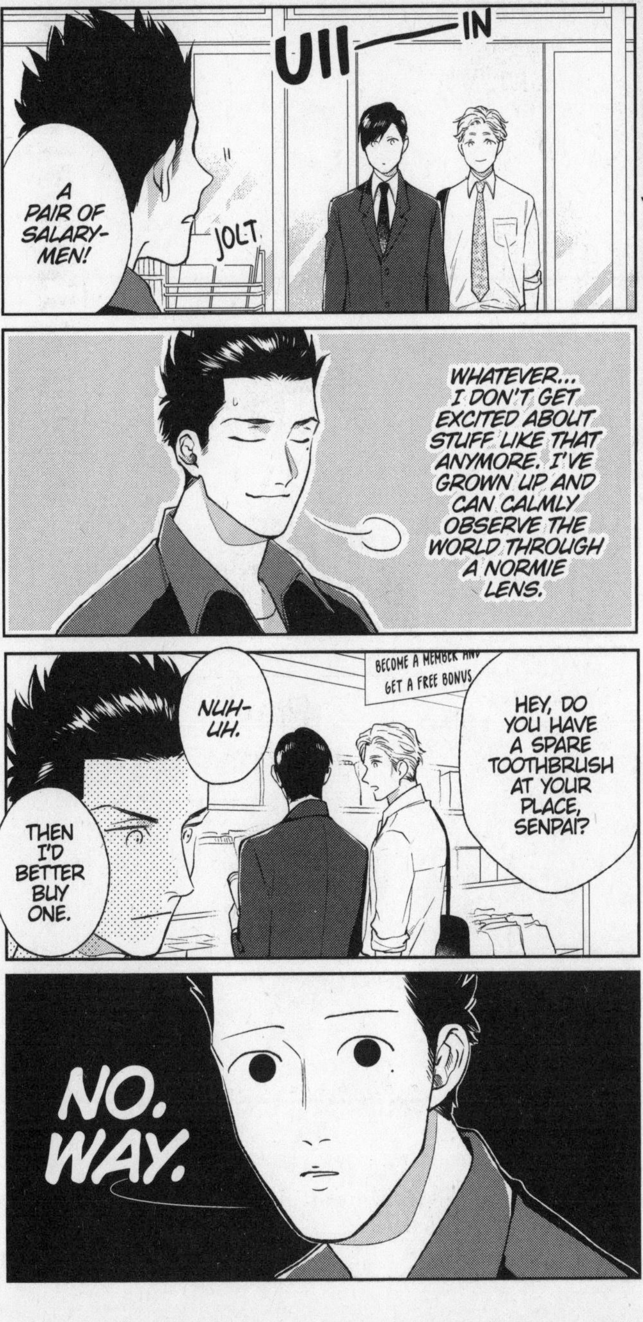
UII—IN
JOLT.
A PAIR OF SALARY-MEN!
WHATEVER... I DON'T GET EXCITED ABOUT STUFF LIKE THAT ANYMORE. I'VE GROWN UP AND CAN CALMLY OBSERVE THE WORLD THROUGH A NORMIE LENS.
HEY, DO YOU HAVE A SPARE TOOTHBRUSH AT YOUR PLACE, SENPAI?
BECOME A MEMBER
GET A FREE BONUS
NUH-UH.
THEN I'D BETTER BUY ONE.
NO. WAY.

LEADING ME ON

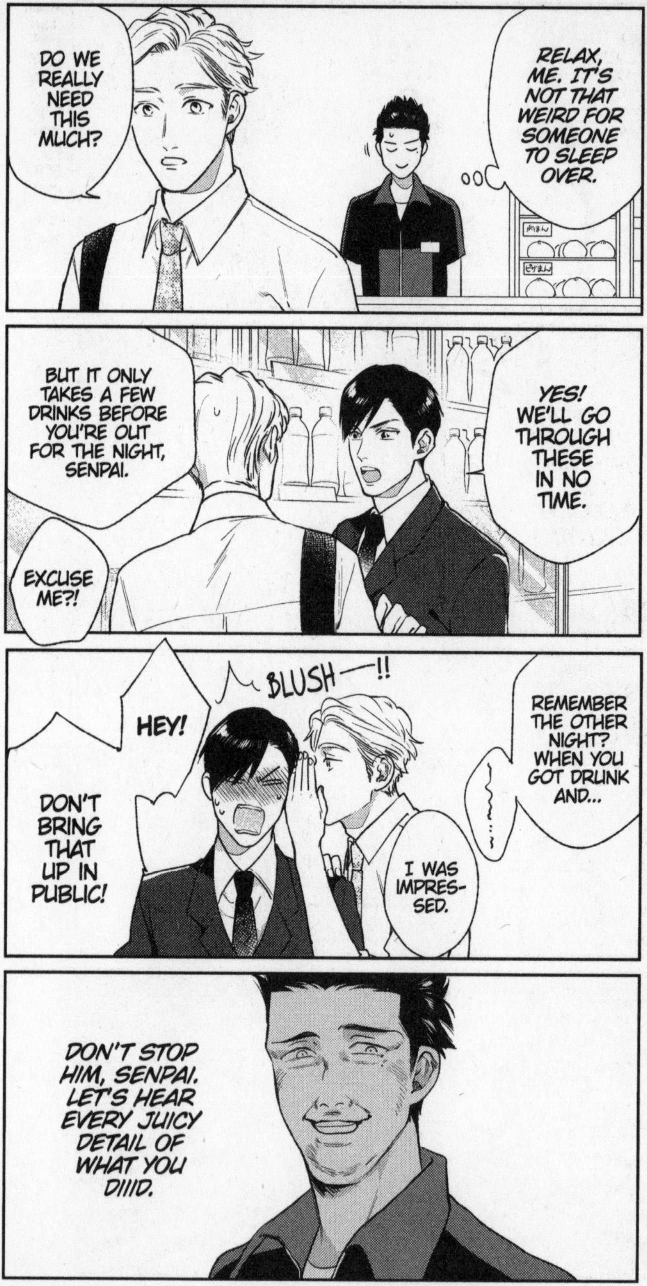
RELAX, ME. IT'S NOT THAT WEIRD FOR SOMEONE TO SLEEP OVER.
肉まん
ピザまん
DO WE REALLY NEED THIS MUCH?
YES! WE'LL GO THROUGH THESE IN NO TIME.
BUT IT ONLY TAKES A FEW DRINKS BEFORE YOU'RE OUT FOR THE NIGHT, SENPAI.
EXCUSE ME?!
REMEMBER THE OTHER NIGHT? WHEN YOU GOT DRUNK AND...
I WAS IMPRESSED.
BLUSH—!!
HEY!
DON'T BRING THAT UP IN PUBLIC!
DON'T STOP HIM, SENPAI. LET'S HEAR EVERY JUICY DETAIL OF WHAT YOU DIIID.

THAT NAILS IT

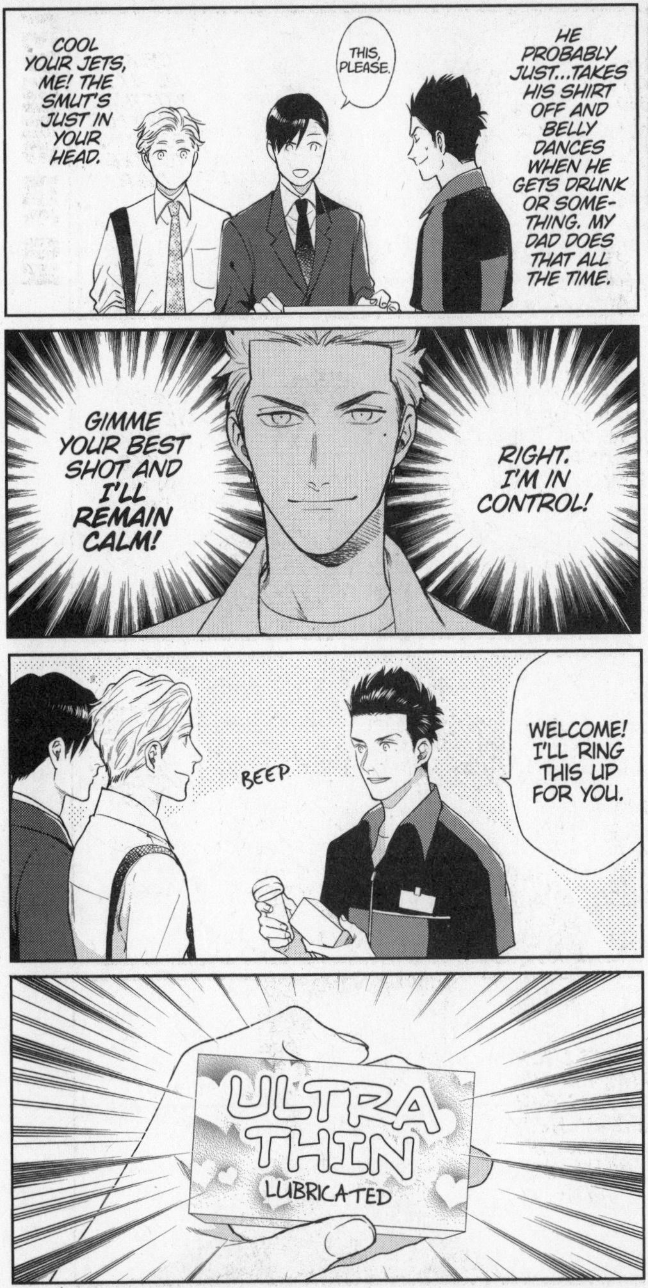
HE PROBABLY JUST...TAKES HIS SHIRT OFF AND BELLY DANCES WHEN HE GETS DRUNK OR SOME-THING. MY DAD DOES THAT ALL THE TIME.
THIS, PLEASE.
COOL YOUR JETS, ME! THE SMUT'S JUST IN YOUR HEAD.
RIGHT. I'M IN CONTROL!
GIMME YOUR BEST SHOT AND I'LL REMAIN CALM!
WELCOME! I'LL RING THIS UP FOR YOU.
BEEP
ULTRA THIN
LUBRICATED

NO TRUST

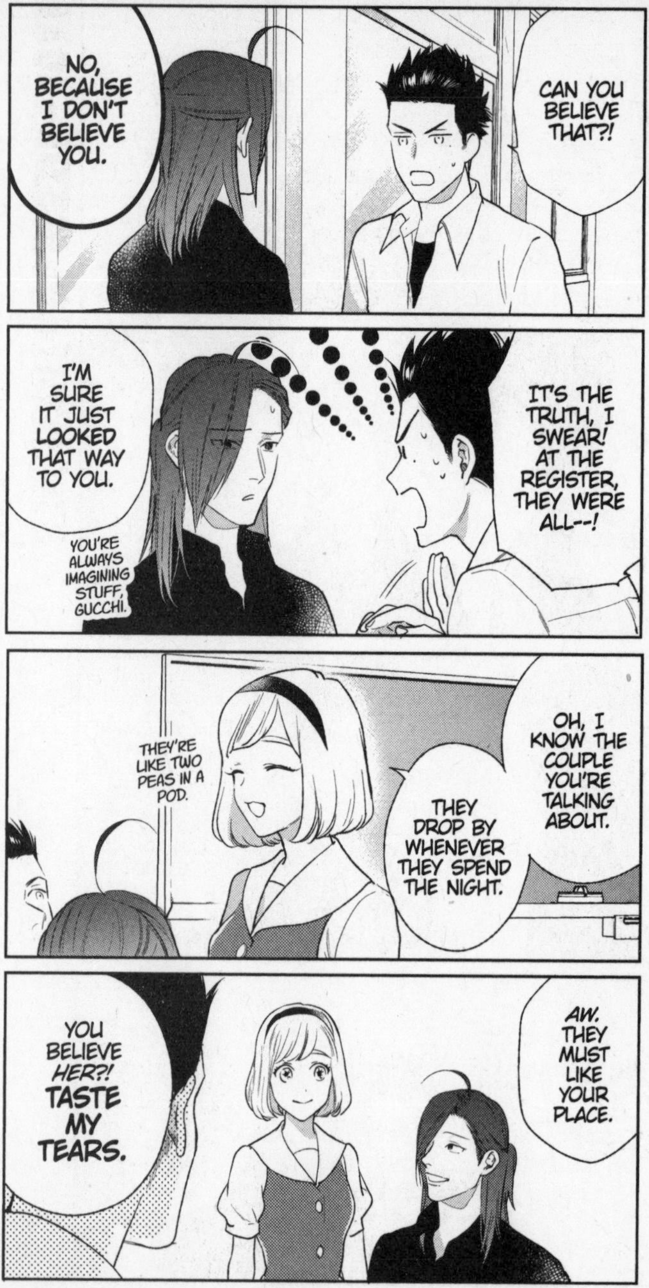
CAN YOU BELIEVE THAT?!
NO, BECAUSE I DON'T BELIEVE YOU.
IT'S THE TRUTH, I SWEAR! AT THE REGISTER, THEY WERE ALL--!
I'M SURE IT JUST LOOKED THAT WAY TO YOU.
YOU'RE ALWAYS IMAGINING STUFF, GUCCHI.
OH, I KNOW THE COUPLE YOU'RE TALKING ABOUT.
THEY DROP BY WHENEVER THEY SPEND THE NIGHT.
THEY'RE LIKE TWO PEAS IN A POD.
AW. THEY MUST LIKE YOUR PLACE.
YOU BELIEVE *HER?!* TASTE MY TEARS.

I LOVE SEEING YOU FLUSTERED

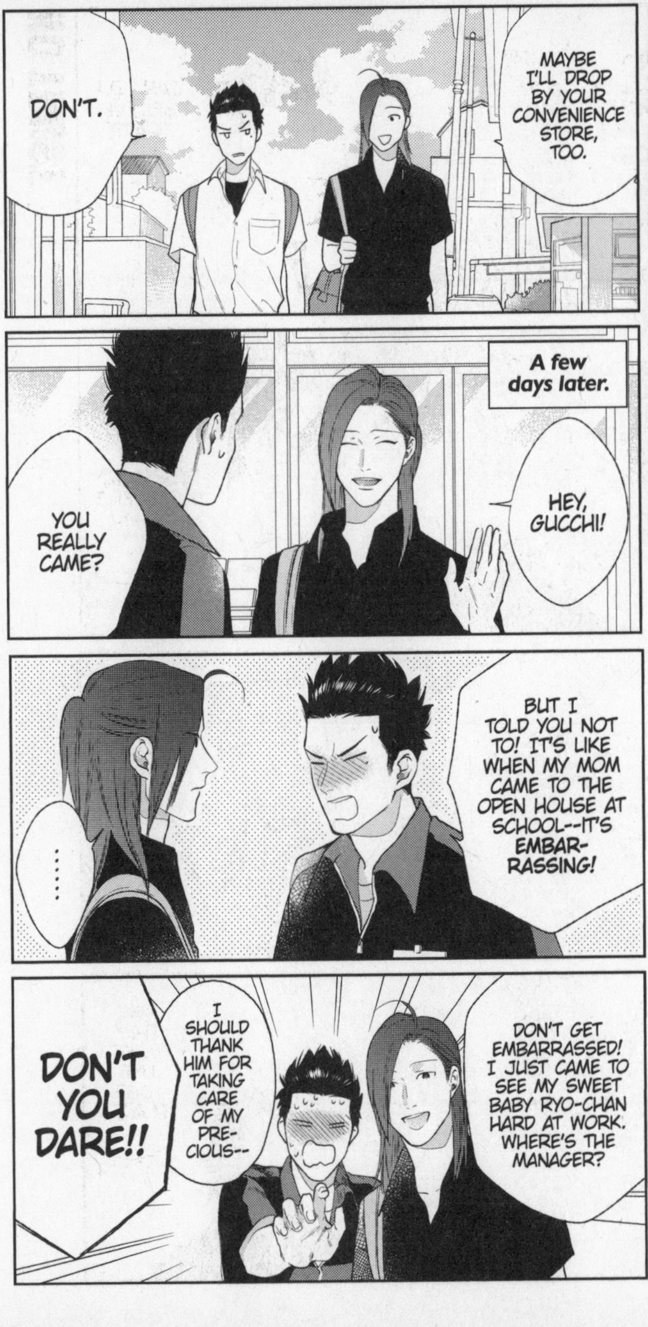
MAYBE I'LL DROP BY YOUR CONVENIENCE STORE, TOO.
DON'T.
A few days later.
HEY, GUCCHI!
YOU REALLY CAME?
BUT I TOLD YOU NOT TO! IT'S LIKE WHEN MY MOM CAME TO THE OPEN HOUSE AT SCHOOL--IT'S EMBARRASSING!
......
DON'T GET EMBARRASSED! I JUST CAME TO SEE MY SWEET BABY RYO-CHAN HARD AT WORK. WHERE'S THE MANAGER?
I SHOULD THANK HIM FOR TAKING CARE OF MY PRECIOUS--
DON'T YOU DARE!!

ALL GONE

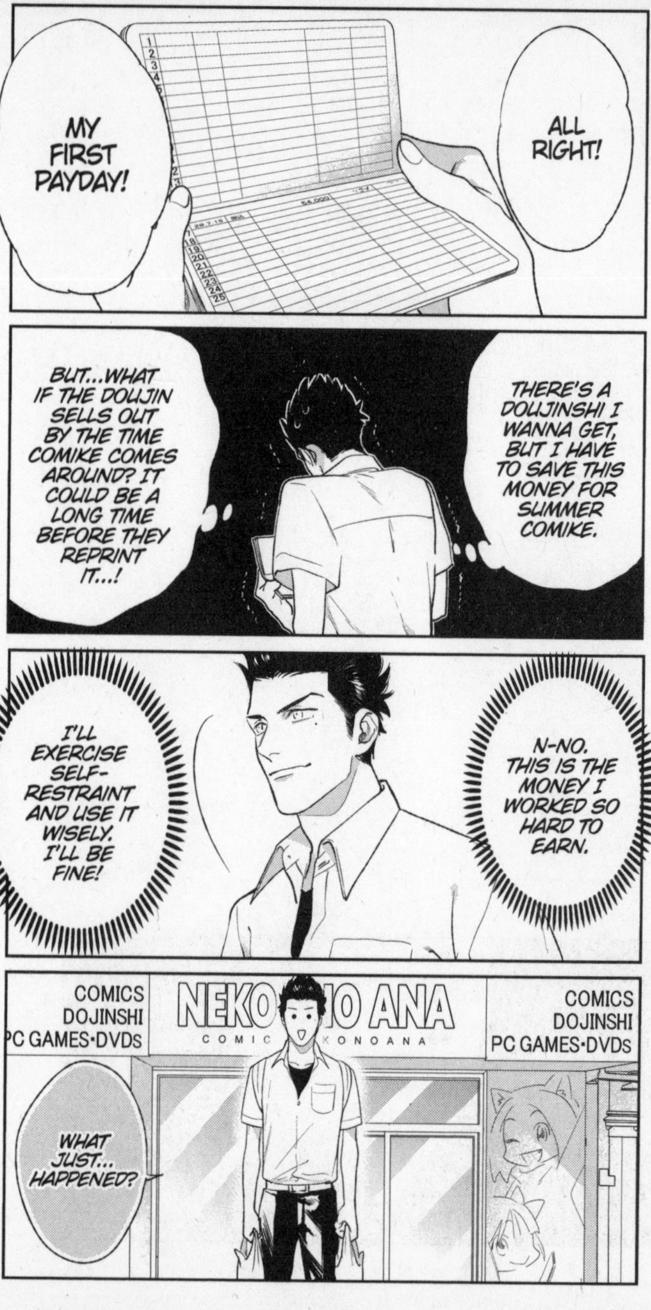
ALL RIGHT!
MY FIRST PAYDAY!
THERE'S A DOUJINSHI I WANNA GET, BUT I HAVE TO SAVE THIS MONEY FOR SUMMER COMIKE.
BUT...WHAT IF THE DOUJIN SELLS OUT BY THE TIME COMIKE COMES AROUND? IT COULD BE A LONG TIME BEFORE THEY REPRINT IT...!
N-NO. THIS IS THE MONEY I WORKED SO HARD TO EARN.
I'LL EXERCISE SELF-RESTRAINT AND USE IT WISELY. I'LL BE FINE!
COMICS DOJINSHI PC GAMES•DVDS
COMICS DOJINSHI PC GAMES•DVDS
WHAT JUST... HAPPENED?

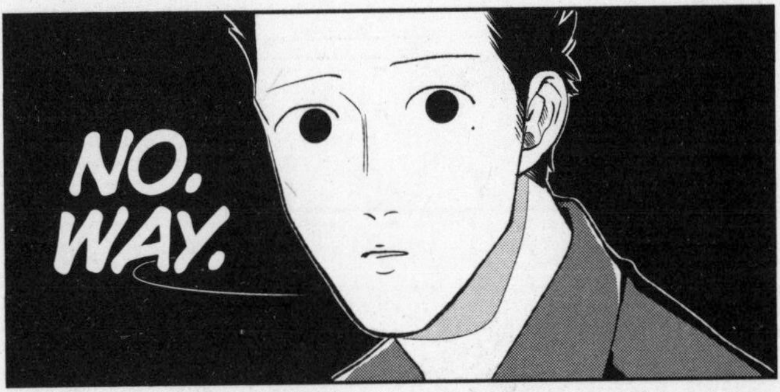
NO. WAY.

K

F S

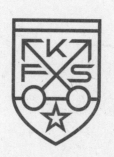

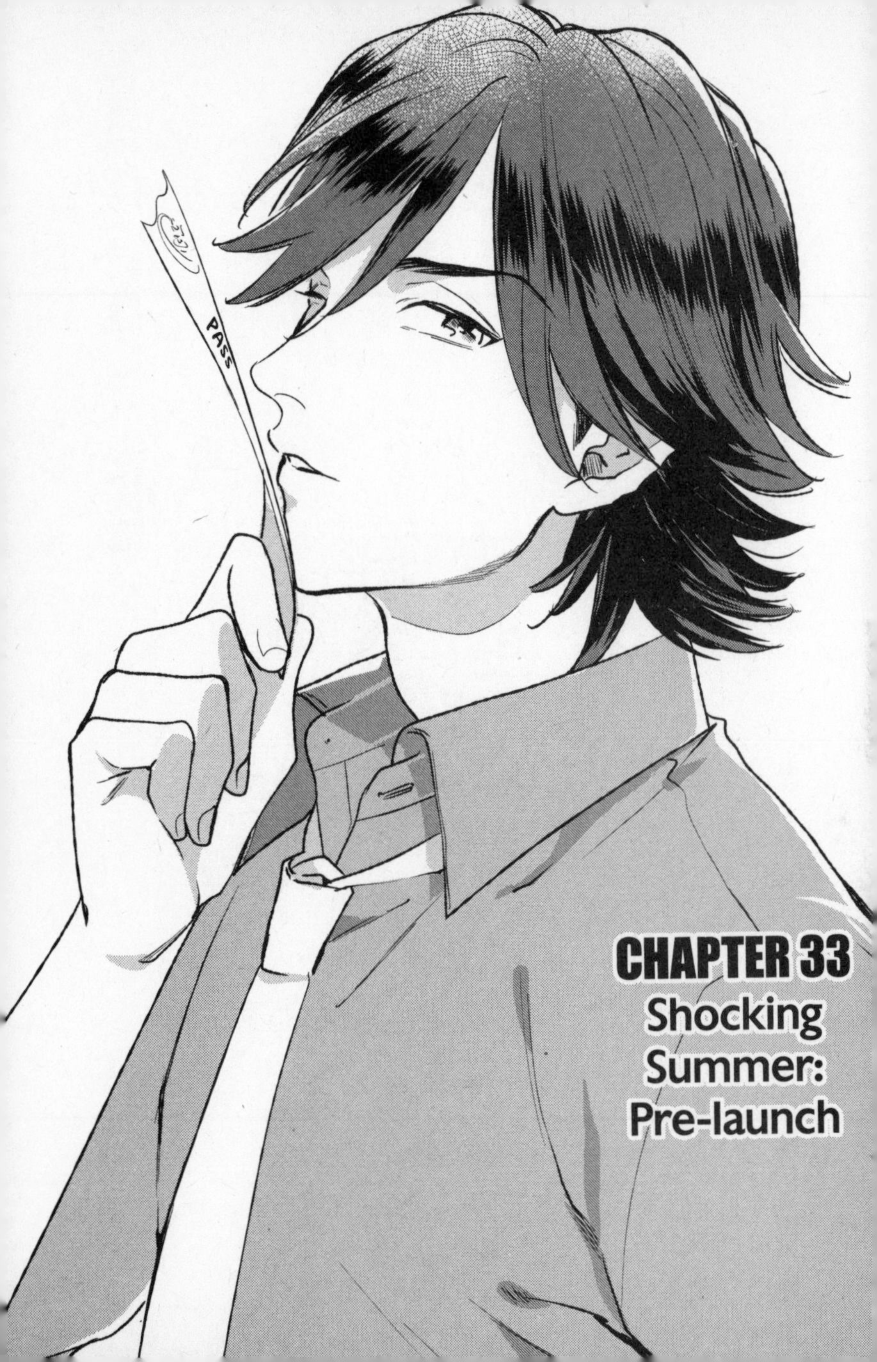
PASS

CHAPTER 33
Shocking Summer: Pre-launch

SOMEONE TRANSLATE PLEASE

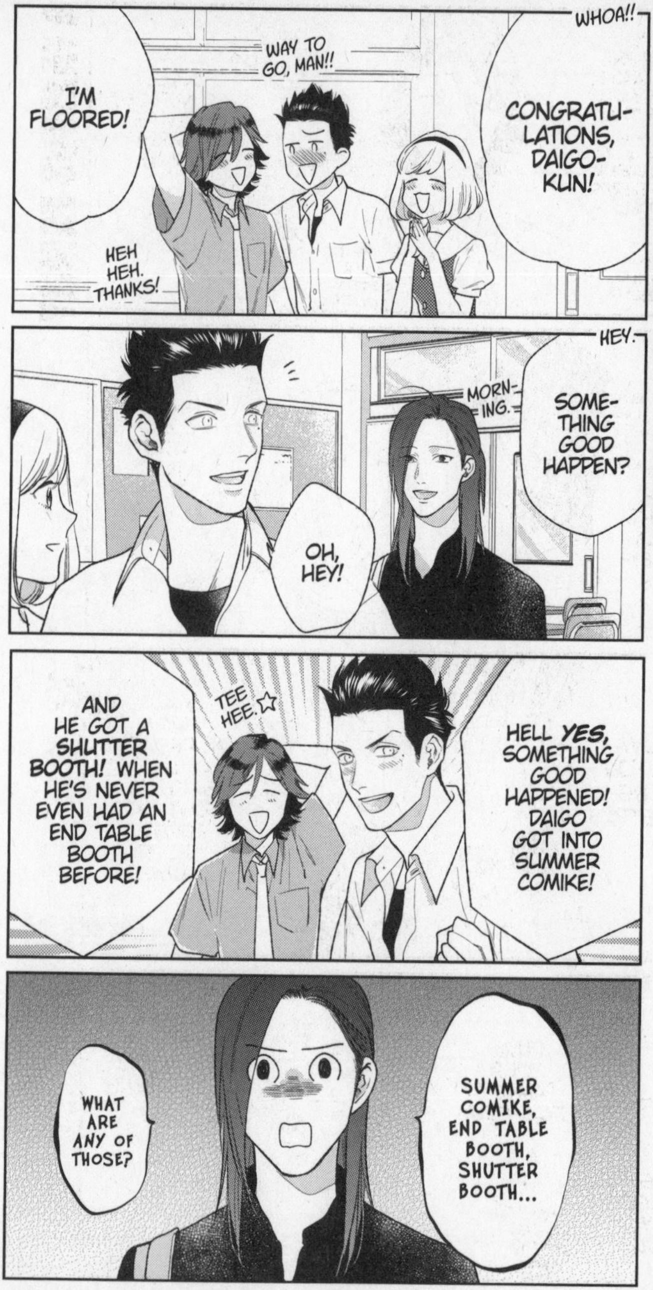
WHOA!! CONGRATULATIONS, DAIGO-KUN!
WAY TO GO, MAN!!
I'M FLOORED!
HEH HEH. THANKS!
HEY. SOMETHING GOOD HAPPEN?
MORNING.
OH, HEY!
HELL YES, SOMETHING GOOD HAPPENED! DAIGO GOT INTO SUMMER COMIKE!
TEE HEE.☆
AND HE GOT A SHUTTER BOOTH! WHEN HE'S NEVER EVEN HAD AN END TABLE BOOTH BEFORE!
SUMMER COMIKE, END TABLE BOOTH, SHUTTER BOOTH...
WHAT ARE ANY OF THOSE?

A FAMOUS FAMILY

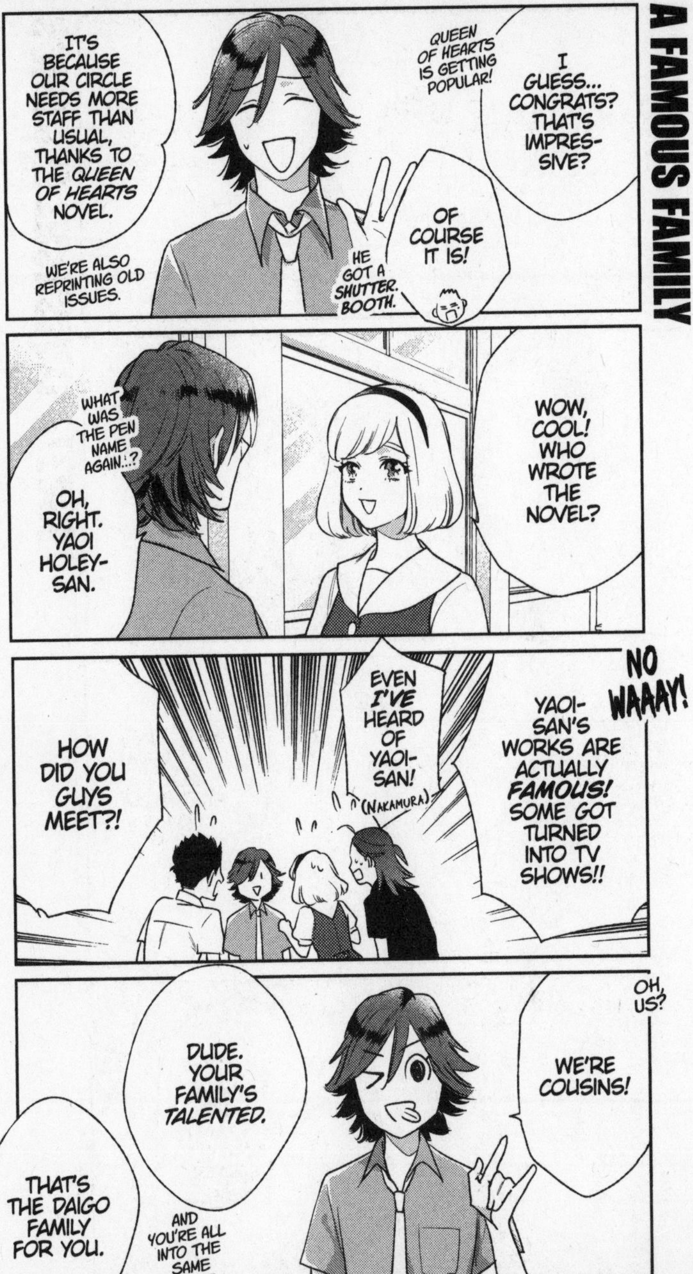
I GUESS... CONGRATS? THAT'S IMPRESSIVE?
QUEEN OF HEARTS IS GETTING POPULAR!
OF COURSE IT IS!
HE GOT A SHUTTER BOOTH.
IT'S BECAUSE OUR CIRCLE NEEDS MORE STAFF THAN USUAL, THANKS TO THE *QUEEN OF HEARTS* NOVEL.
WE'RE ALSO REPRINTING OLD ISSUES.
WOW, COOL! WHO WROTE THE NOVEL?
WHAT WAS THE PEN NAME AGAIN...?
OH, RIGHT. YAOI HOLEY-SAN.
NO WAAAY!
YAOI-SAN'S WORKS ARE ACTUALLY *FAMOUS!* SOME GOT TURNED INTO TV SHOWS!!
EVEN *I'VE* HEARD OF YAOI-SAN!
(NAKAMURA)
HOW DID YOU GUYS MEET?!
OH, US?
WE'RE COUSINS!
DUDE. YOUR FAMILY'S *TALENTED.*
THAT'S THE DAIGO FAMILY FOR YOU.
AND YOU'RE ALL INTO THE SAME STUFF.

DON'T TAKE IT LIGHTLY

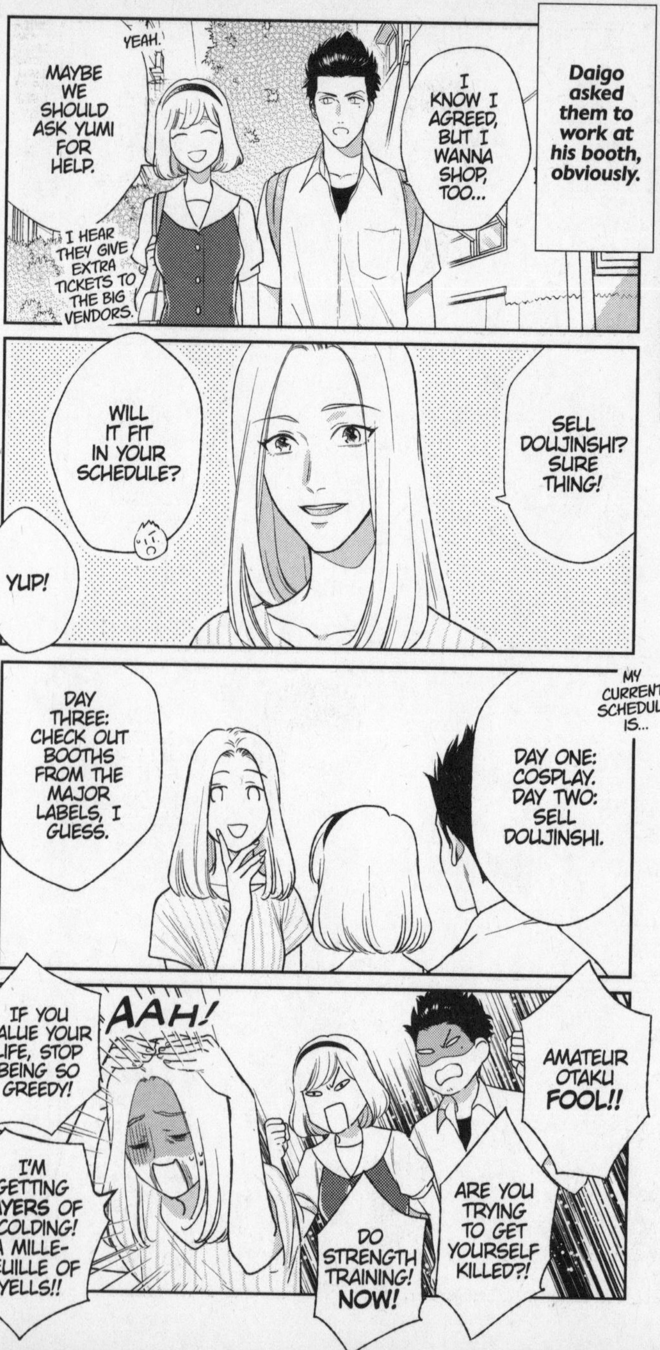
Daigo asked them to work at his booth, obviously.
I KNOW I AGREED, BUT I WANNA SHOP, TOO...
YEAH.
MAYBE WE SHOULD ASK YUMI FOR HELP.
I HEAR THEY GIVE EXTRA TICKETS TO THE BIG VENDORS.
SELL DOUJINSHI? SURE THING!
WILL IT FIT IN YOUR SCHEDULE?
YUP!
MY CURRENT SCHEDULE IS...
DAY ONE: COSPLAY. DAY TWO: SELL DOUJINSHI.
DAY THREE: CHECK OUT BOOTHS FROM THE MAJOR LABELS, I GUESS.
AMATEUR OTAKU FOOL!!
AAH!
IF YOU VALUE YOUR LIFE, STOP BEING SO GREEDY!
ARE YOU TRYING TO GET YOURSELF KILLED?!
DO STRENGTH TRAINING! NOW!
I'M GETTING LAYERS OF SCOLDING! A MILLE-FEUILLE OF YELLS!!

PRIDE

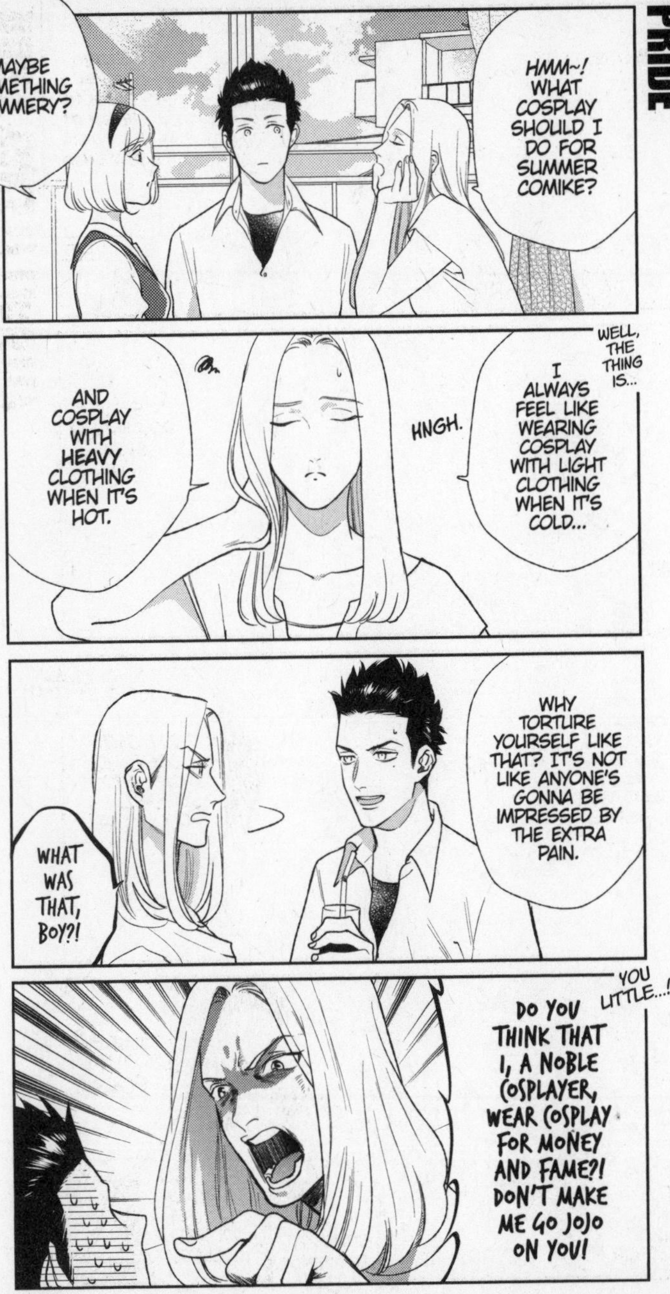
HMM~! WHAT COSPLAY SHOULD I DO FOR SUMMER COMIKE?
MAYBE SOMETHING SUMMERY?
WELL, THE THING IS...
I ALWAYS FEEL LIKE WEARING COSPLAY WITH LIGHT CLOTHING WHEN IT'S COLD...
HNGH.
AND COSPLAY WITH HEAVY CLOTHING WHEN IT'S HOT.
WHY TORTURE YOURSELF LIKE THAT? IT'S NOT LIKE ANYONE'S GONNA BE IMPRESSED BY THE EXTRA PAIN.
WHAT WAS THAT, BOY?!
YOU LITTLE...!!
DO YOU THINK THAT I, A NOBLE COSPLAYER, WEAR COSPLAY FOR MONEY AND FAME?! DON'T MAKE ME GO JOJO ON YOU!

EXTRA CHARGE? NO PROBLEM!

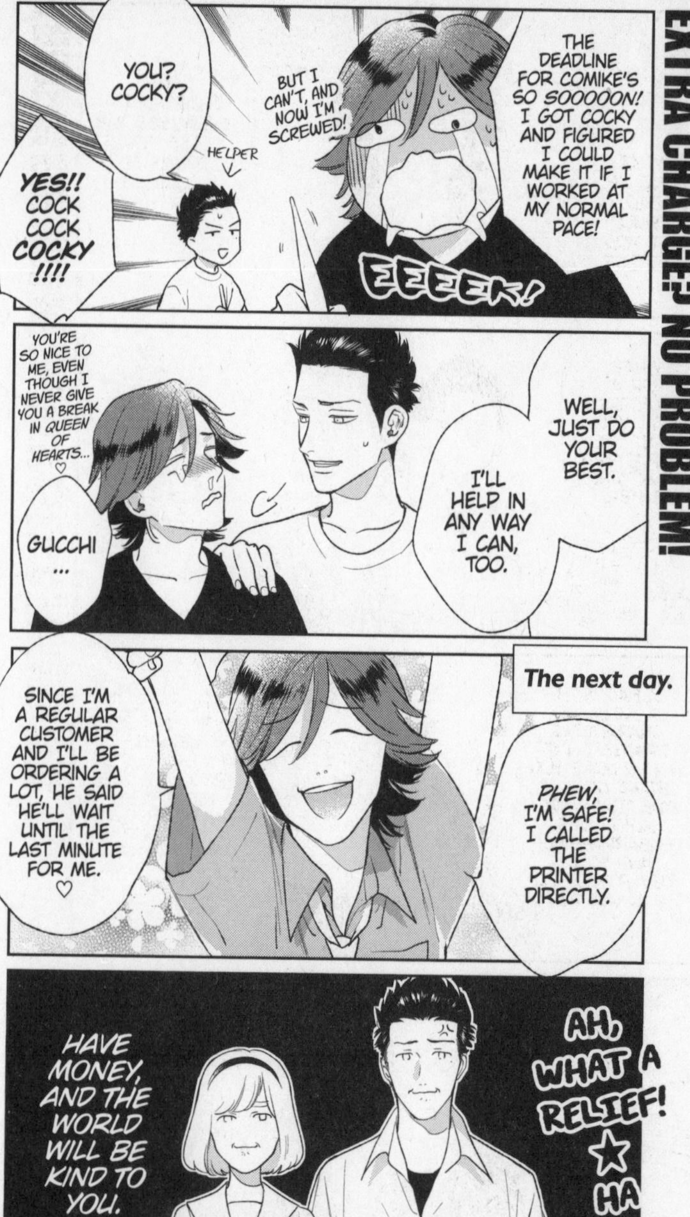
THE DEADLINE FOR COMIKE'S SO SOOOOON! I GOT COCKY AND FIGURED I COULD MAKE IT IF I WORKED AT MY NORMAL PACE!
EEEEK!
BUT I CAN'T, AND NOW I'M SCREWED!
YOU? COCKY?
HELPER
YES!! COCK COCK COCKY !!!!
WELL, JUST DO YOUR BEST.
I'LL HELP IN ANY WAY I CAN, TOO.
YOU'RE SO NICE TO ME, EVEN THOUGH I NEVER GIVE YOU A BREAK IN QUEEN OF HEARTS... ♡
GUCCHI ...
The next day.
PHEW, I'M SAFE! I CALLED THE PRINTER DIRECTLY.
SINCE I'M A REGULAR CUSTOMER AND I'LL BE ORDERING A LOT, HE SAID HE'LL WAIT UNTIL THE LAST MINUTE FOR ME. ♡
AH, WHAT A RELIEF! ☆ HA HA!
HAVE MONEY, AND THE WORLD WILL BE KIND TO YOU.

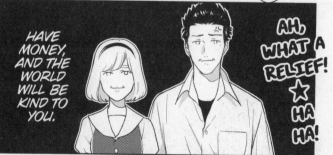

THE DIFFERENCE BETWEEN MEN AND WOMEN

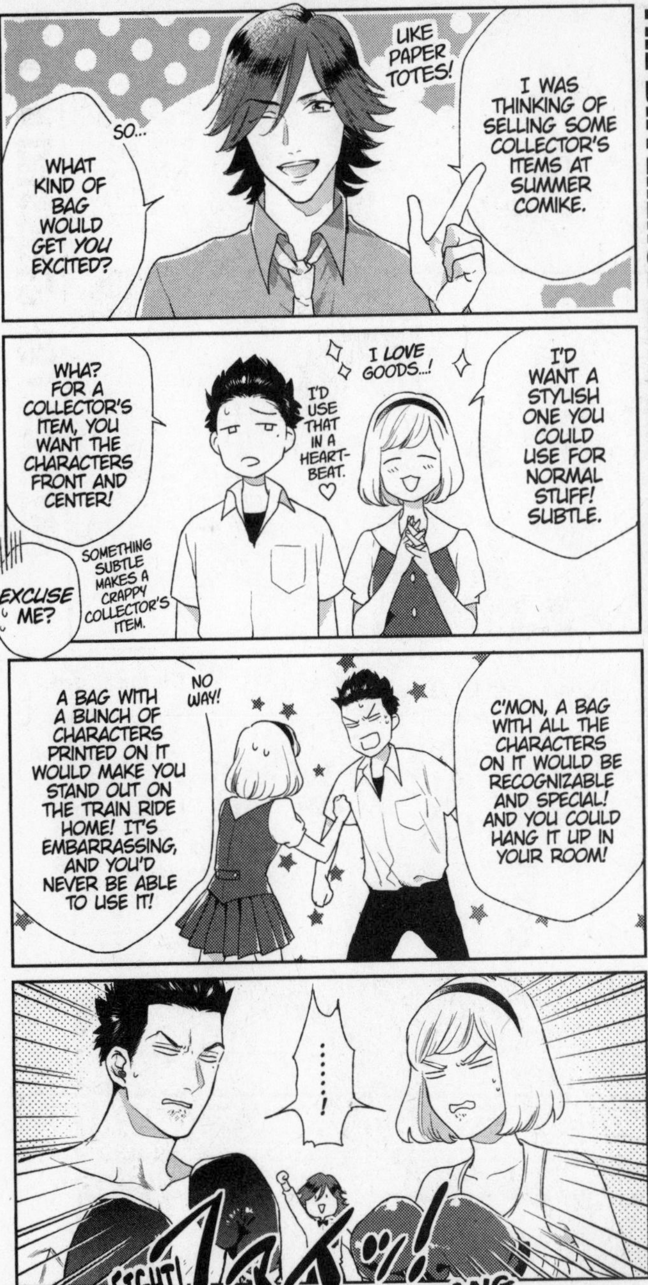
I WAS THINKING OF SELLING SOME COLLECTOR'S ITEMS AT SUMMER COMIKE.
LIKE PAPER TOTES!
SO...
WHAT KIND OF BAG WOULD GET *YOU* EXCITED?
I'D WANT A STYLISH ONE YOU COULD USE FOR NORMAL STUFF! SUBTLE.
I *LOVE* GOODS...!
I'D USE THAT IN A HEART-BEAT. ♡
WHA? FOR A COLLECTOR'S ITEM, YOU WANT THE CHARACTERS FRONT AND CENTER!
SOMETHING SUBTLE MAKES A CRAPPY COLLECTOR'S ITEM.
EXCUSE ME?
C'MON, A BAG WITH ALL THE CHARACTERS ON IT WOULD BE RECOGNIZABLE AND SPECIAL! AND YOU COULD HANG IT UP IN YOUR ROOM!
NO WAY!
A BAG WITH A BUNCH OF CHARACTERS PRINTED ON IT WOULD MAKE YOU STAND OUT ON THE TRAIN RIDE HOME! IT'S EMBARRASSING, AND YOU'D NEVER BE ABLE TO USE IT!
......!
FIGHT!
CLANG

AND THE WINNER IS...

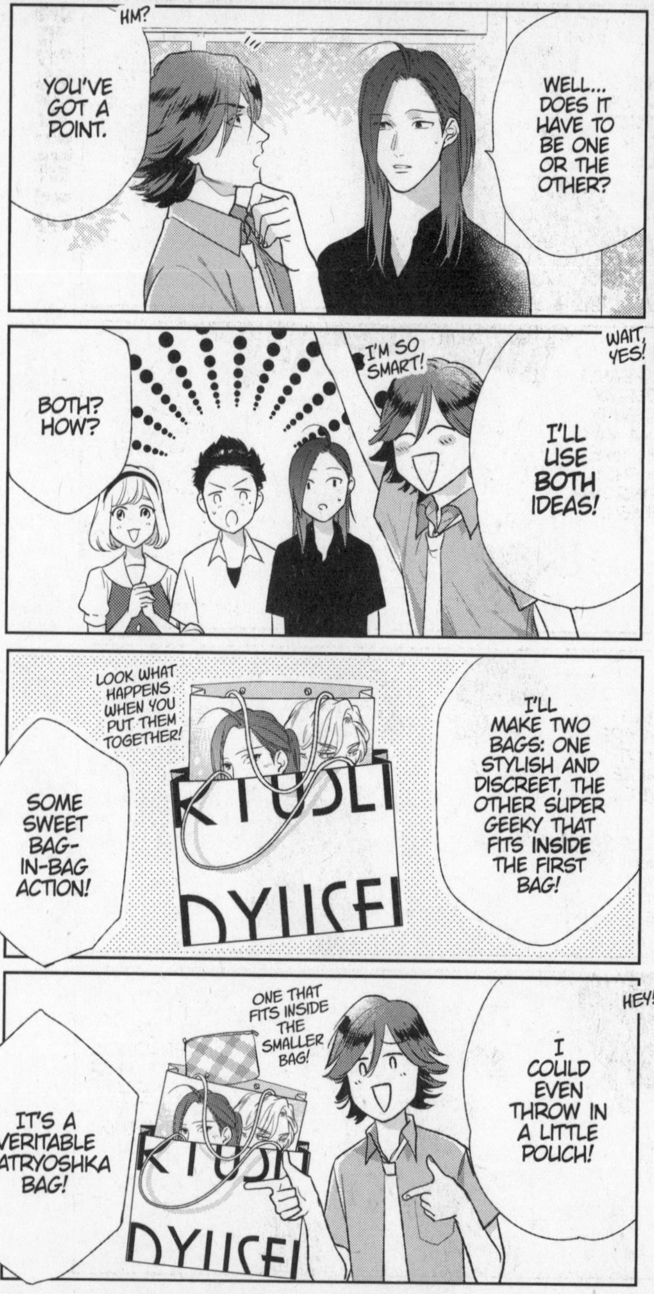
WELL... DOES IT HAVE TO BE ONE OR THE OTHER?
HM?
YOU'VE GOT A POINT.
WAIT, YES!
I'LL USE BOTH IDEAS!
I'M SO SMART!
BOTH? HOW?
I'LL MAKE TWO BAGS: ONE STYLISH AND DISCREET, THE OTHER SUPER GEEKY THAT FITS INSIDE THE FIRST BAG!
LOOK WHAT HAPPENS WHEN YOU PUT THEM TOGETHER!
SOME SWEET BAG-IN-BAG ACTION!
HEY!
I COULD EVEN THROW IN A LITTLE POUCH!
ONE THAT FITS INSIDE THE SMALLER BAG!
IT'S A VERITABLE MATRYOSHKA BAG!

SPECIALISTS

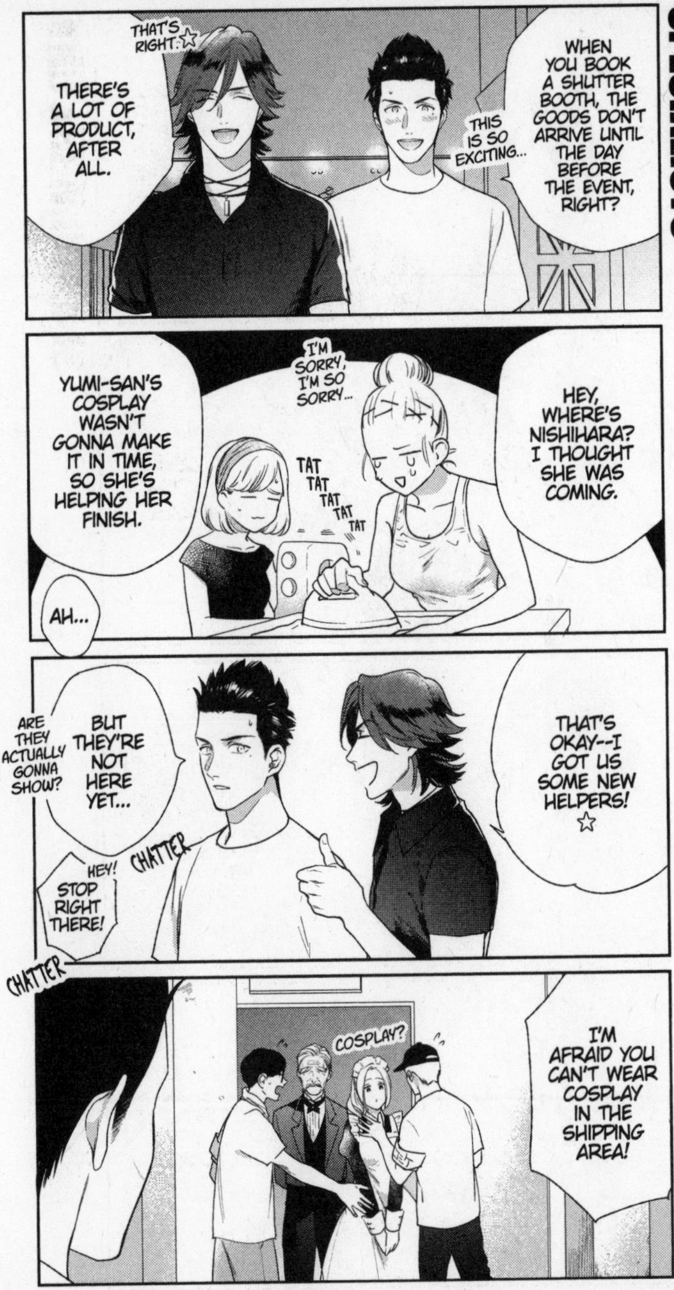
WHEN YOU BOOK A SHUTTER BOOTH, THE GOODS DON'T ARRIVE UNTIL THE DAY BEFORE THE EVENT, RIGHT?
THIS IS SO EXCITING...
THAT'S RIGHT.☆
THERE'S A LOT OF PRODUCT, AFTER ALL.
HEY, WHERE'S NISHIHARA? I THOUGHT SHE WAS COMING.
I'M SORRY, I'M SO SORRY...
TAT TAT TAT TAT TAT
YUMI-SAN'S COSPLAY WASN'T GONNA MAKE IT IN TIME, SO SHE'S HELPING HER FINISH.
AH...
THAT'S OKAY--I GOT US SOME NEW HELPERS! ☆
BUT THEY'RE NOT HERE YET...
ARE THEY ACTUALLY GONNA SHOW?
CHATTER
HEY! STOP RIGHT THERE!
CHATTER
I'M AFRAID YOU CAN'T WEAR COSPLAY IN THE SHIPPING AREA!
COSPLAY?

GOING OVERBOARD

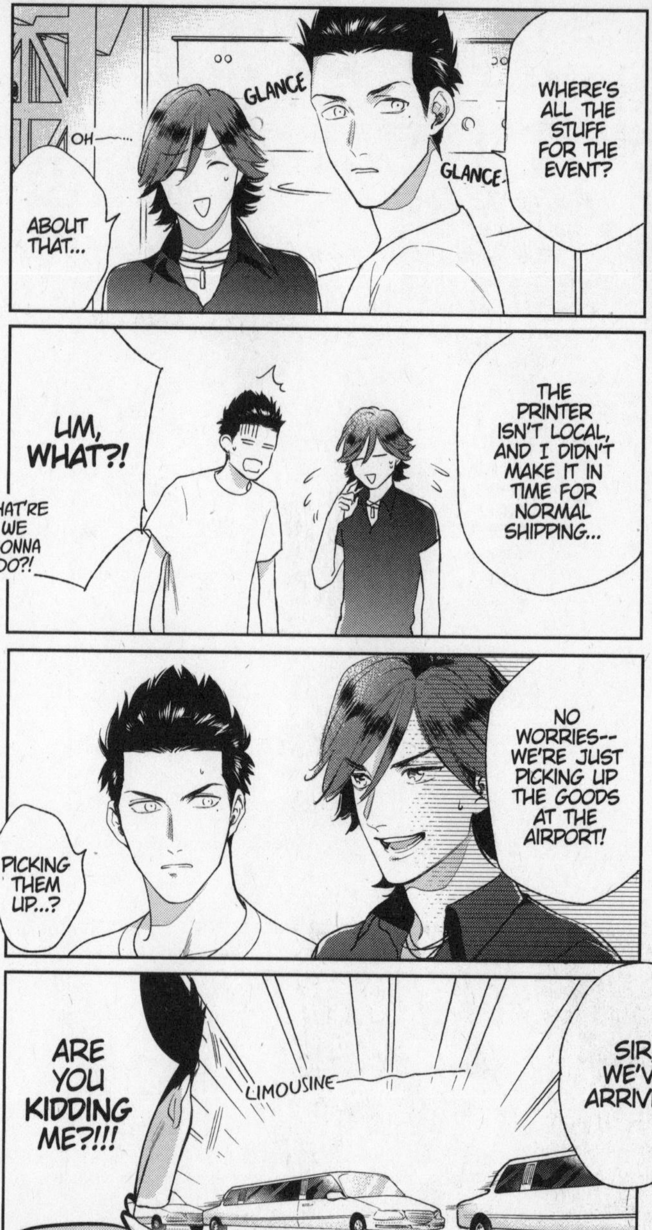
WHERE'S ALL THE STUFF FOR THE EVENT?
GLANCE
GLANCE
OH—...
ABOUT THAT...
THE PRINTER ISN'T LOCAL, AND I DIDN'T MAKE IT IN TIME FOR NORMAL SHIPPING...
UM, WHAT?!
WHAT'RE WE GONNA DO?!
NO WORRIES-- WE'RE JUST PICKING UP THE GOODS AT THE AIRPORT!
PICKING THEM UP...?
SIR, WE'VE ARRIVED!
LIMOUSINE
ARE YOU KIDDING ME?!!!

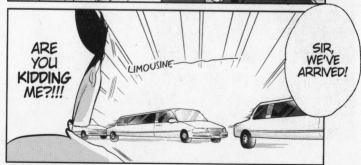

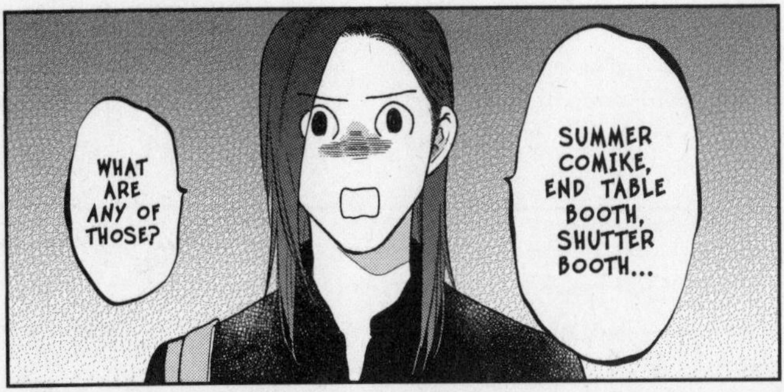
SUMMER COMIKE, END TABLE BOOTH, SHUTTER BOOTH...
WHAT ARE ANY OF THOSE?

K F S

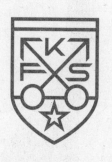

CHAPTER 34
Shocking Summer: The Main Feature

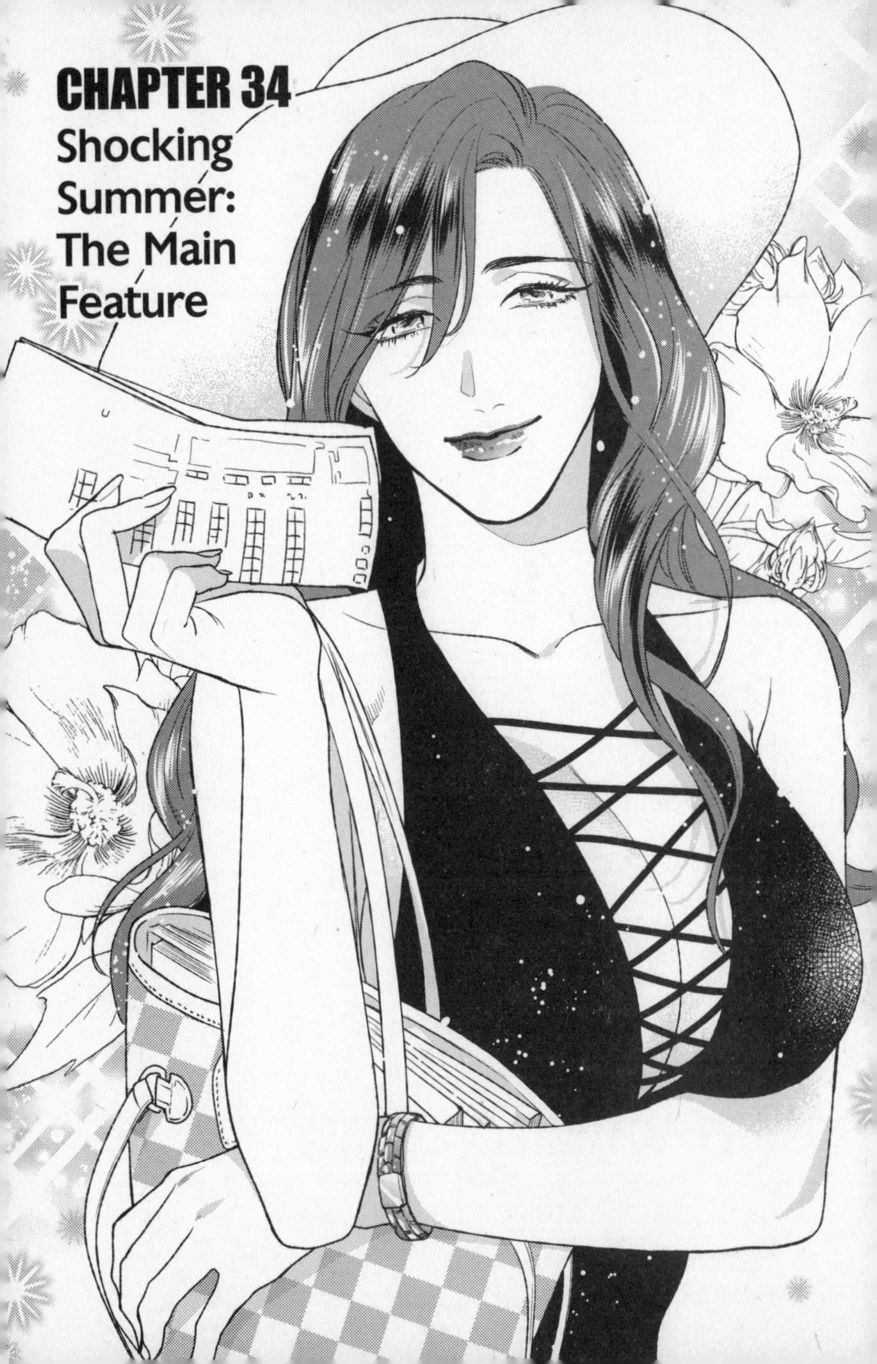

IS HE TRYING TO PISS US OFF?

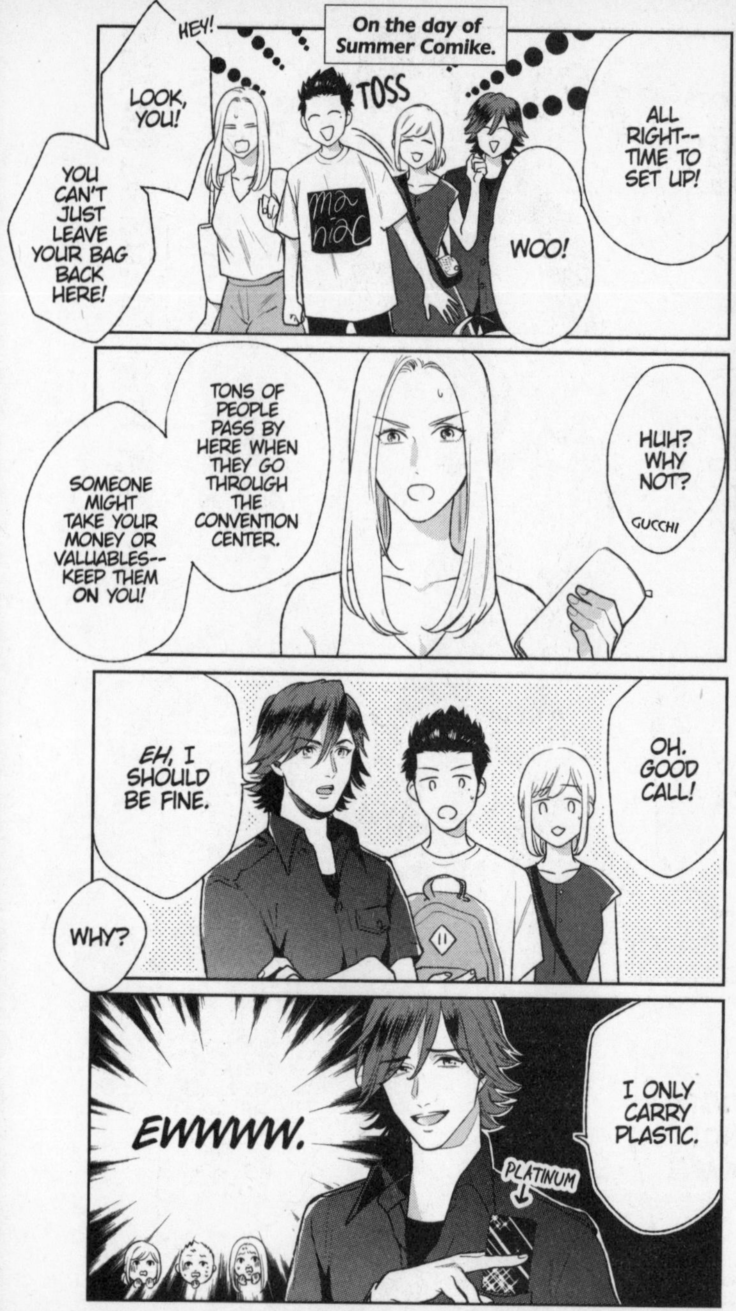
On the day of Summer Comike.
ALL RIGHT--TIME TO SET UP!
WOO!
TOSS
HEY!
LOOK, YOU!
YOU CAN'T JUST LEAVE YOUR BAG BACK HERE!
HUH? WHY NOT?
GUCCHI
TONS OF PEOPLE PASS BY HERE WHEN THEY GO THROUGH THE CONVENTION CENTER.
SOMEONE MIGHT TAKE YOUR MONEY OR VALUABLES--KEEP THEM ON YOU!
OH. GOOD CALL!
EH, I SHOULD BE FINE.
WHY?
I ONLY CARRY PLASTIC.
PLATINUM
EWWWW.

SAY NO TO BUYING FOR MINORS!

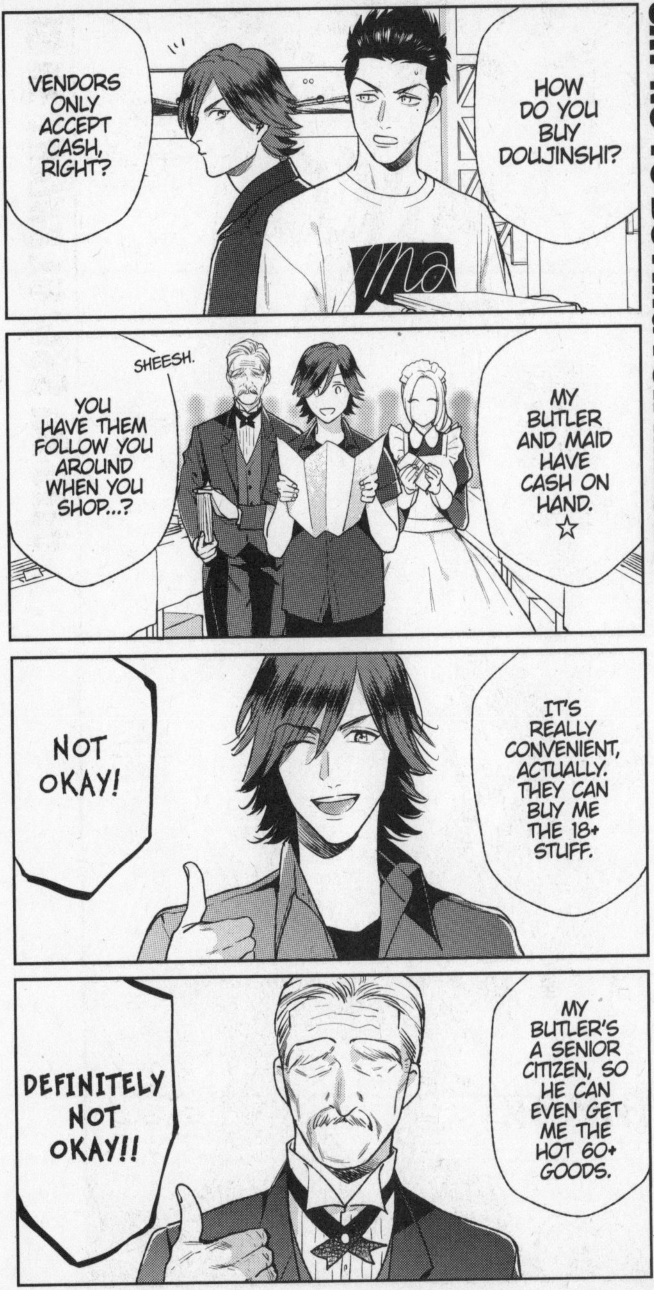
HOW DO YOU BUY DOUJINSHI?
VENDORS ONLY ACCEPT CASH, RIGHT?
MY BUTLER AND MAID HAVE CASH ON HAND. ☆
SHEESH.
YOU HAVE THEM FOLLOW YOU AROUND WHEN YOU SHOP...?
IT'S REALLY CONVENIENT, ACTUALLY. THEY CAN BUY ME THE 18+ STUFF.
NOT OKAY!
MY BUTLER'S A SENIOR CITIZEN, SO HE CAN EVEN GET ME THE HOT 60+ GOODS.
DEFINITELY NOT OKAY!!

JUST POINT TO WHAT YOU WANT

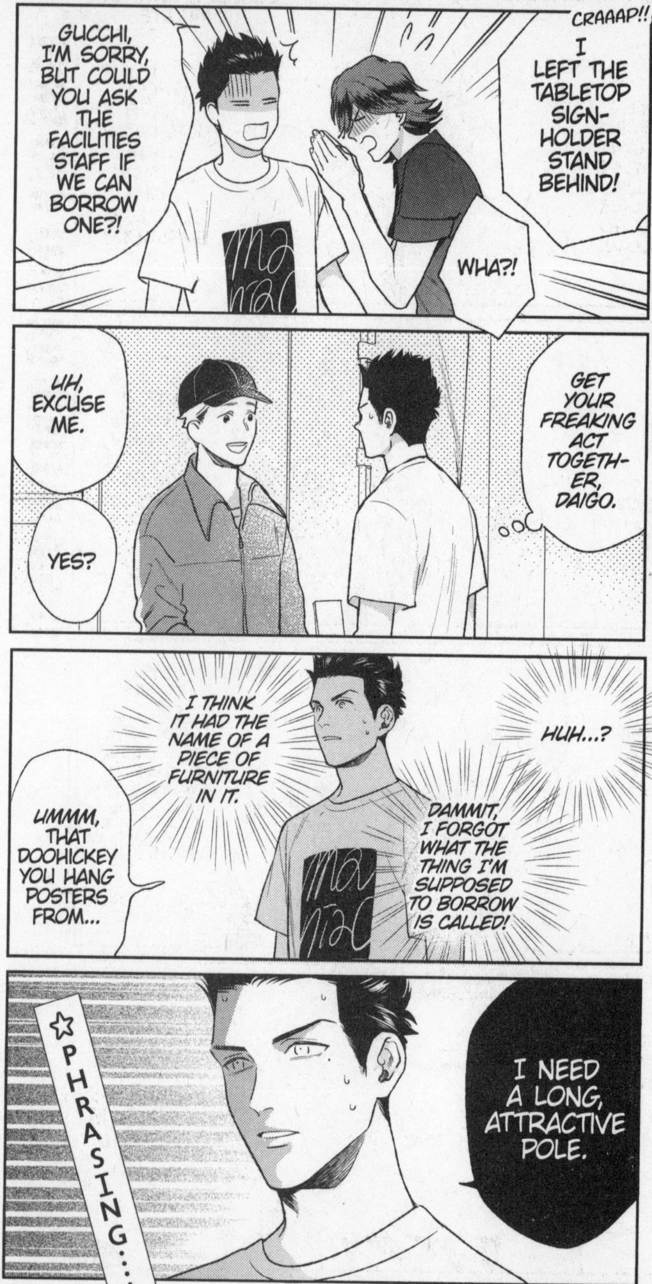
CRAAAP!!
I LEFT THE TABLETOP SIGN-HOLDER STAND BEHIND!
GUCCHI, I'M SORRY, BUT COULD YOU ASK THE FACILITIES STAFF IF WE CAN BORROW ONE?!
WHA?!
GET YOUR FREAKING ACT TOGETHER, DAIGO.
UH, EXCUSE ME.
YES?
HUH...?
I THINK IT HAD THE NAME OF A PIECE OF FURNITURE IN IT.
DAMMIT, I FORGOT WHAT THE THING I'M SUPPOSED TO BORROW IS CALLED!
UMMM, THAT DOOHICKEY YOU HANG POSTERS FROM...
I NEED A LONG, ATTRACTIVE POLE.
☆PHRASING...!

FANS CAN TELL, NO MATTER WHAT

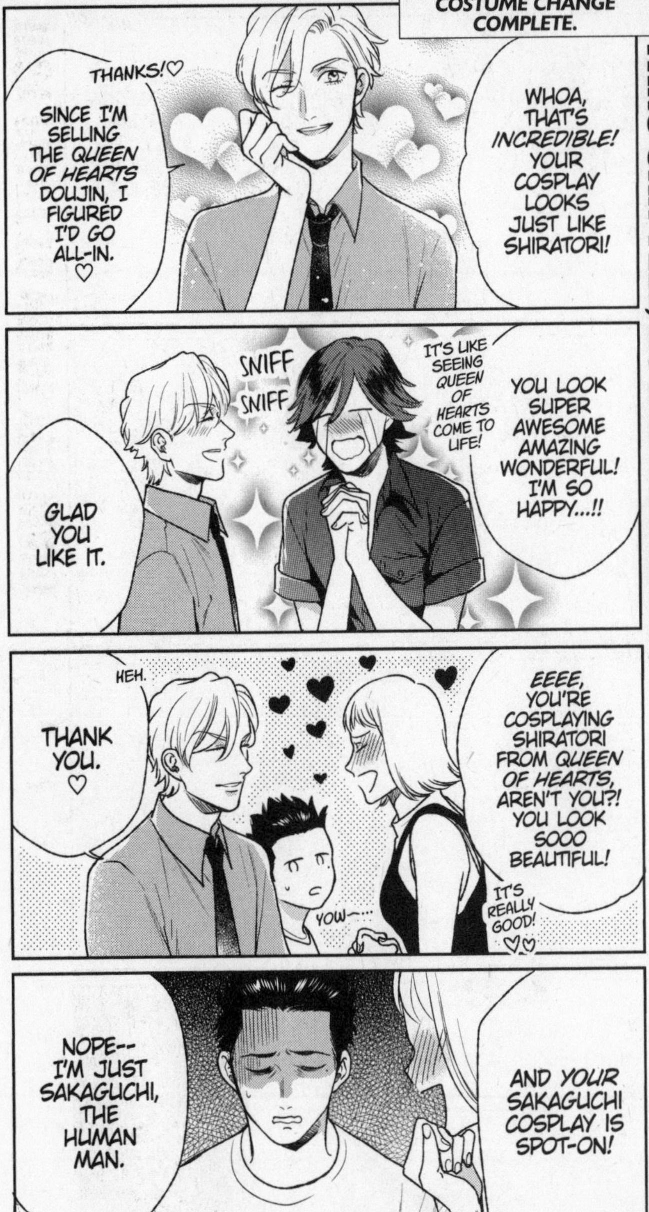
COSTUME CHANGE COMPLETE.
WHOA, THAT'S INCREDIBLE! YOUR COSPLAY LOOKS JUST LIKE SHIRATORI!
THANKS! ♡
SINCE I'M SELLING THE QUEEN OF HEARTS DOUJIN, I FIGURED I'D GO ALL-IN. ♡
YOU LOOK SUPER AWESOME AMAZING WONDERFUL! I'M SO HAPPY...!!
IT'S LIKE SEEING QUEEN OF HEARTS COME TO LIFE!
SNIFF
SNIFF
GLAD YOU LIKE IT.
EEEE, YOU'RE COSPLAYING SHIRATORI FROM QUEEN OF HEARTS, AREN'T YOU?! YOU LOOK SOOO BEAUTIFUL!
IT'S REALLY GOOD! ♡♡
YOW~...
HEH.
THANK YOU. ♡
AND YOUR SAKAGUCHI COSPLAY IS SPOT-ON!
NOPE-- I'M JUST SAKAGUCHI, THE HUMAN MAN.

STYLE

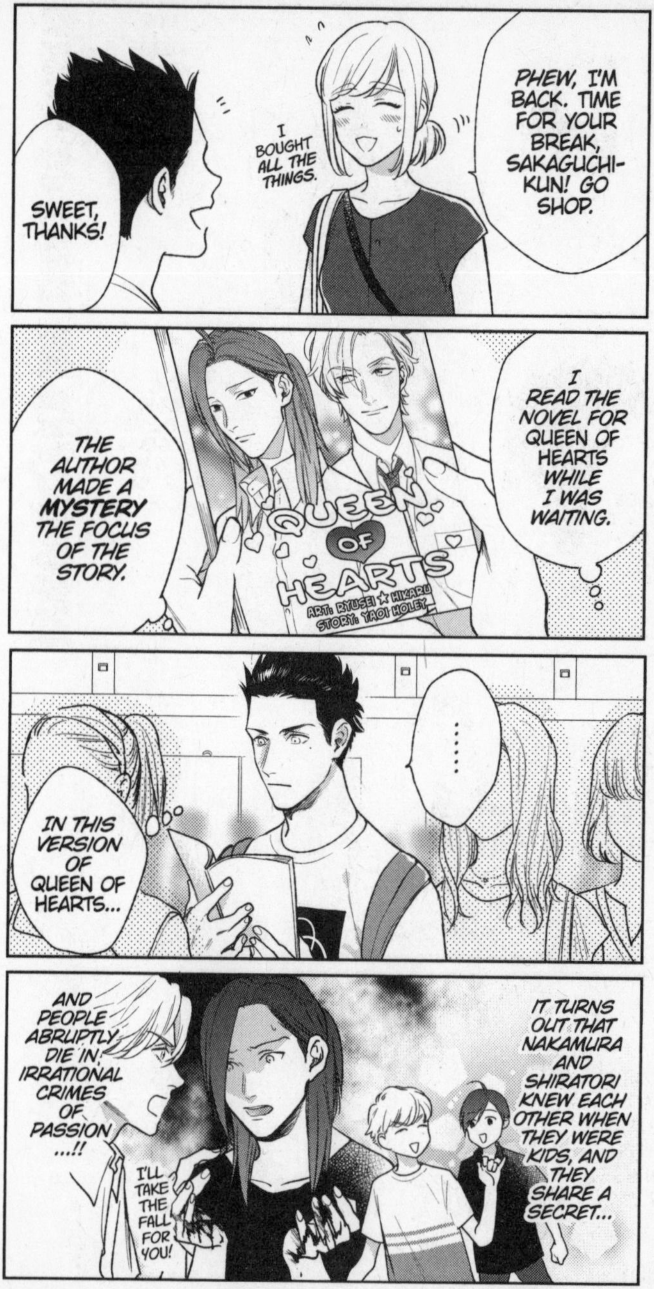
PHEW, I'M BACK. TIME FOR YOUR BREAK, SAKAGUCHI-KUN! GO SHOP.
I BOUGHT ALL THE THINGS.
SWEET, THANKS!
I READ THE NOVEL FOR QUEEN OF HEARTS WHILE I WAS WAITING.
THE AUTHOR MADE A **MYSTERY** THE FOCUS OF THE STORY.
QUEEN OF HEARTS
ART: RYUSEI ☆ HIKARU
STORY: YAOI HOLEY
......
IN THIS VERSION OF QUEEN OF HEARTS...
IT TURNS OUT THAT NAKAMURA AND SHIRATORI KNEW EACH OTHER WHEN THEY WERE KIDS, AND THEY SHARE A SECRET...
AND PEOPLE ABRUPTLY DIE IN IRRATIONAL CRIMES OF PASSION...!!
I'LL TAKE THE FALL FOR YOU!

GORGEOUS THROUGH AND THROUGH

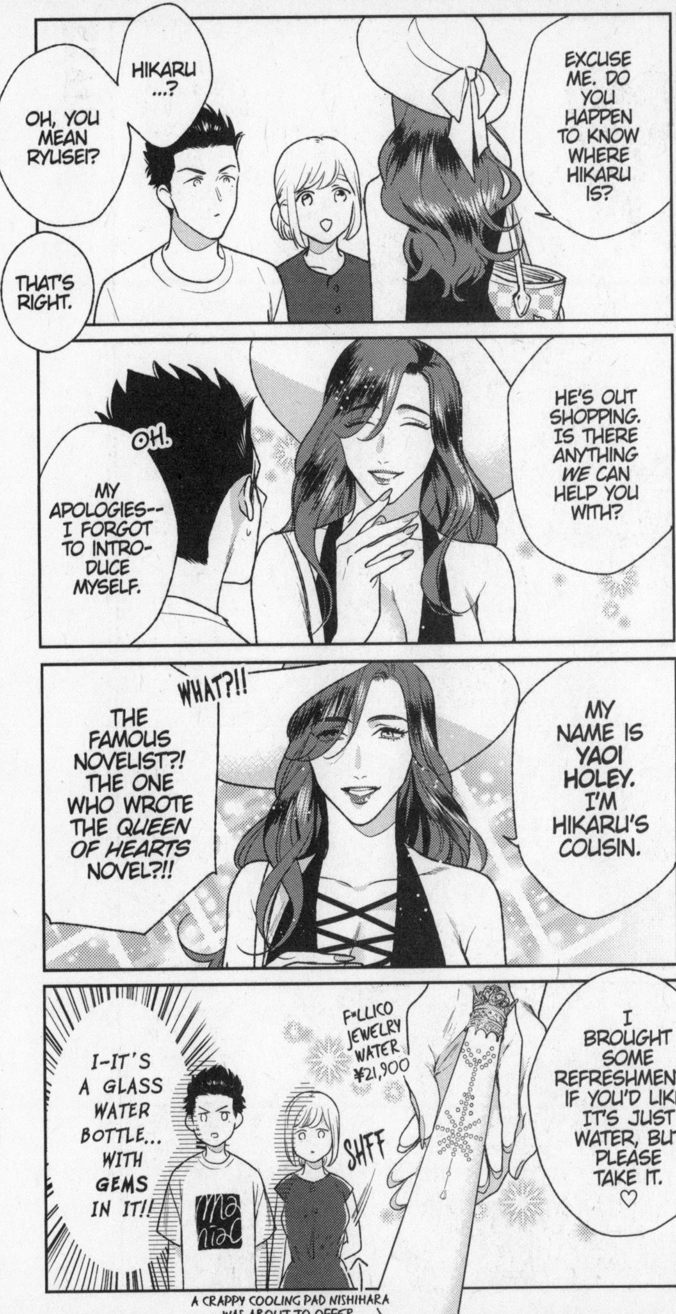
EXCUSE ME. DO YOU HAPPEN TO KNOW WHERE HIKARU IS?
HIKARU ...?
OH, YOU MEAN RYUSEI?
THAT'S RIGHT.
HE'S OUT SHOPPING. IS THERE ANYTHING *WE* CAN HELP YOU WITH?
OH.
MY APOLOGIES-- I FORGOT TO INTRO-DUCE MYSELF.
MY NAME IS YAOI HOLEY. I'M HIKARU'S COUSIN.
WHAT?!!
THE FAMOUS NOVELIST?! THE ONE WHO WROTE THE *QUEEN OF HEARTS* NOVEL?!!
I BROUGHT SOME REFRESHMENTS, IF YOU'D LIKE. IT'S JUST WATER, BUT PLEASE TAKE IT. ♡
F*LLICO JEWELRY WATER ¥21,900
SHFF
I-IT'S A GLASS WATER BOTTLE... WITH GEMS IN IT!!

A CRAPPY COOLING PAD NISHIHARA WAS ABOUT TO OFFER.

PEARLS BEFORE SWINE

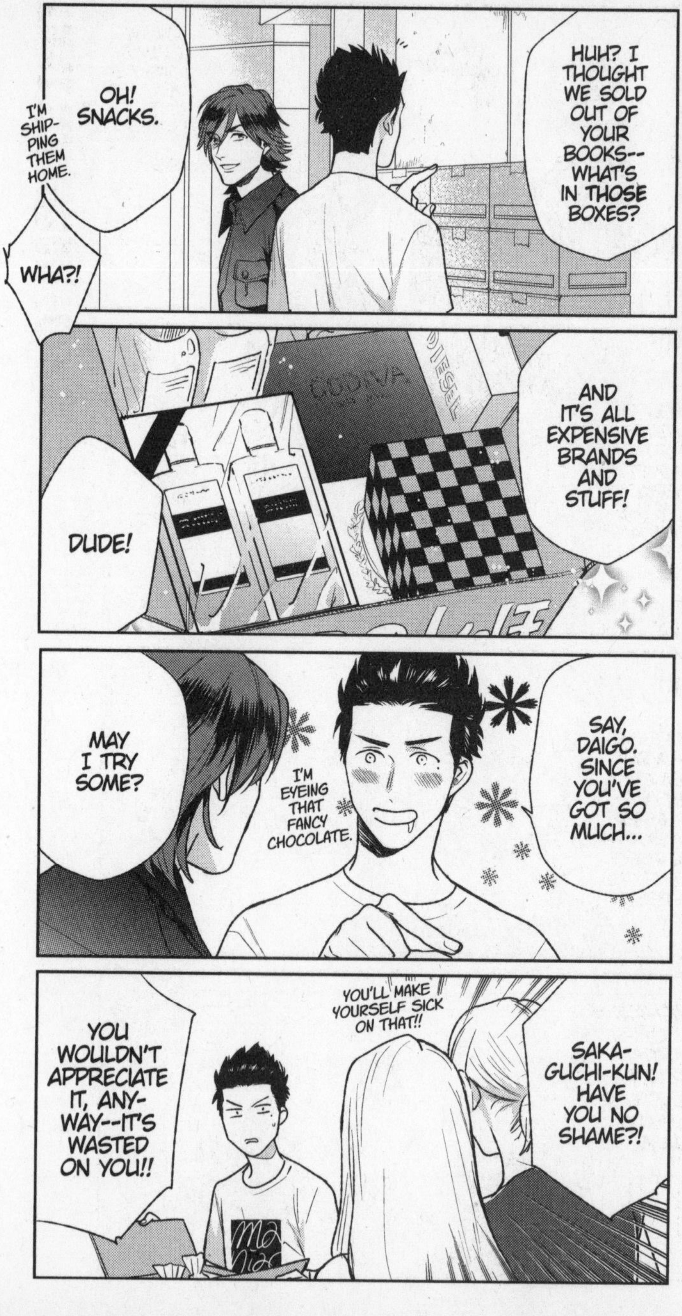
HUH? I THOUGHT WE SOLD OUT OF YOUR BOOKS--WHAT'S IN THOSE BOXES?
OH! SNACKS.
I'M SHIPPING THEM HOME.
WHA?!
AND IT'S ALL EXPENSIVE BRANDS AND STUFF!
DIESEL
GODIVA
DUDE!
SAY, DAIGO. SINCE YOU'VE GOT SO MUCH...
I'M EYEING THAT FANCY CHOCOLATE.
MAY I TRY SOME?
SAKAGUCHI-KUN! HAVE YOU NO SHAME?!
YOU'LL MAKE YOURSELF SICK ON THAT!!
YOU WOULDN'T APPRECIATE IT, ANYWAY--IT'S WASTED ON YOU!!

THAT'S A WRAP, FOLKS!

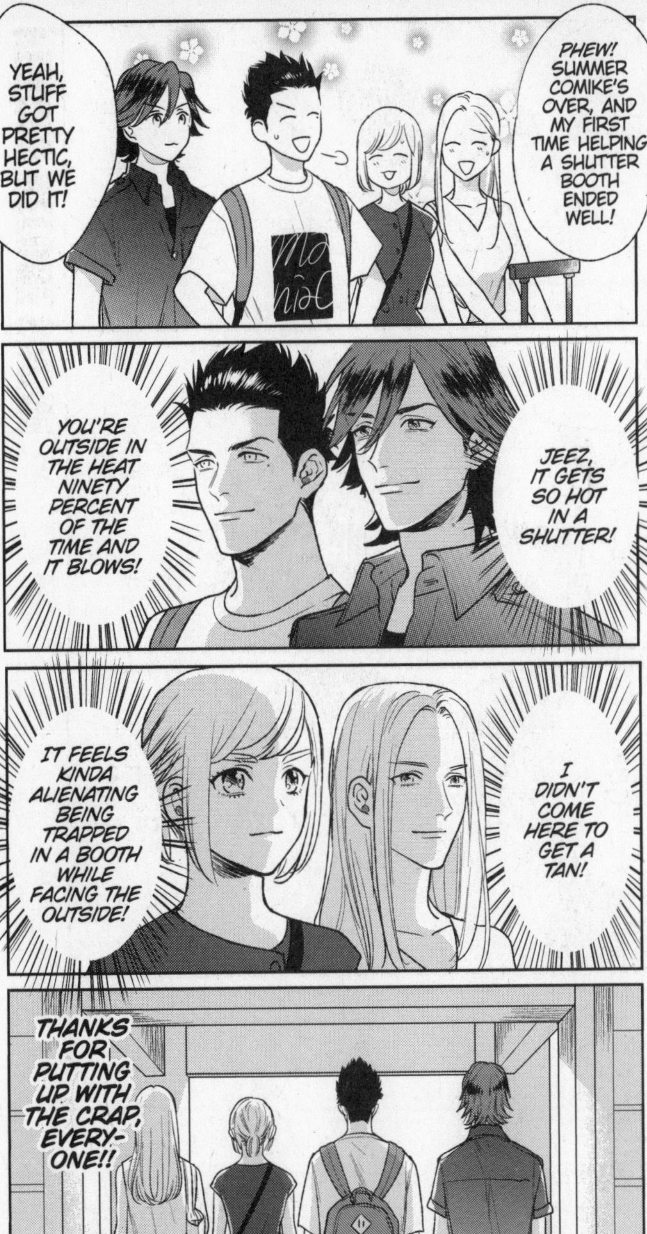
PHEW! SUMMER COMIKE'S OVER, AND MY FIRST TIME HELPING A SHUTTER BOOTH ENDED WELL!
YEAH, STUFF GOT PRETTY HECTIC, BUT WE DID IT!
JEEZ, IT GETS SO HOT IN A SHUTTER!
YOU'RE OUTSIDE IN THE HEAT NINETY PERCENT OF THE TIME AND IT BLOWS!
I DIDN'T COME HERE TO GET A TAN!
IT FEELS KINDA ALIENATING BEING TRAPPED IN A BOOTH WHILE FACING THE OUTSIDE!
THANKS FOR PUTTING UP WITH THE CRAP, EVERY-ONE!!

HALF OF WHAT I GET FROM MY JOB

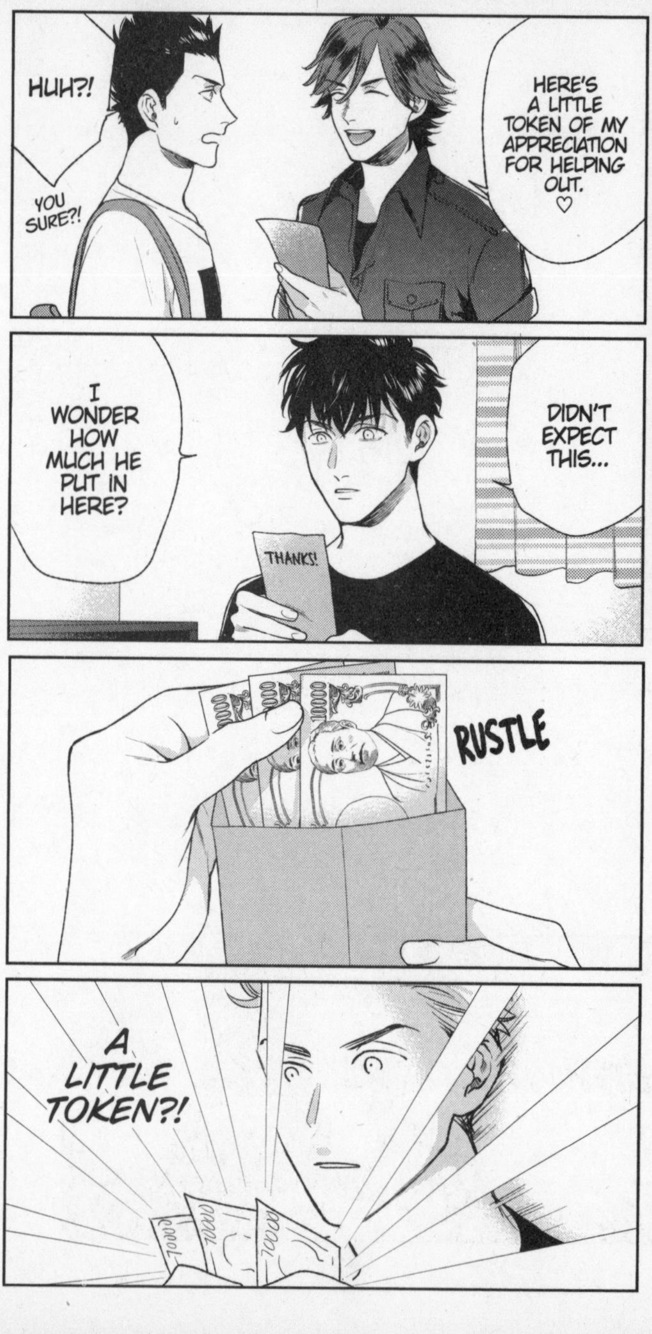
HERE'S A LITTLE TOKEN OF MY APPRECIATION FOR HELPING OUT. ♡
HUH?!
YOU SURE?!
DIDN'T EXPECT THIS...
THANKS!
I WONDER HOW MUCH HE PUT IN HERE?
RUSTLE
A LITTLE TOKEN?!

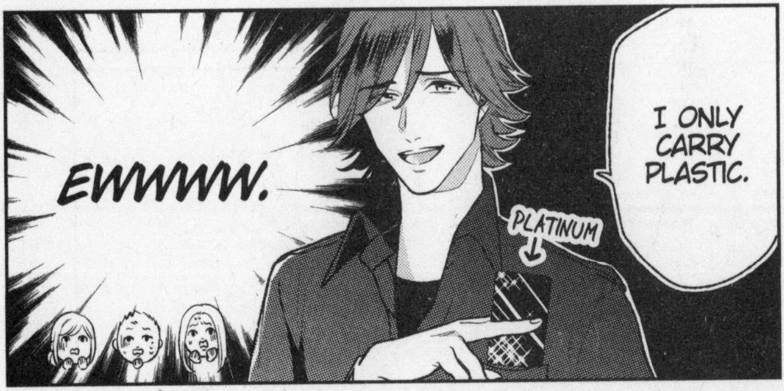
I ONLY CARRY PLASTIC.
PLATINUM
EWWWW.

KFS

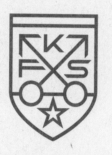

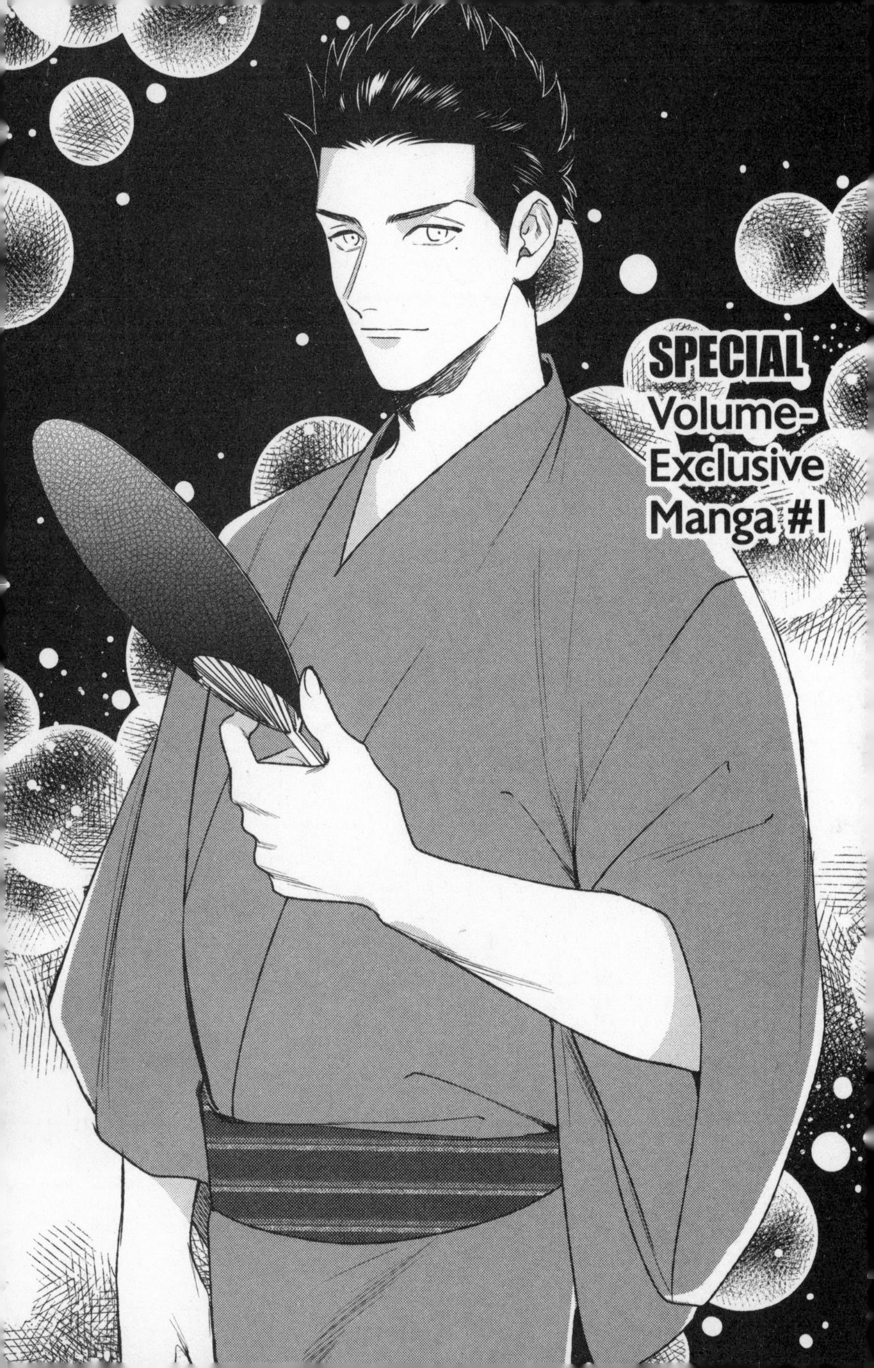
SPECIAL
Volume-
Exclusive
Manga #1

SUMMER IS EVENT SEASON

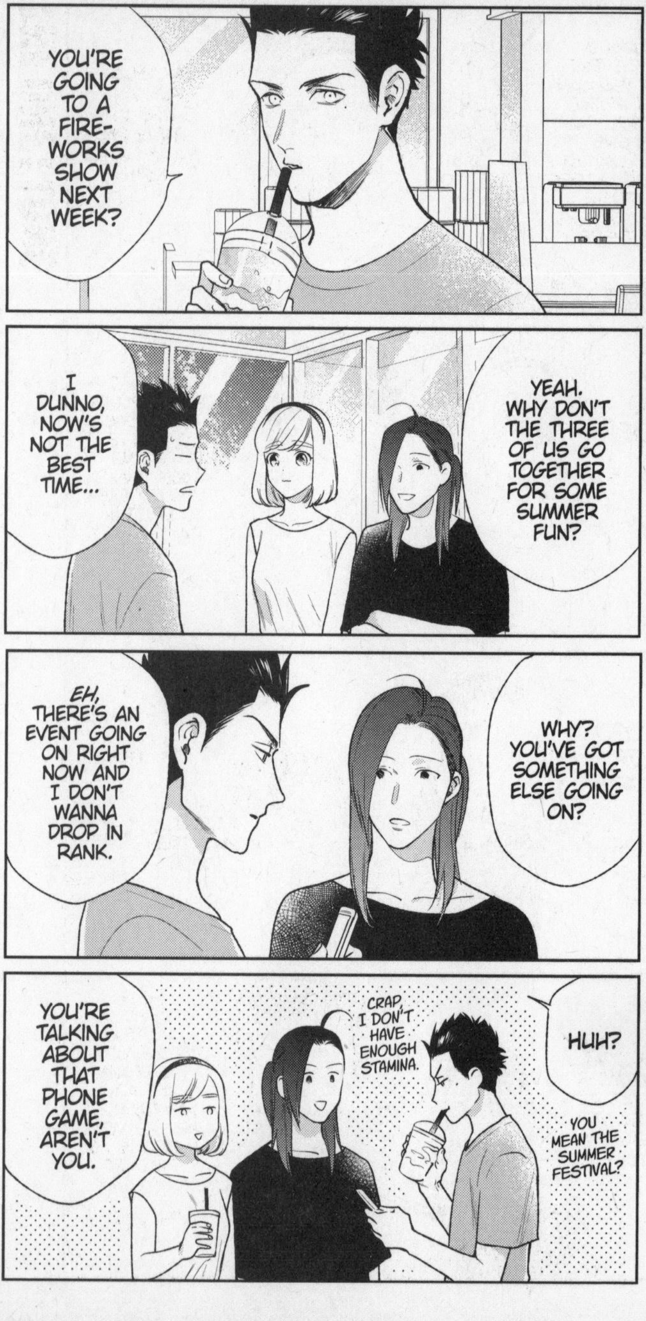
YOU'RE GOING TO A FIRE-WORKS SHOW NEXT WEEK?
YEAH. WHY DON'T THE THREE OF US GO TOGETHER FOR SOME SUMMER FUN?
I DUNNO, NOW'S NOT THE BEST TIME...
WHY? YOU'VE GOT SOMETHING ELSE GOING ON?
EH, THERE'S AN EVENT GOING ON RIGHT NOW AND I DON'T WANNA DROP IN RANK.
HUH?
YOU MEAN THE SUMMER FESTIVAL?
CRAP, I DON'T HAVE ENOUGH STAMINA.
YOU'RE TALKING ABOUT THAT PHONE GAME, AREN'T YOU.

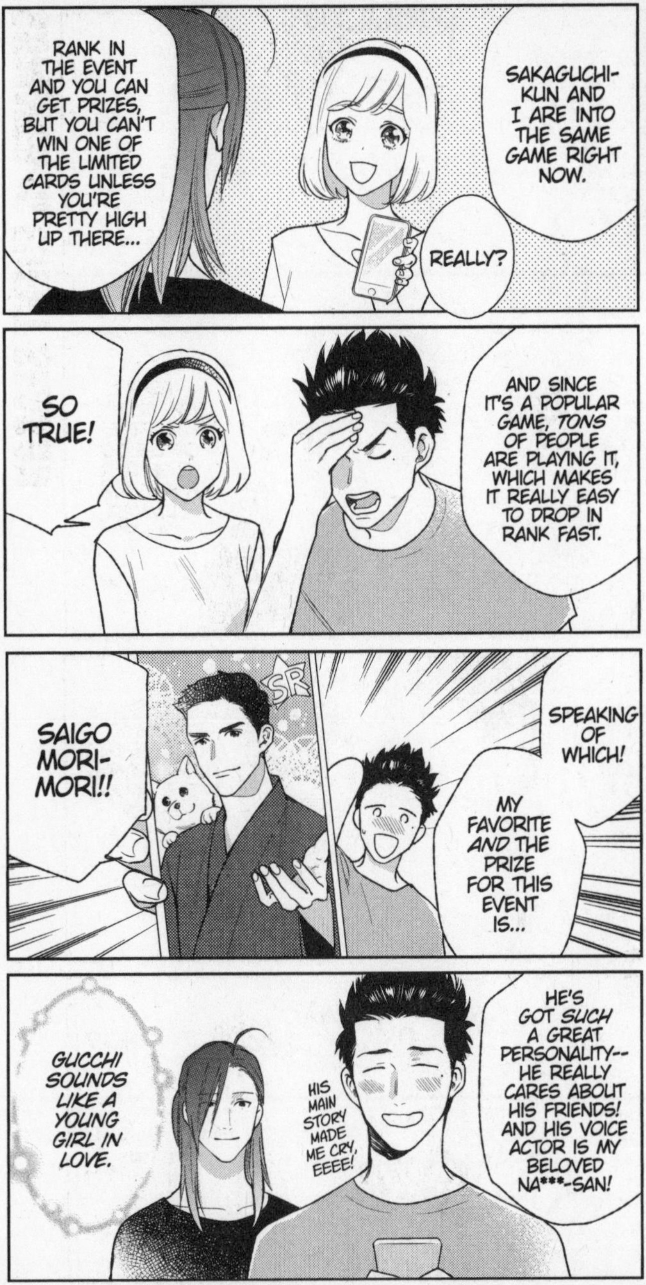
SAKAGUCHI-KUN AND I ARE INTO THE SAME GAME RIGHT NOW.
REALLY?
RANK IN THE EVENT AND YOU CAN GET PRIZES, BUT YOU CAN'T WIN ONE OF THE LIMITED CARDS UNLESS YOU'RE PRETTY HIGH UP THERE...
AND SINCE IT'S A POPULAR GAME, *TONS* OF PEOPLE ARE PLAYING IT, WHICH MAKES IT REALLY EASY TO DROP IN RANK FAST.
SO TRUE!
SPEAKING OF WHICH!
MY FAVORITE *AND* THE PRIZE FOR THIS EVENT IS...
SAIGO MORI-MORI!!
SR
HE'S GOT *SUCH* A GREAT PERSONALITY--HE REALLY CARES ABOUT HIS FRIENDS! AND HIS VOICE ACTOR IS MY BELOVED NA***-SAN!
HIS MAIN STORY MADE ME CRY, EEEE!
GUCCHI SOUNDS LIKE A YOUNG GIRL IN LOVE.

I WANT YOU

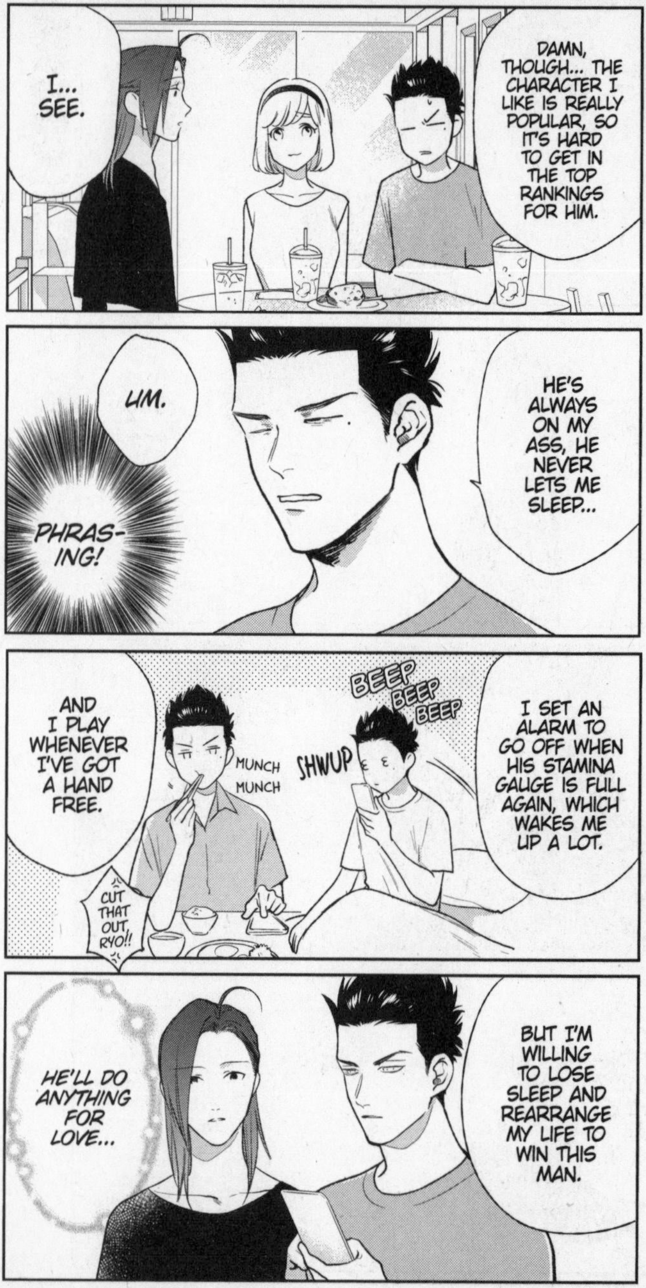
DAMN, THOUGH... THE CHARACTER I LIKE IS REALLY POPULAR, SO IT'S HARD TO GET IN THE TOP RANKINGS FOR HIM.
I... SEE.
HE'S ALWAYS ON MY ASS, HE NEVER LETS ME SLEEP...
UM.
PHRAS-ING!
I SET AN ALARM TO GO OFF WHEN HIS STAMINA GAUGE IS FULL AGAIN, WHICH WAKES ME UP A LOT.
BEEP BEEP BEEP
SHWUP
MUNCH MUNCH
AND I PLAY WHENEVER I'VE GOT A HAND FREE.
CUT THAT OUT, RYO!!
BUT I'M WILLING TO LOSE SLEEP AND REARRANGE MY LIFE TO WIN THIS MAN.
HE'LL DO ANYTHING FOR LOVE...

I WAS COUNTING ON YOU!

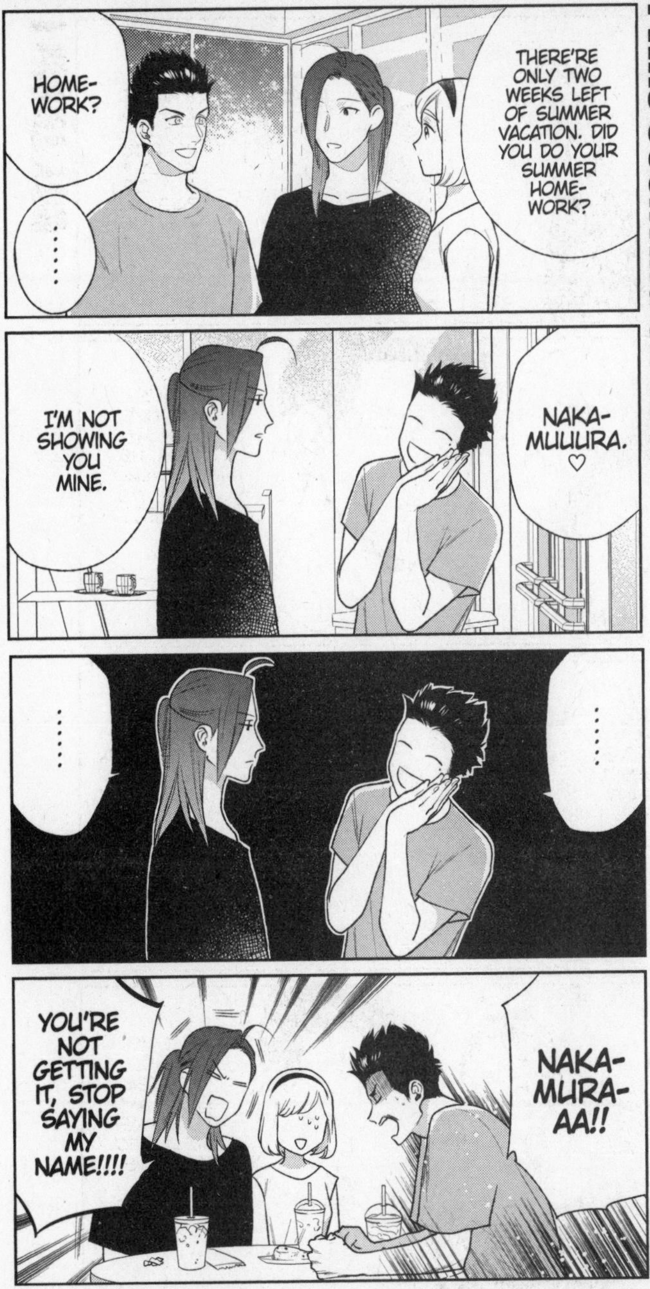
THERE'RE ONLY TWO WEEKS LEFT OF SUMMER VACATION. DID YOU DO YOUR SUMMER HOME-WORK?
HOME-WORK?
......
NAKA-MUUURA. ♡
I'M NOT SHOWING YOU MINE.
......
......
NAKA-MURA-AA!!
YOU'RE NOT GETTING IT, STOP SAYING MY NAME!!!!

WHY ARE YOU SO ADAMANT?

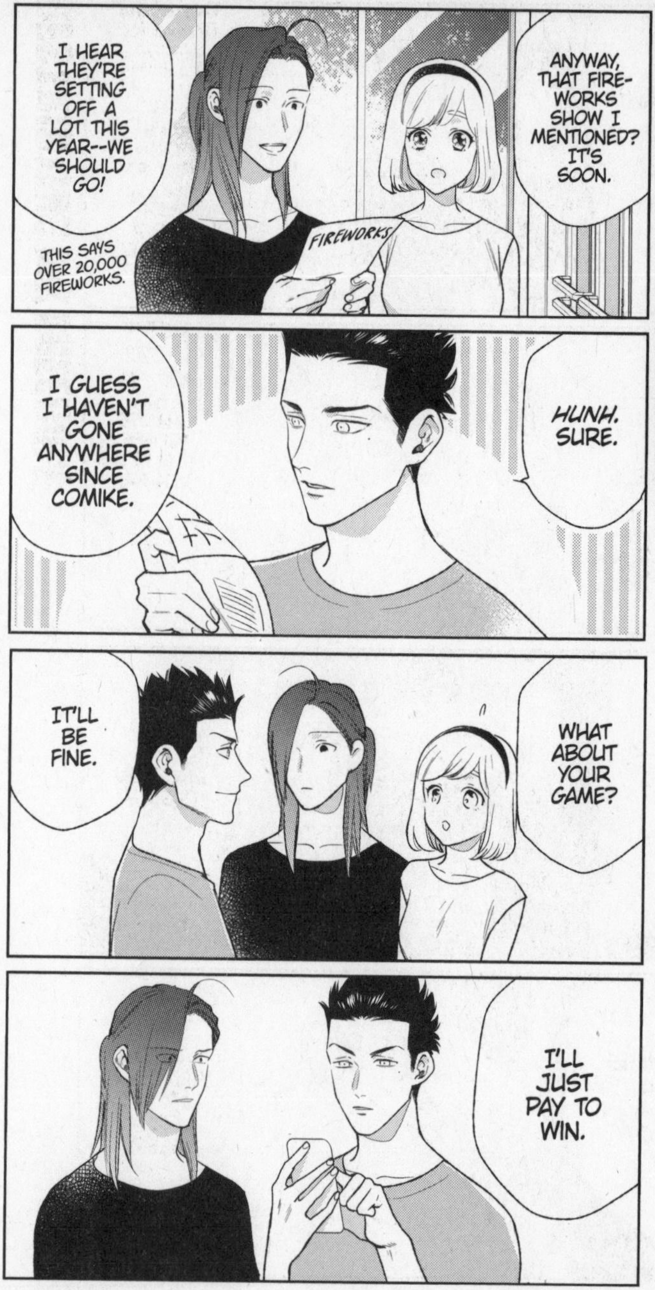
ANYWAY, THAT FIRE-WORKS SHOW I MENTIONED? IT'S SOON.
I HEAR THEY'RE SETTING OFF A LOT THIS YEAR--WE SHOULD GO!
FIREWORKS
THIS SAYS OVER 20,000 FIREWORKS.
HUNH. SURE.
I GUESS I HAVEN'T GONE ANYWHERE SINCE COMIKE.
WHAT ABOUT YOUR GAME?
IT'LL BE FINE.
I'LL JUST PAY TO WIN.

RESTRICTING MY FREEDOM

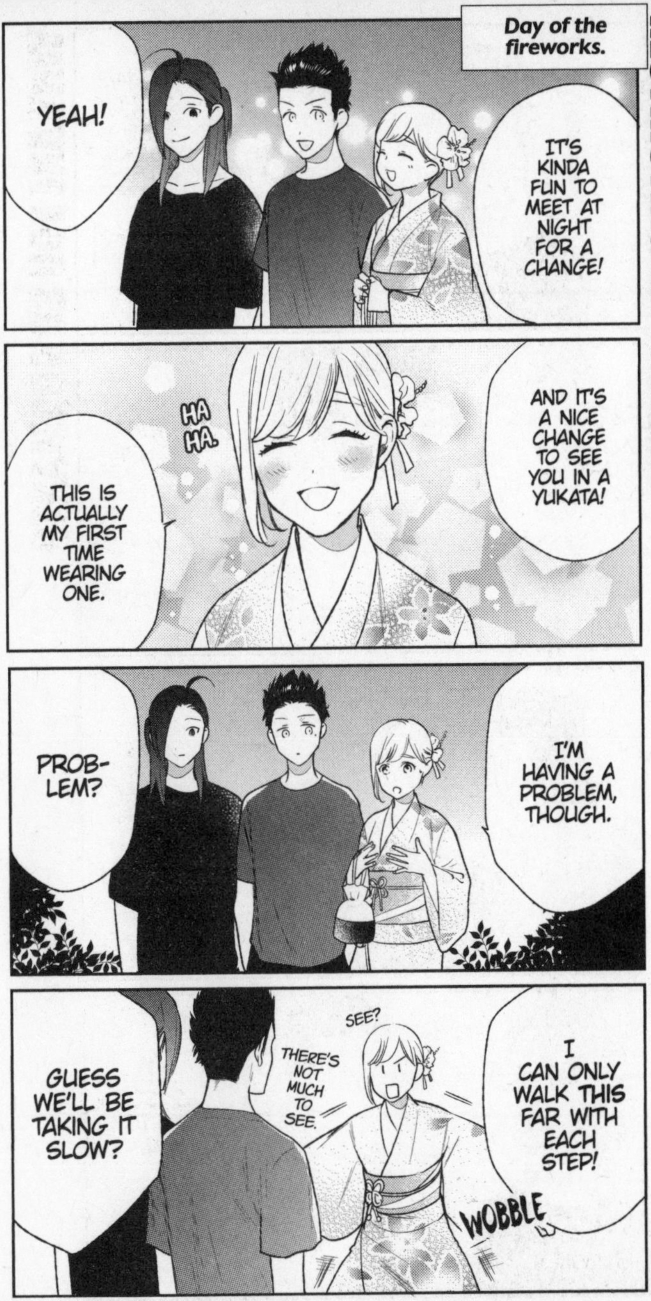
Day of the fireworks.
IT'S KINDA FUN TO MEET AT NIGHT FOR A CHANGE!
YEAH!
AND IT'S A NICE CHANGE TO SEE YOU IN A YUKATA!
HA HA.
THIS IS ACTUALLY MY FIRST TIME WEARING ONE.
I'M HAVING A PROBLEM, THOUGH.
PROB-LEM?
I CAN ONLY WALK THIS FAR WITH EACH STEP!
SEE?
THERE'S NOT MUCH TO SEE.
WOBBLE
GUESS WE'LL BE TAKING IT SLOW?

CHOICES, CHOICES

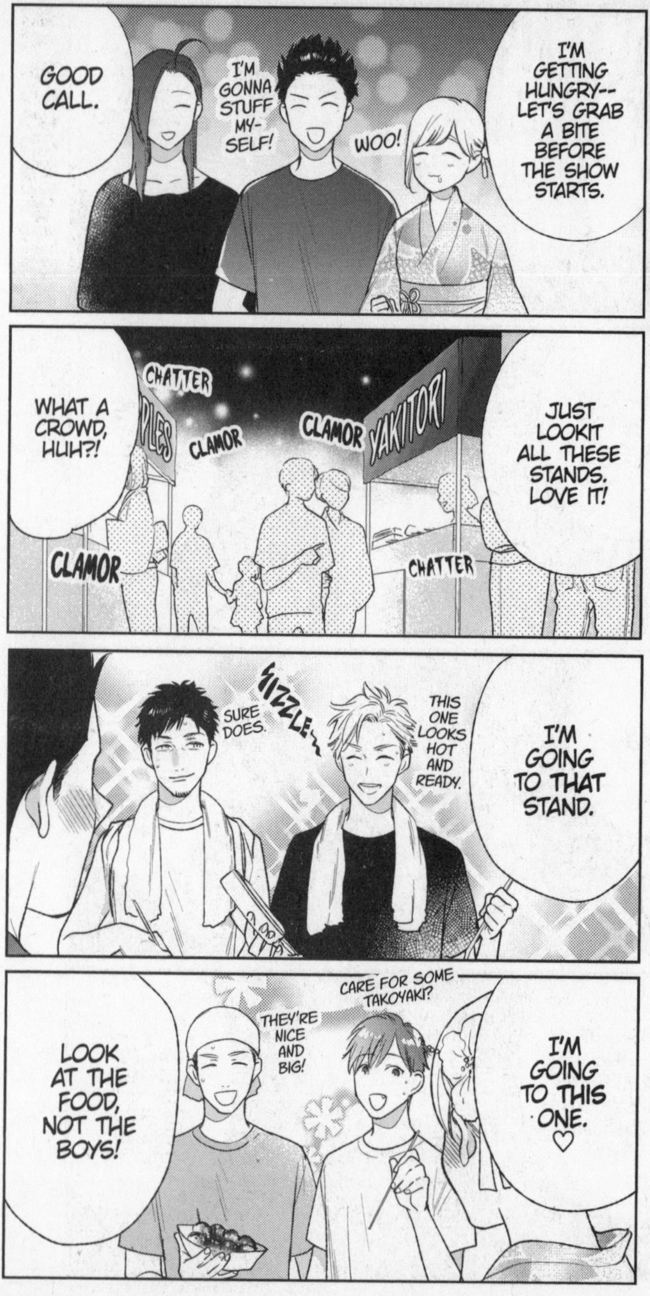

I'M GETTING HUNGRY-- LET'S GRAB A BITE BEFORE THE SHOW STARTS.
WOO!
I'M GONNA STUFF MY-SELF!
GOOD CALL.
JUST LOOKIT ALL THESE STANDS. LOVE IT!
YAKITORI
CLAMOR
CHATTER
CLAMOR
CHATTER
WHAT A CROWD, HUH?!
CLAMOR
I'M GOING TO THAT STAND.
THIS ONE LOOKS HOT AND READY.
SIZZLE
SURE DOES.
I'M GOING TO THIS ONE. ♡
CARE FOR SOME TAKOYAKI?
THEY'RE NICE AND BIG!
LOOK AT THE FOOD, NOT THE BOYS!

BY ASSOCIATION

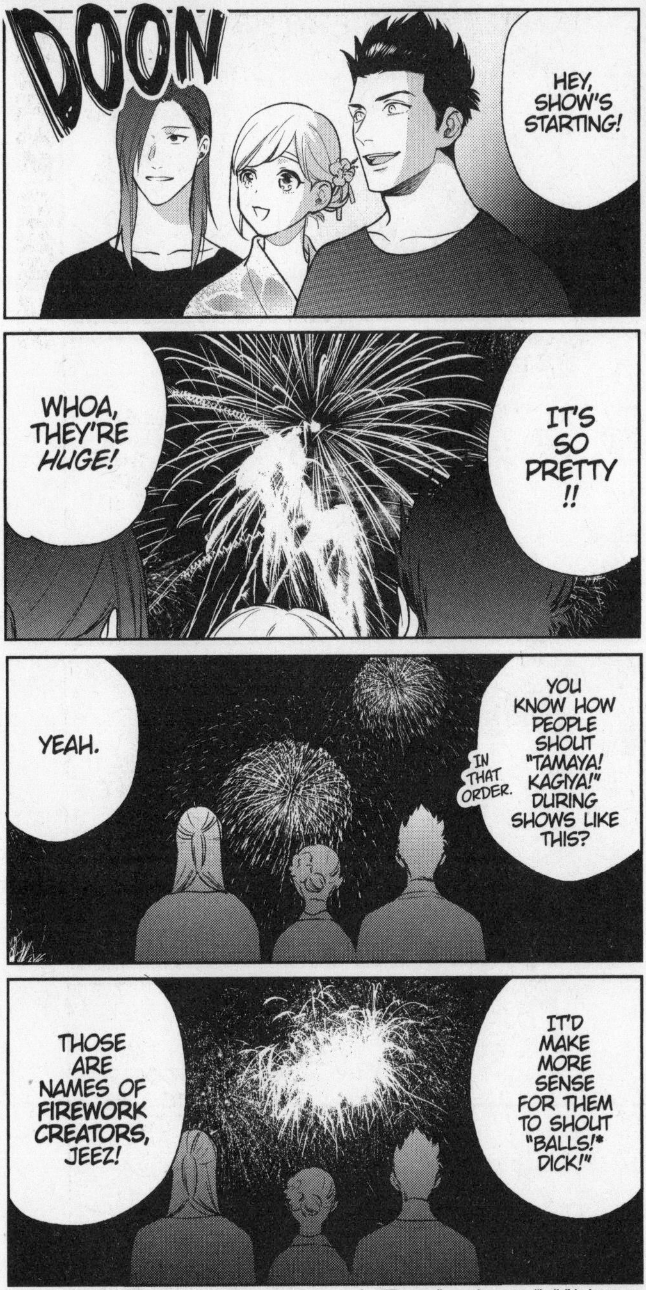
HEY, SHOW'S STARTING!
DOON
IT'S SO PRETTY !!
WHOA, THEY'RE *HUGE!*
YOU KNOW HOW PEOPLE SHOUT "TAMAYA! KAGIYA!" DURING SHOWS LIKE THIS?
IN THAT ORDER.
YEAH.
IT'D MAKE MORE SENSE FOR THEM TO SHOUT "BALLS!* DICK!"
THOSE ARE NAMES OF FIREWORK CREATORS, JEEZ!

*"Tama ya" can also mean "balls" in Japanese.

LEAVE THEM BE

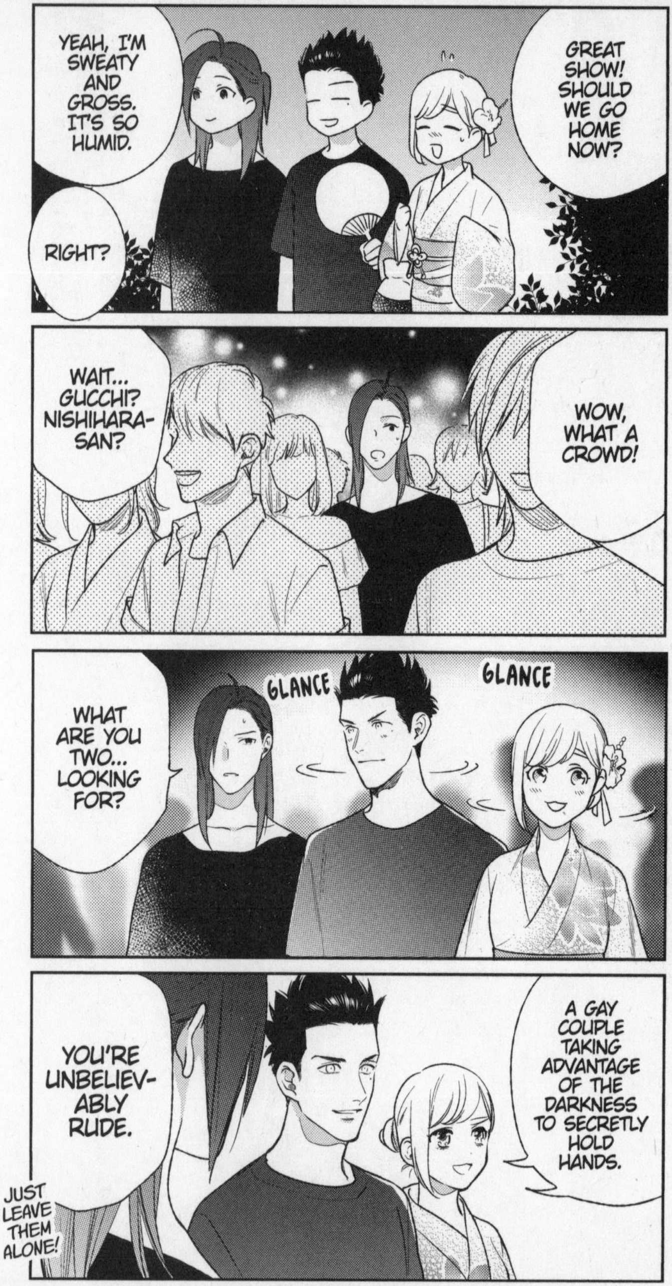
GREAT SHOW! SHOULD WE GO HOME NOW?
YEAH, I'M SWEATY AND GROSS. IT'S SO HUMID.
RIGHT?
WOW, WHAT A CROWD!
WAIT... GUCCHI? NISHIHARA-SAN?
GLANCE
GLANCE
WHAT ARE YOU TWO... LOOKING FOR?
A GAY COUPLE TAKING ADVANTAGE OF THE DARKNESS TO SECRETLY HOLD HANDS.
YOU'RE UNBELIEV-ABLY RUDE.
JUST LEAVE THEM ALONE!

FKS

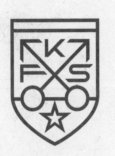

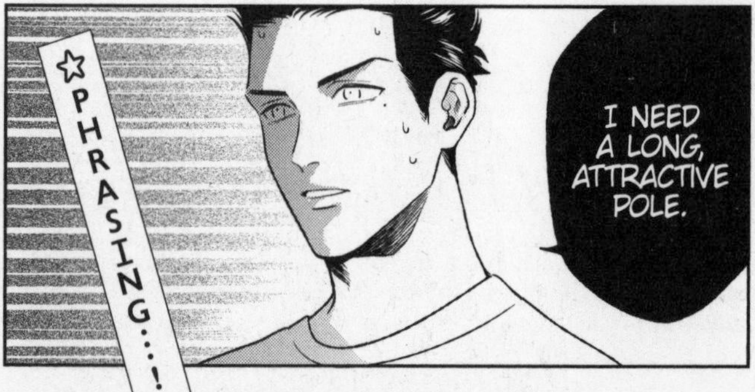
I NEED A LONG, ATTRACTIVE POLE.
☆PHRASING...!

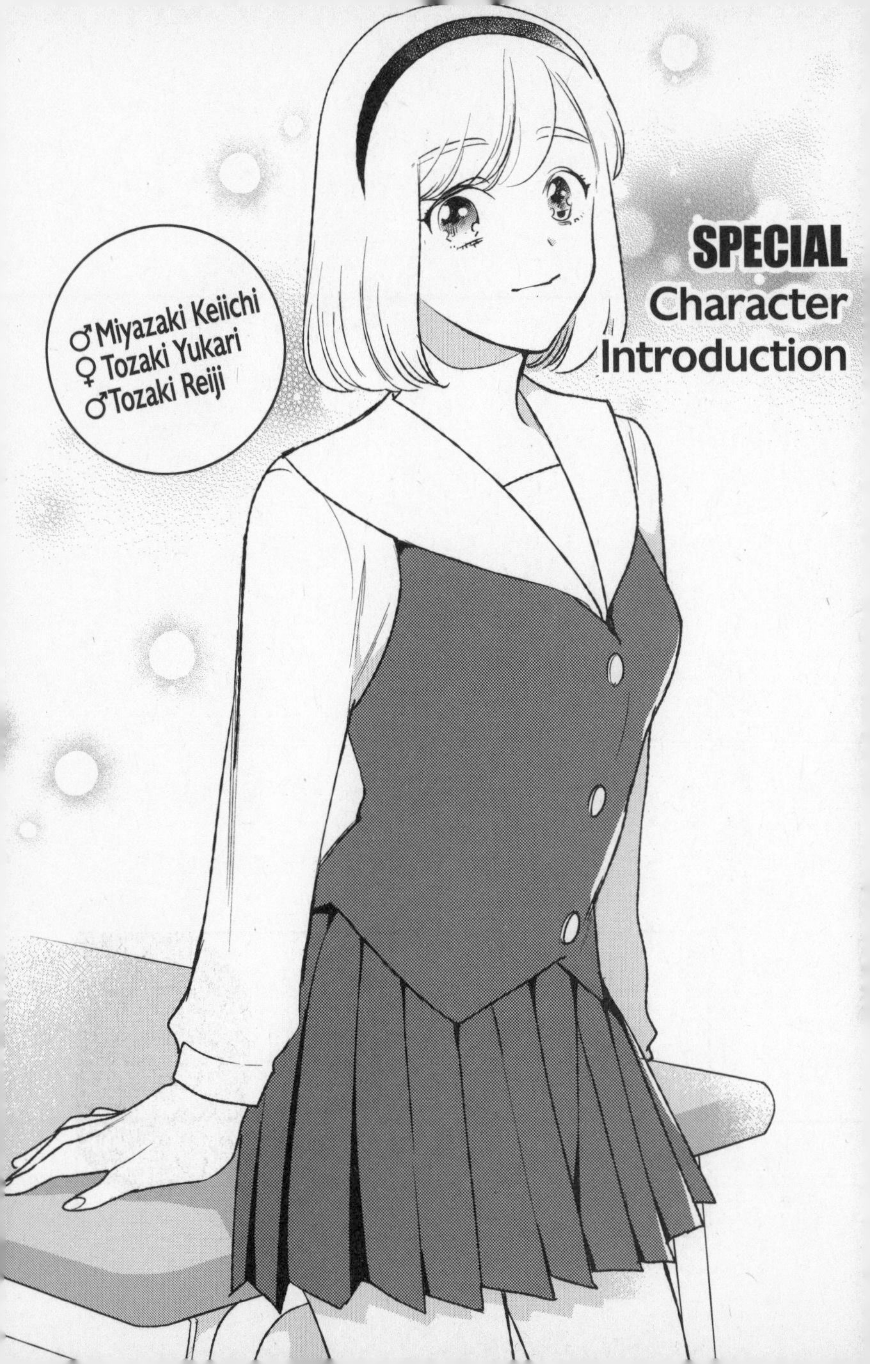
SPECIAL
Character
Introduction
♂Miyazaki Keiichi
♀Tozaki Yukari
♂Tozaki Reiji

HARD WORKER WHO TAKES AN ALARMING NUMBER OF PAINKILLERS

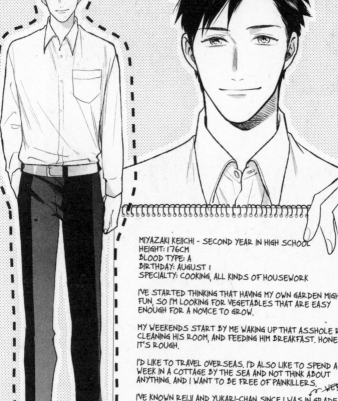

MIYAZAKI KEIICHI - SECOND YEAR IN HIGH SCHOOL
HEIGHT: 176CM
BLOOD TYPE: A
BIRTHDAY: AUGUST 1
SPECIALTY: COOKING, ALL KINDS OF HOUSEWORK

I'VE STARTED THINKING THAT HAVING MY OWN GARDEN MIGHT BE
FUN, SO I'M LOOKING FOR VEGETABLES THAT ARE EASY
ENOUGH FOR A NOVICE TO GROW.

MY WEEKENDS START BY ME WAKING UP THAT ASSHOLE REIJI,
CLEANING HIS ROOM, AND FEEDING HIM BREAKFAST. HONESTLY,
IT'S ROUGH.

I'D LIKE TO TRAVEL OVERSEAS. I'D ALSO LIKE TO SPEND A
WEEK IN A COTTAGE BY THE SEA AND NOT THINK ABOUT
ANYTHING. AND I WANT TO BE FREE OF PAINKILLERS.

WE'RE BESTIES!

I'VE KNOWN REIJI AND YUKARI-CHAN SINCE I WAS IN GRADE
SCHOOL.

YUKARI TOZAKI ♀

A SHRINE MAIDEN VICIOUSLY FIGHTING HER BROTHER FOR LOVE

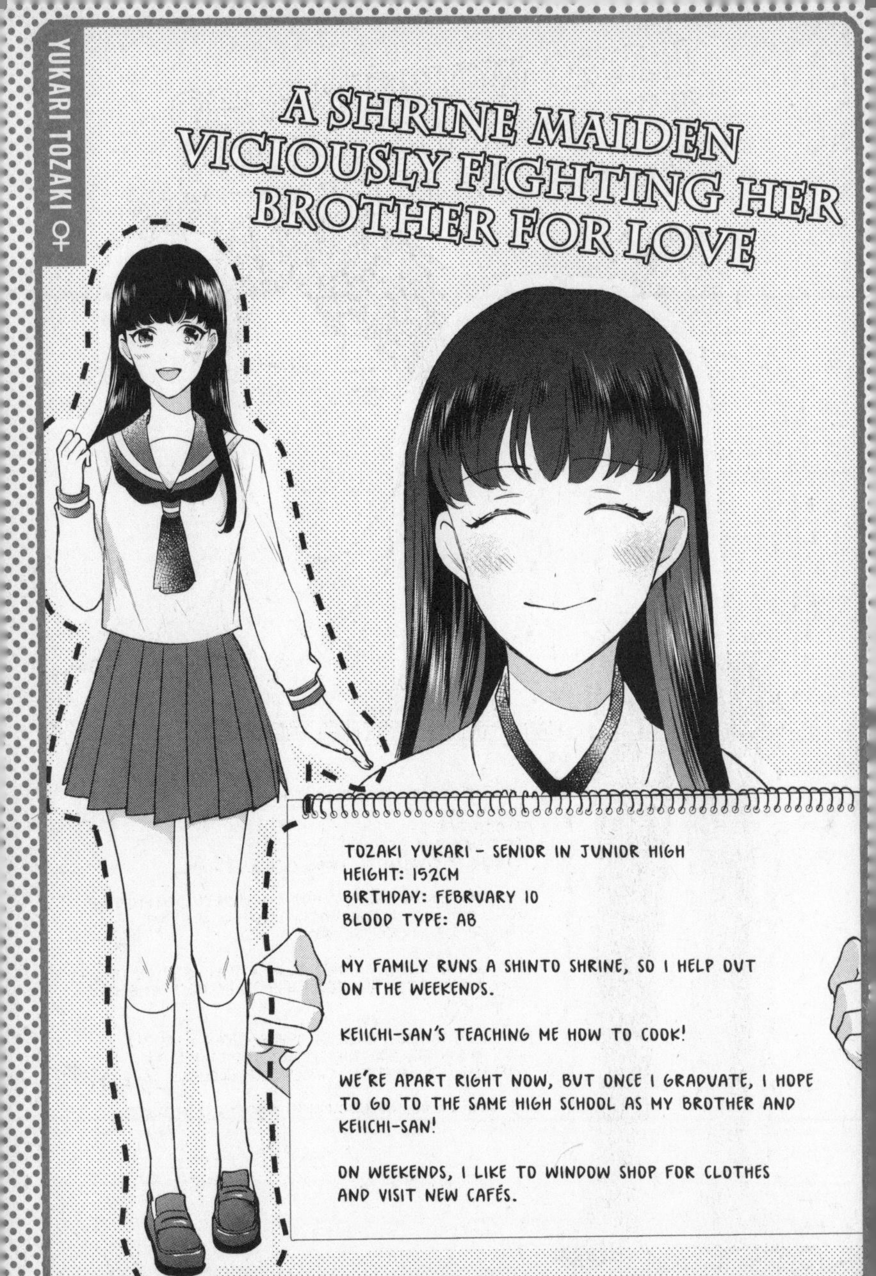

TOZAKI YUKARI - SENIOR IN JUNIOR HIGH
HEIGHT: 152CM
BIRTHDAY: FEBRUARY 10
BLOOD TYPE: AB

MY FAMILY RUNS A SHINTO SHRINE, SO I HELP OUT ON THE WEEKENDS.

KEIICHI-SAN'S TEACHING ME HOW TO COOK!

WE'RE APART RIGHT NOW, BUT ONCE I GRADUATE, I HOPE TO GO TO THE SAME HIGH SCHOOL AS MY BROTHER AND KEIICHI-SAN!

ON WEEKENDS, I LIKE TO WINDOW SHOP FOR CLOTHES AND VISIT NEW CAFÉS.

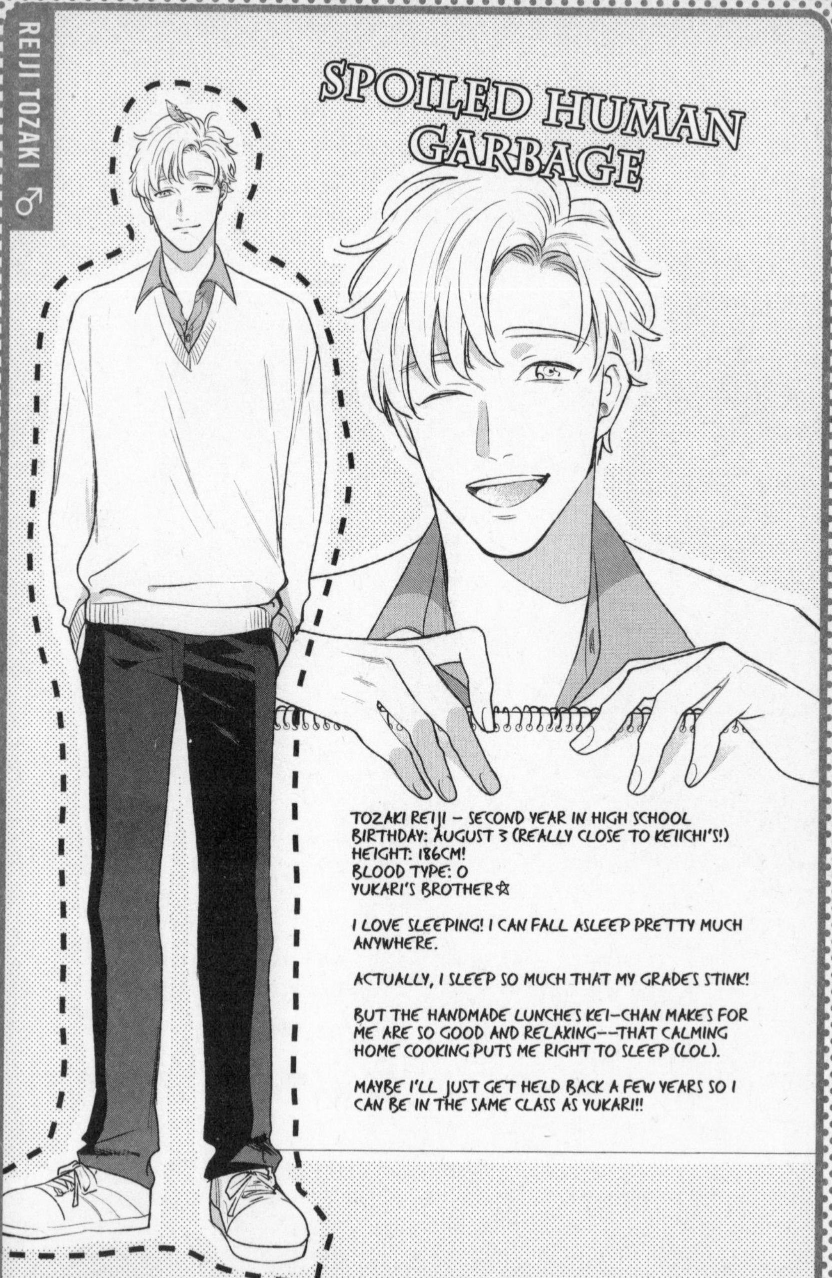
REIJI TOZAKI ♂
SPOILED HUMAN GARBAGE
TOZAKI REIJI – SECOND YEAR IN HIGH SCHOOL
BIRTHDAY: AUGUST 3 (REALLY CLOSE TO KEIICHI'S!)
HEIGHT: 186CM!
BLOOD TYPE: O
YUKARI'S BROTHER☆
I LOVE SLEEPING! I CAN FALL ASLEEP PRETTY MUCH ANYWHERE.
ACTUALLY, I SLEEP SO MUCH THAT MY GRADES STINK!
BUT THE HANDMADE LUNCHES KEI-CHAN MAKES FOR ME ARE SO GOOD AND RELAXING--THAT CALMING HOME COOKING PUTS ME RIGHT TO SLEEP (LOL).
MAYBE I'LL JUST GET HELD BACK A FEW YEARS SO I CAN BE IN THE SAME CLASS AS YUKARI!!

K
F S

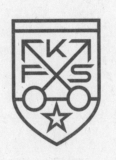

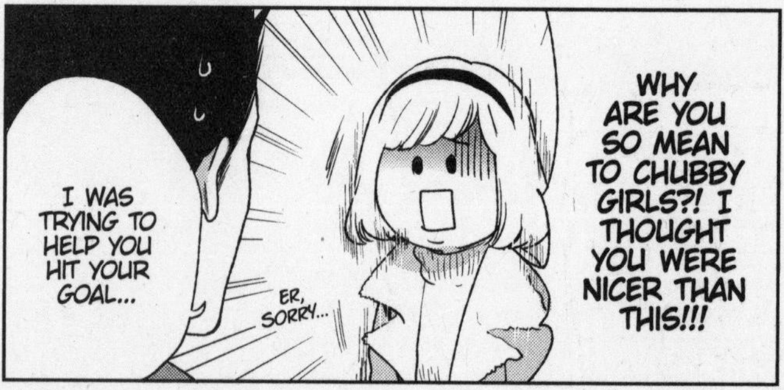
WHY ARE YOU SO MEAN TO CHUBBY GIRLS?! I THOUGHT YOU WERE NICER THAN THIS!!!
I WAS TRYING TO HELP YOU HIT YOUR GOAL...
ER, SORRY...

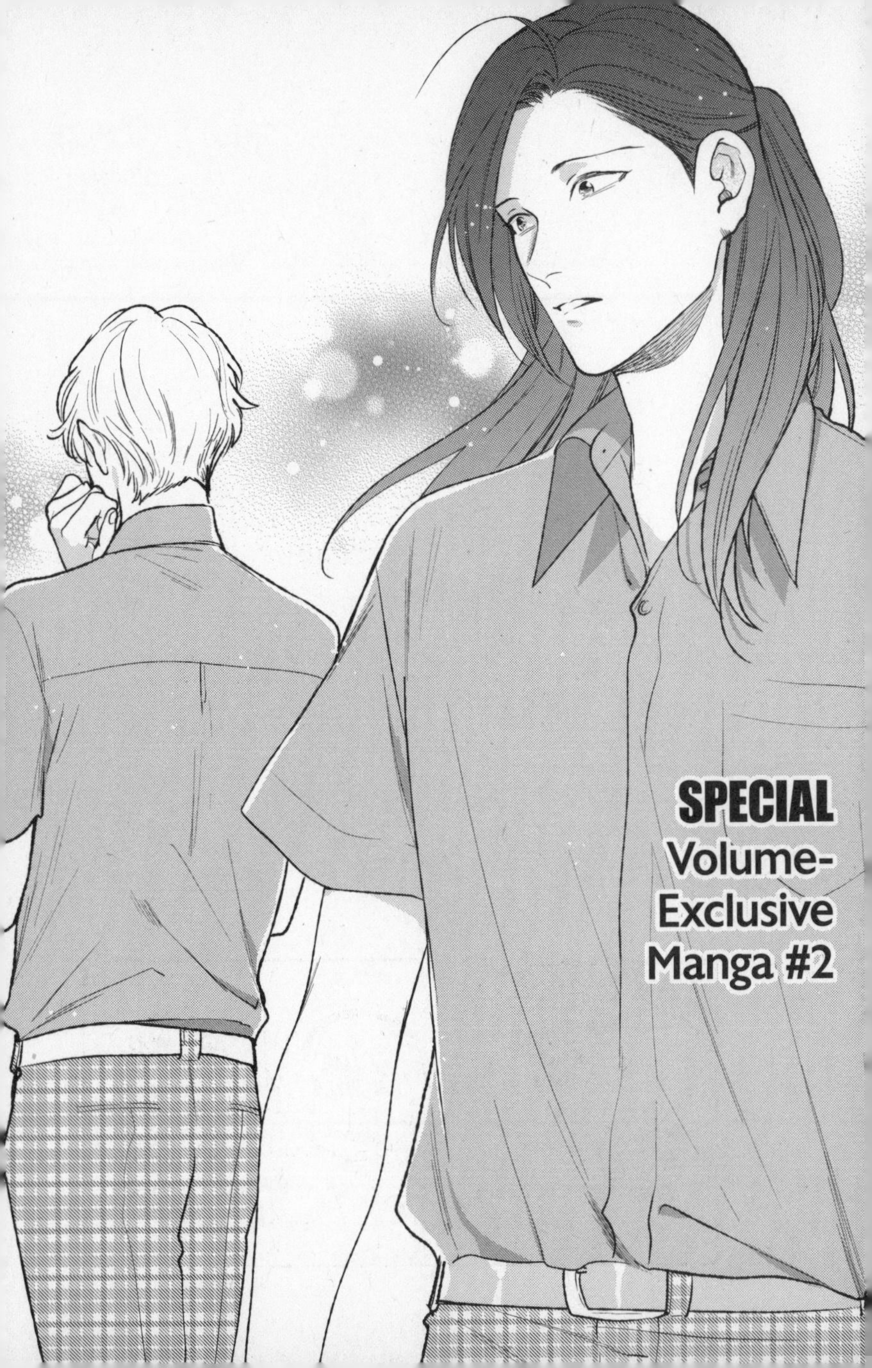
SPECIAL
Volume-Exclusive Manga #2

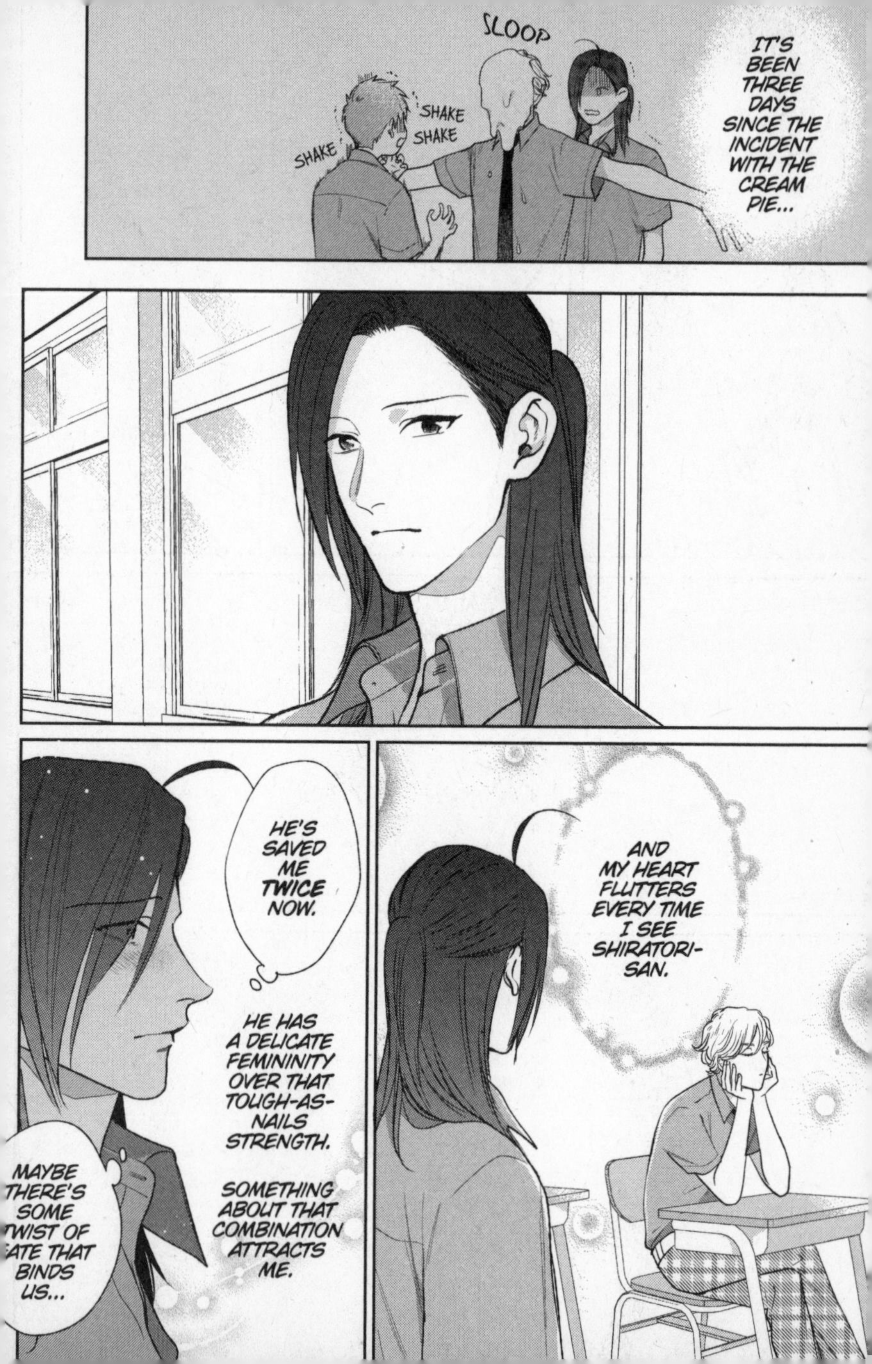
IT'S BEEN THREE DAYS SINCE THE INCIDENT WITH THE CREAM PIE...
SLOOP
SHAKE SHAKE
SHAKE
AND MY HEART FLUTTERS EVERY TIME I SEE SHIRATORI-SAN.
HE'S SAVED ME TWICE NOW.
HE HAS A DELICATE FEMININITY OVER THAT TOUGH-AS-NAILS STRENGTH.
SOMETHING ABOUT THAT COMBINATION ATTRACTS ME.
MAYBE THERE'S SOME WIST OF ATE THAT BINDS US...

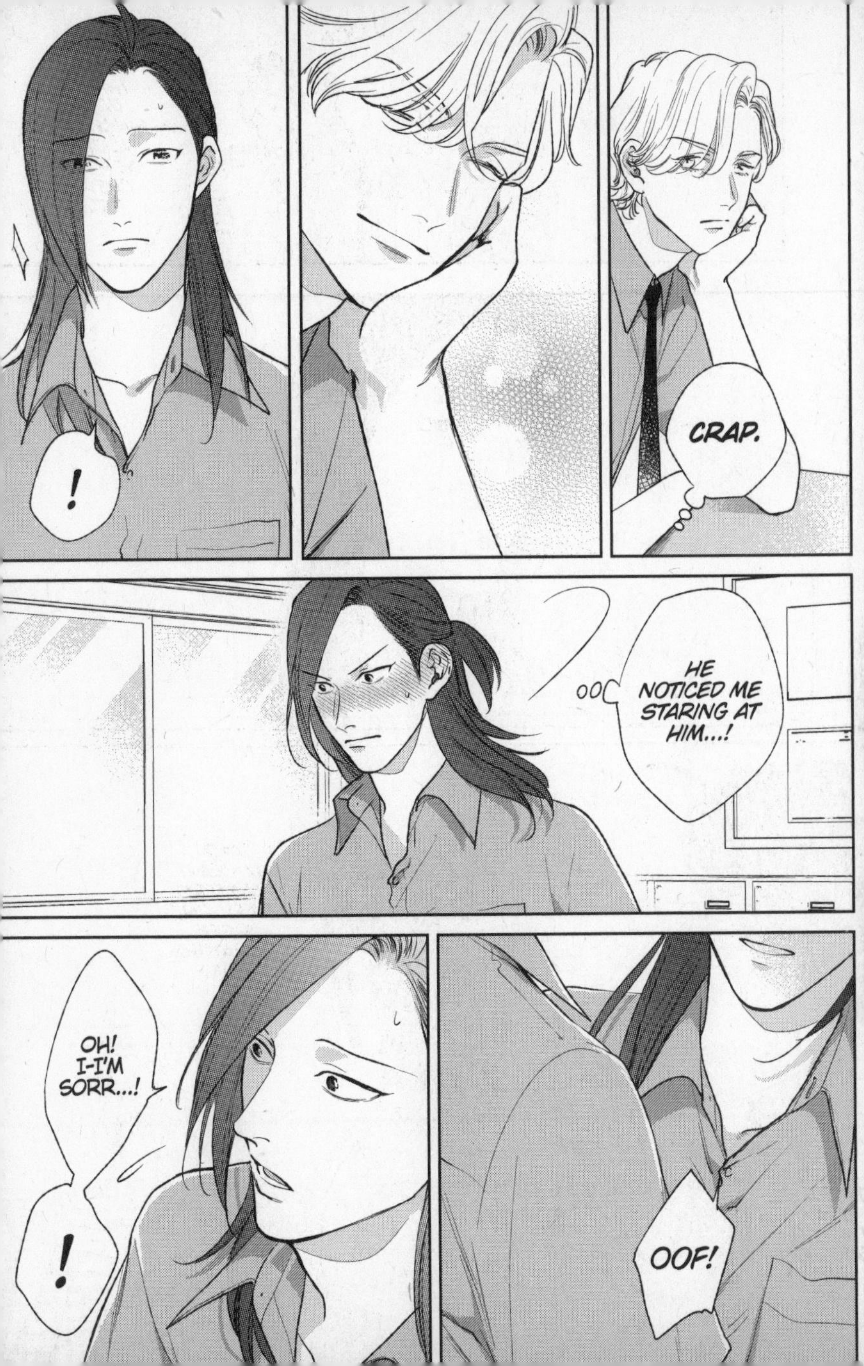
CRAP.
!
HE NOTICED ME STARING AT HIM...!
OOF!
OH! I-I'M SORR...!
!

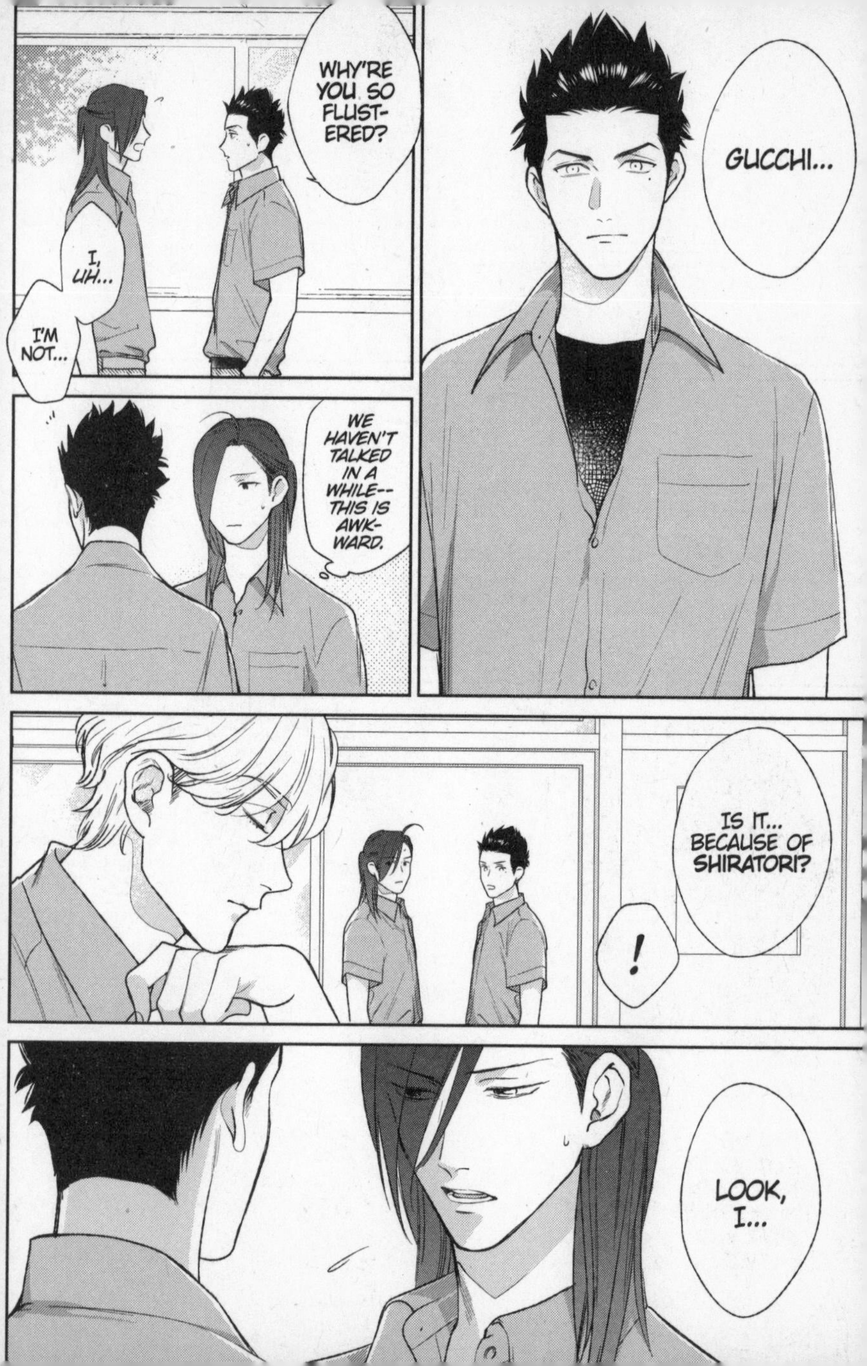
GUCCHI...
WHY'RE YOU SO FLUSTERED?
I, UH...
I'M NOT...
WE HAVEN'T TALKED IN A WHILE-- THIS IS AWKWARD.
IS IT... BECAUSE OF SHIRATORI?
!
LOOK, I...

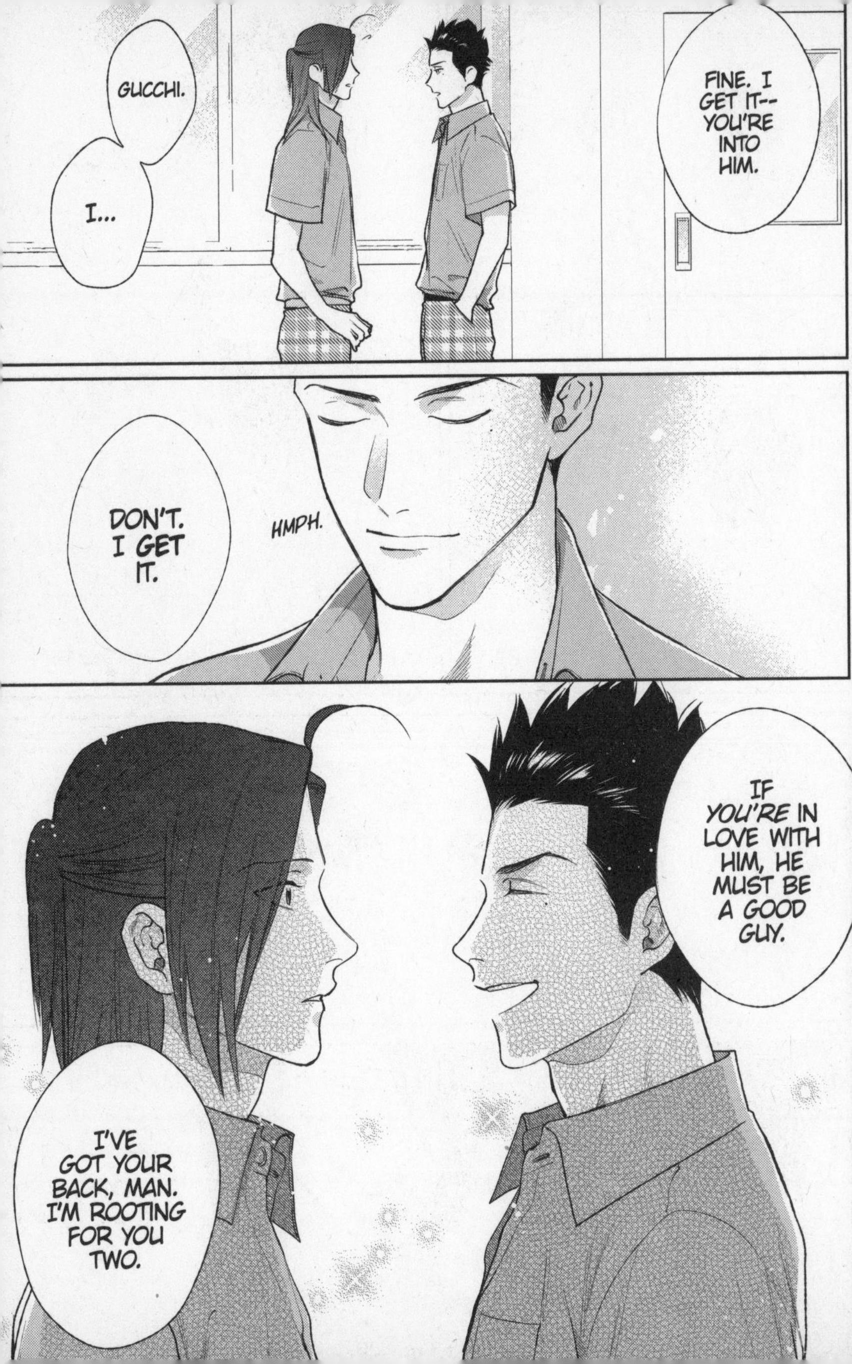
FINE. I GET IT-- YOU'RE INTO HIM.
GUCCHI.
I...
HMPH.
DON'T. I GET IT.
IF *YOU'RE* IN LOVE WITH HIM, HE MUST BE A GOOD GUY.
I'VE GOT YOUR BACK, MAN. I'M ROOTING FOR YOU TWO.

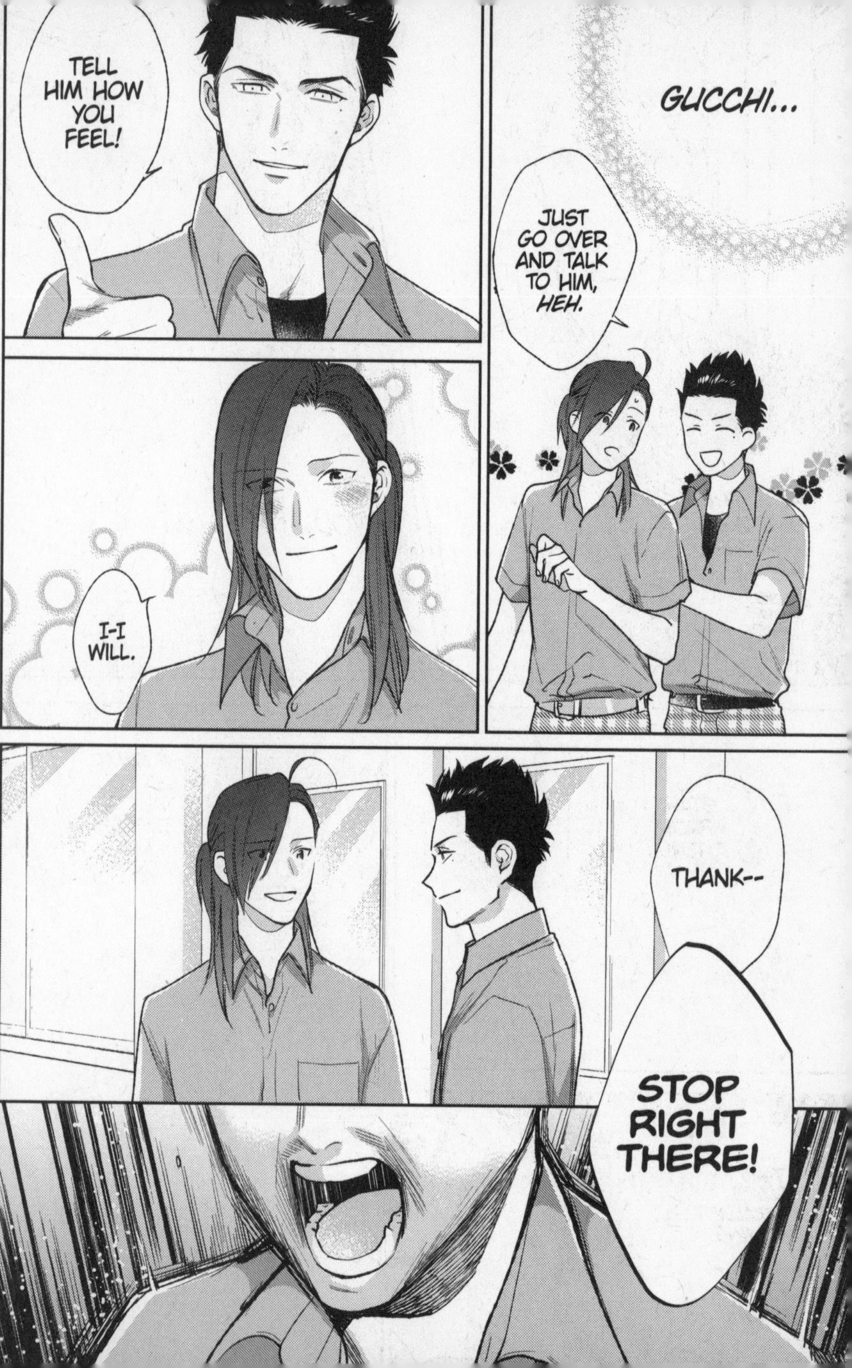
GUCCHI...
JUST GO OVER AND TALK TO HIM, *HEH.*
TELL HIM HOW YOU FEEL!
I-I WILL.
THANK--
STOP RIGHT THERE!

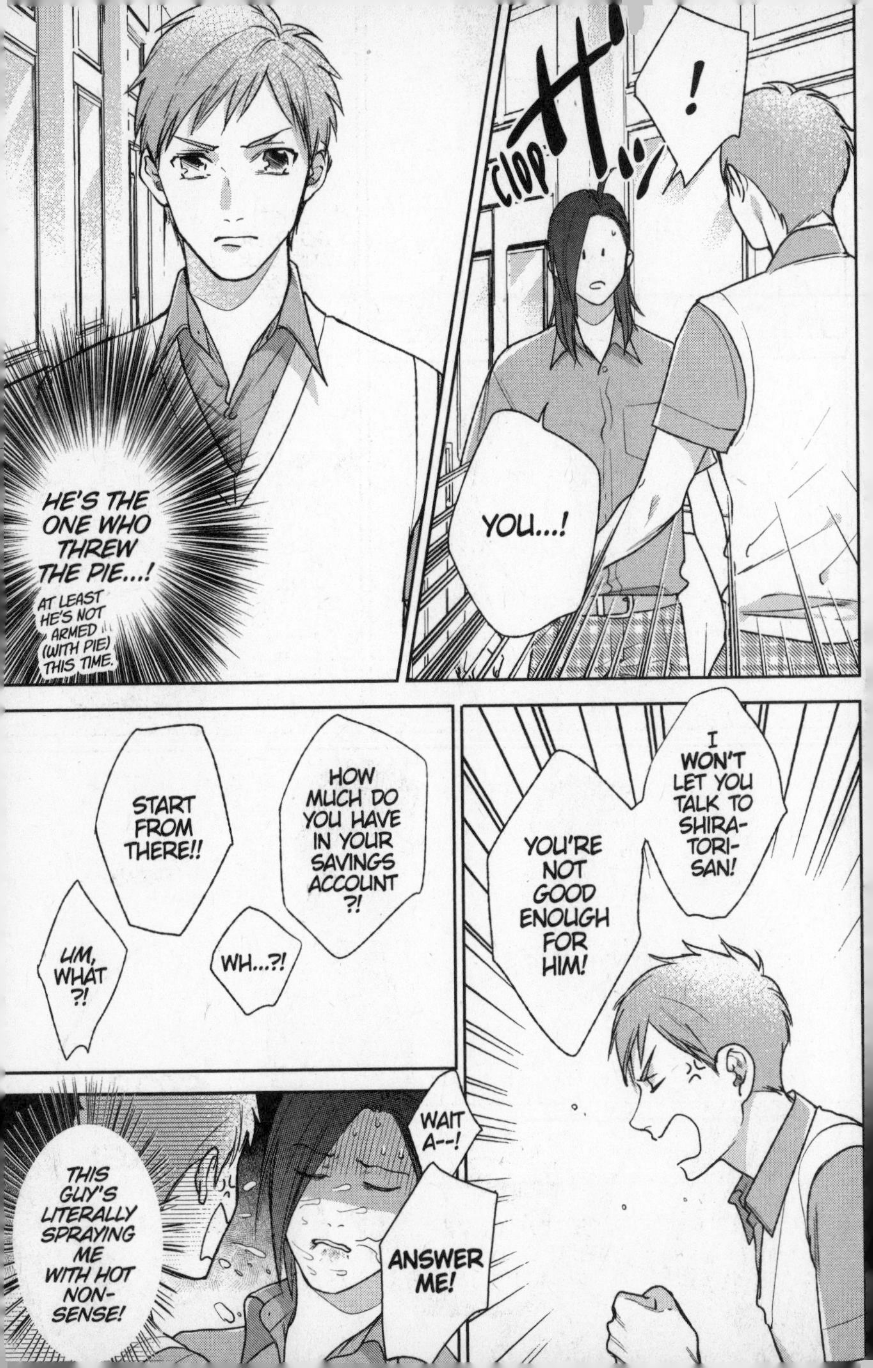
CLOP
!
YOU...!
HE'S THE ONE WHO THREW THE PIE...!
AT LEAST HE'S NOT ARMED (WITH PIE) THIS TIME.
I WON'T LET YOU TALK TO SHIRA-TORI-SAN!
YOU'RE NOT GOOD ENOUGH FOR HIM!
HOW MUCH DO YOU HAVE IN YOUR SAVINGS ACCOUNT?!
START FROM THERE!!
WH...?!
UM, WHAT?!
WAIT A--!
ANSWER ME!
THIS GUY'S LITERALLY SPRAYING ME WITH HOT NON-SENSE!

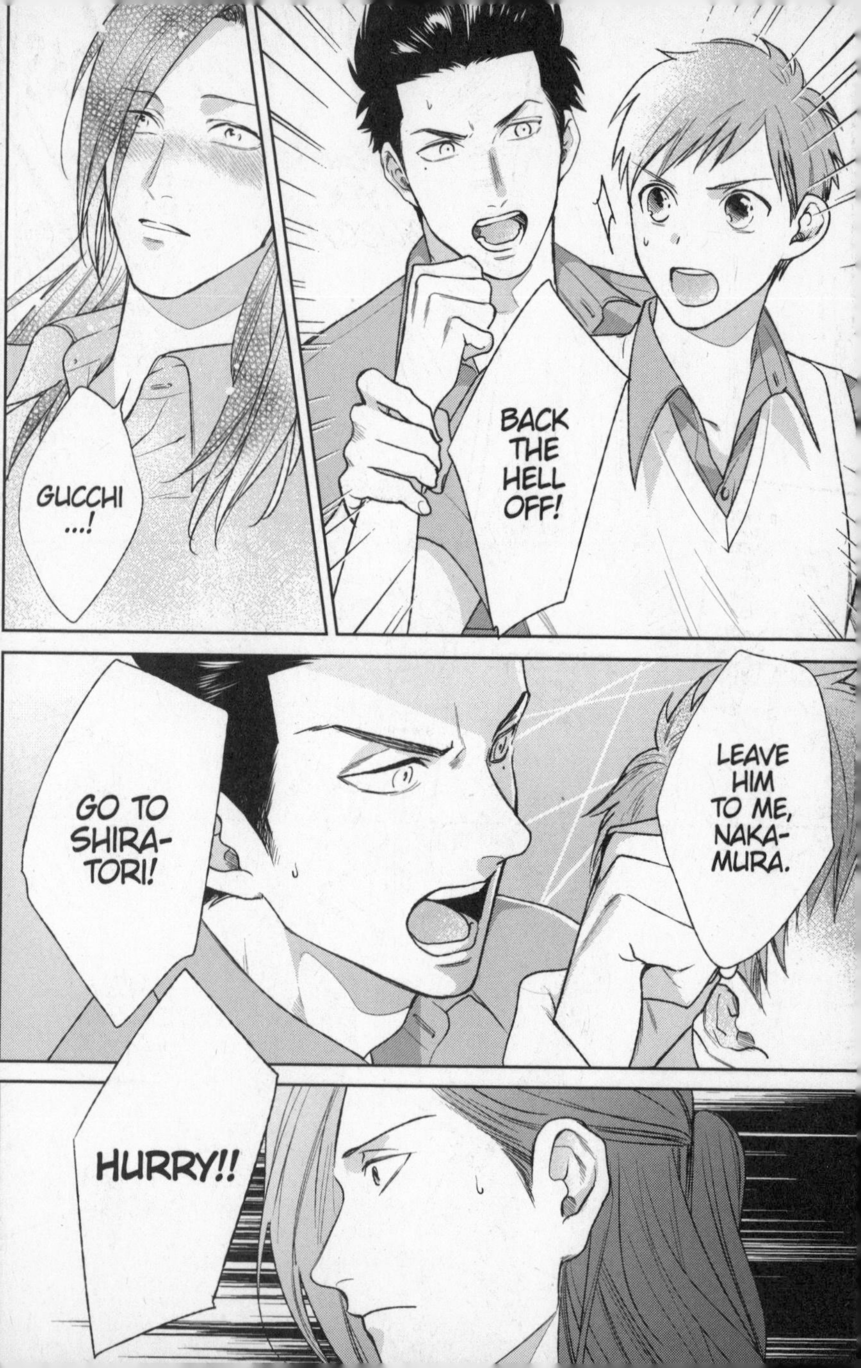
BACK THE HELL OFF!
GUCCHI ...!
LEAVE HIM TO ME, NAKA-MURA.
GO TO SHIRA-TORI!
HURRY!!

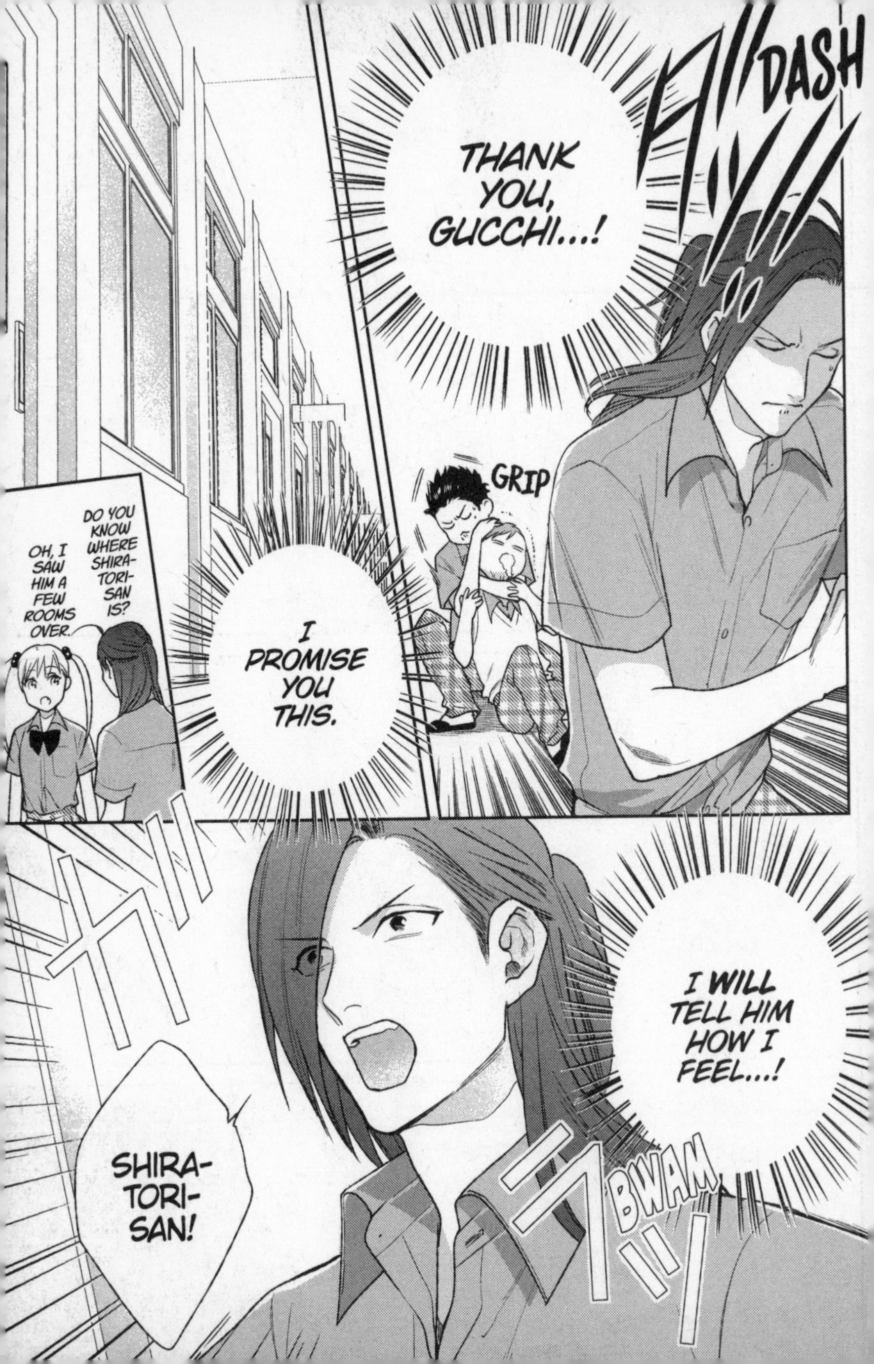
DASH
THANK YOU, GUCCHI...!
GRIP
I PROMISE YOU THIS.
DO YOU KNOW WHERE SHIRA-TORI-SAN IS?
OH, I SAW HIM A FEW ROOMS OVER.
I WILL TELL HIM HOW I FEEL...!
BWAM
SHIRA-TORI-SAN!

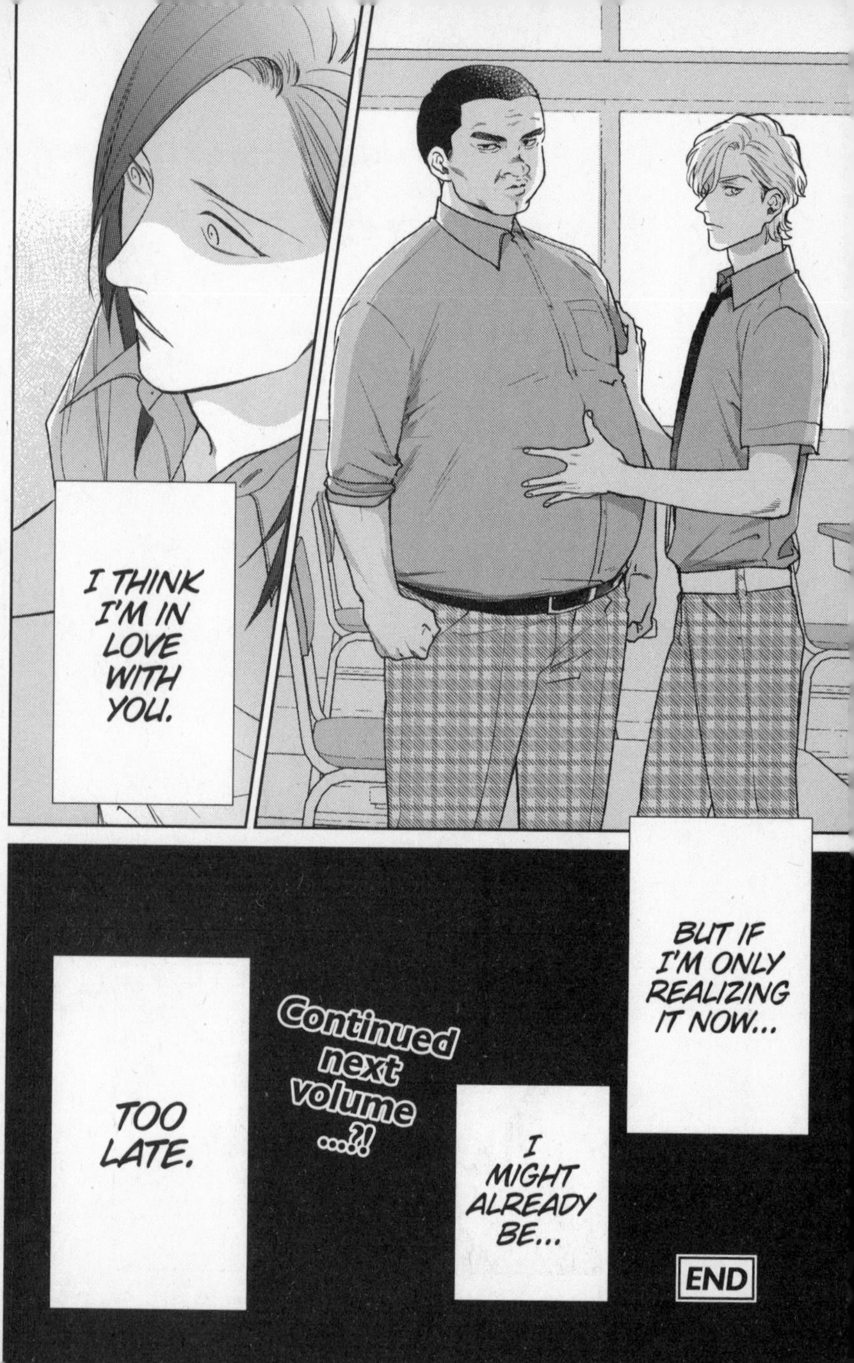
I THINK I'M IN LOVE WITH YOU.
BUT IF I'M ONLY REALIZING IT NOW...
I MIGHT ALREADY BE...
TOO LATE.
Continued next volume ...?!
END

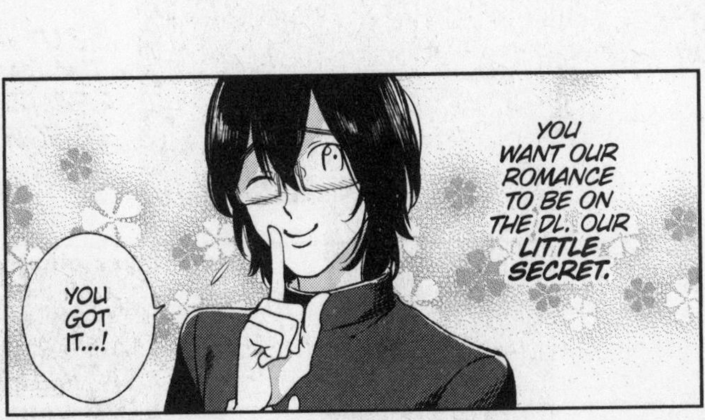
YOU WANT OUR ROMANCE TO BE ON THE DL. OUR LITTLE SECRET.
YOU GOT IT...!

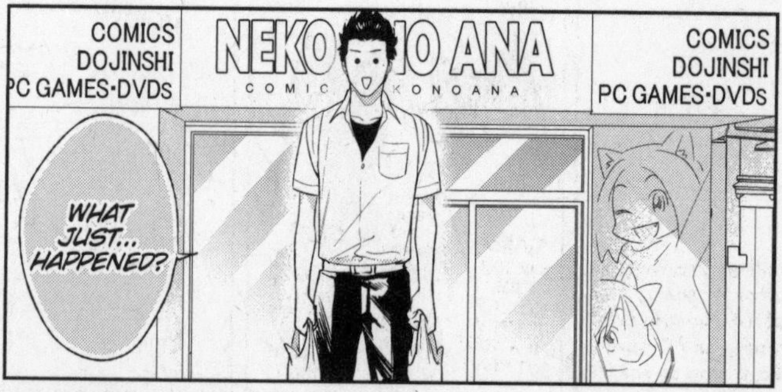
COMICS
DOJINSHI
PC GAMES·DVDs
COMICS
DOJINSHI
PC GAMES·DVDs
WHAT JUST... HAPPENED?

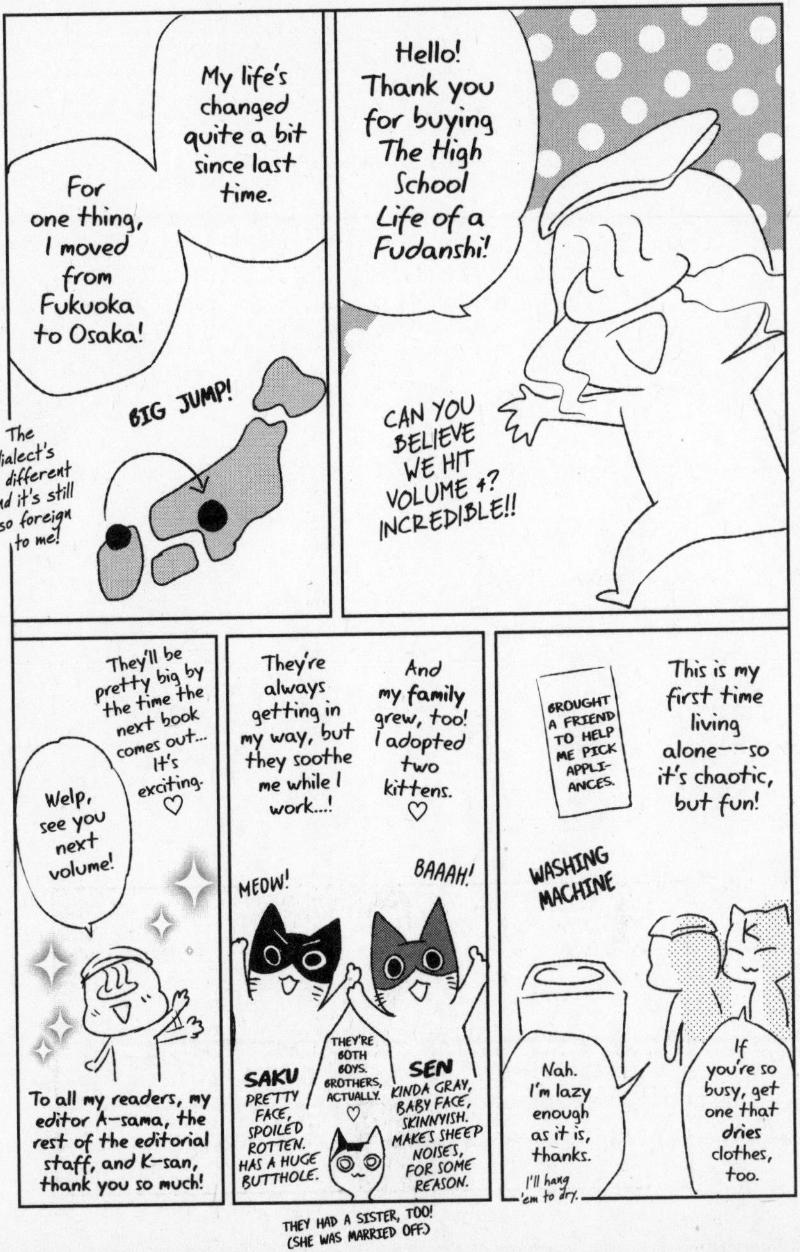
Hello! Thank you for buying The High School Life of a Fudanshi!
CAN YOU BELIEVE WE HIT VOLUME 4? INCREDIBLE!!
My life's changed quite a bit since last time.
For one thing, I moved from Fukuoka to Osaka!
BIG JUMP!
The dialect's so different and it's still so foreign to me!
This is my first time living alone--so it's chaotic, but fun!
BROUGHT A FRIEND TO HELP ME PICK APPLI-ANCES.
WASHING MACHINE
If you're so busy, get one that dries clothes, too.
Nah. I'm lazy enough as it is, thanks.
I'll hang 'em to dry.
And my family grew, too! I adopted two kittens. ♡
They're always getting in my way, but they soothe me while I work...!
BAAAH!
MEOW!
SEN
KINDA GRAY, BABY FACE, SKINNYISH. MAKES SHEEP NOISES, FOR SOME REASON.
THEY'RE BOTH BOYS. BROTHERS, ACTUALLY. ♡
SAKU
PRETTY FACE, SPOILED ROTTEN. HAS A HUGE BUTTHOLE.
THEY HAD A SISTER, TOO! (SHE WAS MARRIED OFF.)
They'll be pretty big by the time the next book comes out... It's exciting. ♡
Welp, see you next volume!
To all my readers, my editor A-sama, the rest of the editorial staff, and K-san, thank you so much!

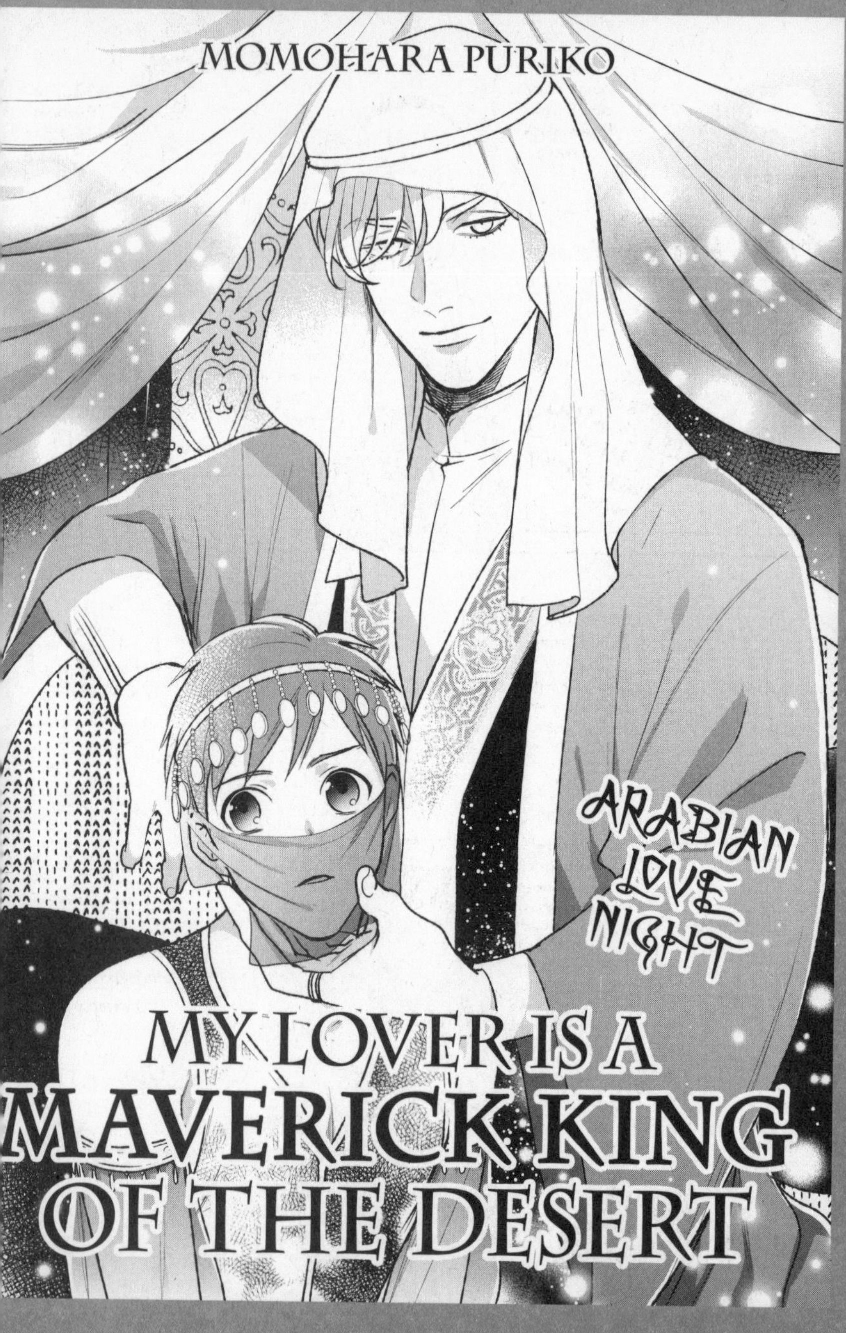
MOMOHARA PURIKO
ARABIAN LOVE NIGHT
MY LOVER IS A MAVERICK KING OF THE DESERT

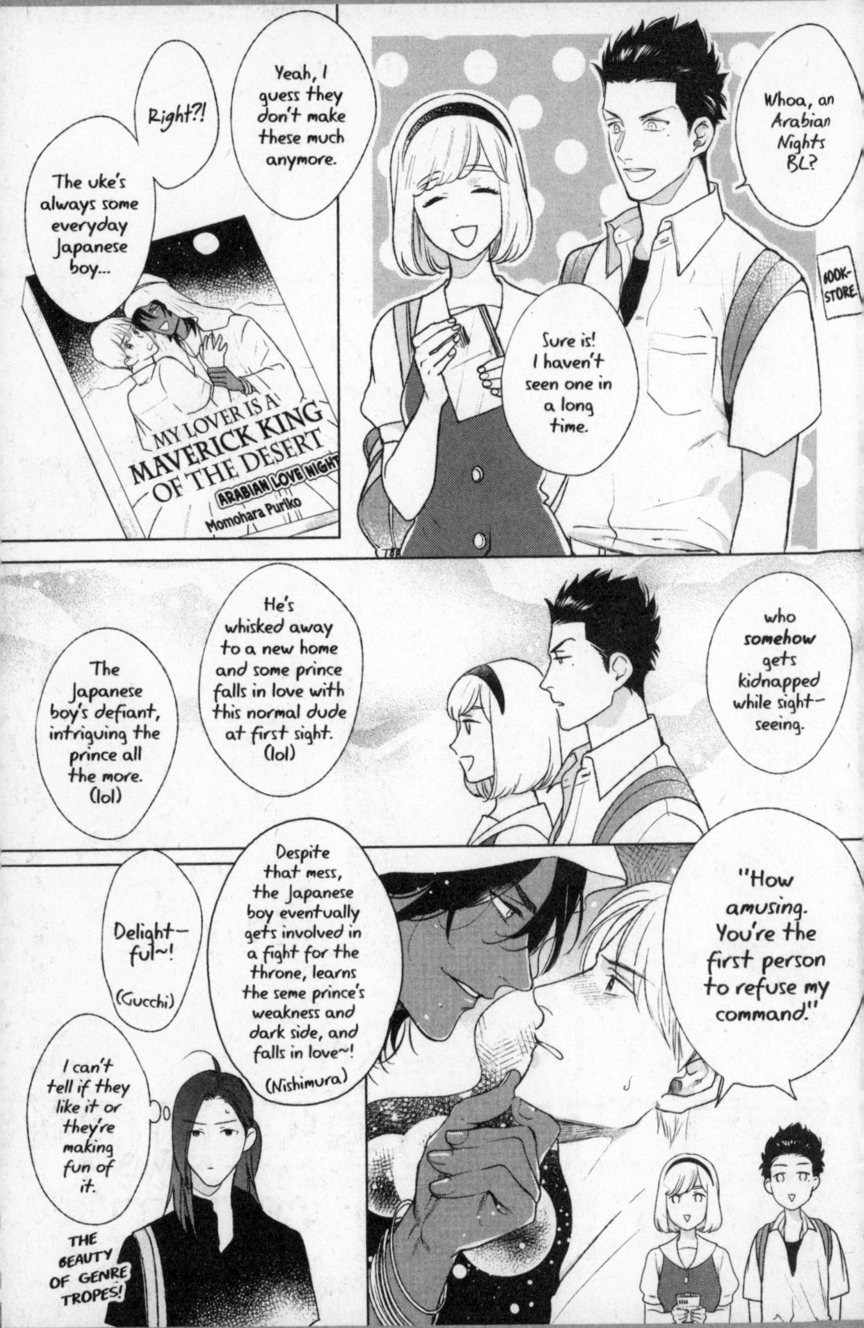
Whoa, an Arabian Nights BL?
BOOK-STORE
Sure is! I haven't seen one in a long time.
Yeah, I guess they don't make these much anymore.
Right?!
The uke's always some everyday Japanese boy...
MY LOVER IS A MAVERICK KING OF THE DESERT
ARABIAN LOVE NIGHT
Momohara Puriko
who somehow gets kidnapped while sight-seeing.
He's whisked away to a new home and some prince falls in love with this normal dude at first sight. (lol)
The Japanese boy's defiant, intriguing the prince all the more. (lol)
"How amusing. You're the first person to refuse my command."
Despite that mess, the Japanese boy eventually gets involved in a fight for the throne, learns the seme prince's weakness and dark side, and falls in love~! (Nishimura)
Delight-ful~! (Gucchi)
I can't tell if they like it or they're making fun of it.
THE BEAUTY OF GENRE TROPES!